D0209378

THE
Lifetime of a Jew

This book IS PUBLISHED
FROM THE PROCEEDS OF
THE LUDWIG VOGELSTEIN
MEMORIAL FUND

The Lifetime of a Jew

THROUGHOUT THE AGES OF JEWISH HISTORY

BY

HAYYIM SCHAUSS

AUTHOR OF *The Jewish Festivals*

New York · UNION OF AMERICAN HEBREW

CONGREGATIONS · mcml

To the memory of

MY BROTHER AND TWO SISTERS
AND THE MEMBERS OF THEIR FAMILIES
WHO WERE MURDERED BY THE GERMANS

Editor's Introduction

The present work on *The Lifetime of a Jew* discusses the significant aspects in the life of the individual Jew from birth to death. The treatment followed in this book is the same so successfully achieved by the author in his previous volume on *The Jewish Festivals*.

To the best of our knowledge this is the first book in which a writer not only gives the historical and ceremonial significance of each of the great events of birth, bar mitsvo, education, marriage, and death, but also traces the observances connected with these events through the centuries and in various lands. The book therefore is a unique contribution to the story of Jewish life.

The author who is steeped in Jewish life and lore approaches his subject critically, yet with warmth, sympathy, and enthusiasm. This twofold treatment is indeed a significant achievement. As a result, the book will serve as a popular reader for young people and adults, as well as a book of study for all those who are interested in the subject.

A word should be said concerning the plan of transliteration followed in this book. Usually schemes of transliteration follow the S'fardic pronunciation. In view of the fact that the Jews in America use mainly the Ashk'nazic pronunciation, many of the Hebrew terms when transliterated in accordance with S'fardic practice strike them as strange, even when these terms are familiar to them in the form commonly employed in conversation among Jews. The plan we have followed is therefore largely popular and phonetic and in accordance with the Ashk'nazic pronunciation with very few exceptions. Where words and phrases have become familiar in the S'fardic form, we have retained them. We hope therefore that the average layman interested in the subject will find the book more readable.

Mention should be made concerning the notes presented by the author in the back of the book. They will be of special interest to students of the subject. They contain important source material, references to scientific literature, comments, and explanations. These should be helpful, as should also the bibliography and glossary there appended.

We trust that an intelligent and sympathetic understanding of the ceremonies connected with the great events in the life of the individual Jew will help our people to appreciate the spiritual ideals that constitute the central thread of that life.

EMANUEL GAMORAN

Preface

This book was written as a companion volume to *The Jewish Festivals*, first published in 1938, following its general style and pattern.

The study of the lifetime of a Jew throughout the ages is based on original research into primary sources. The description, however, of the joyous occasions and celebrations of Jewish family life in Eastern Europe is, with few exceptions, derived from the personal observation of the author as a child in his native town in Lithuania which, together with all other Jewish communities in that land of deeply rooted Jewish life and learning, was destroyed and wiped off the earth by the Germans in 1941. Barring some minor details the description in this book holds true of every Jewish community in Eastern Europe a generation ago.

The author desires to express his acknowledgment and thanks to all who were helpful to him in preparing the book: to Professor Louis Ginzberg of the Jewish Theological Seminary, New York City, for many scholarly remarks on some of the topics treated; to Dr. William G. Braude, Rabbi Leon Fram, and Dr. Solomon B. Freehof of the Commission on Jewish Education for reading the manuscript and making many valuable suggestions; to Mr. M. Myer Singer for the splendid typography and physical make-up of the book; to Dr. Franz Landsberger, Curator of the Museum, and Mr. Isaac Goldberg, Administrative Secretary of the Library, of the Hebrew Union College; and to Mrs. Philip Dreifus and Mrs. M. Myer Singer for many important changes in language and style and for their help in preparing the manuscript for the printer. His boundless gratitude is due to Dr. Emanuel Gamoran who worked hard and painstakingly in editing the book and without whose extended friendship the book would not have been written.

The writer mentions with deep sorrow the late Rabbi Louis Feinberg who read the manuscript in its final revision and made a number of helpful suggestions. He is also grateful to the librarians of the Jewish division of the New York Public Library and of the library of the Jewish Theological Seminary of America for help rendered in the course of his writing.

He regrets that limits of space made it necessary for him to be selective in his references to sources and to scientific literature.

H. S.

Contents

PART FOUR

DEATH, FUNERAL, BURIAL, AND MOURNING

List of Illustrations

The Lifetime of a Jew

Introduction

A Panorama of Jewish Life . . . In these pages we shall present a panorama of Jewish life throughout the ages of Jewish history. It is not the life of the Jewish people as a whole that will be depicted, but the life of the individual Jew, of the average individual within the circle of his family and of the community in which he lived, commencing with his birth and concluding with the memorial services and prayers for him after his death. Between birth and death, we shall be concerned with the solemn moments which mark the milestones in his life. All these occasions in man's career on earth are marked by symbolic rites and religious ceremonies. They have, since ancient times, been surrounded by popular customs intended to bring good luck to the individual and to safeguard his welfare. These rites and ceremonies, customs and beliefs, which lend form and color to the Jewish way of life, will be traced through the various epochs of Jewish history, and in the light of the non-Jewish environment in which the Jews lived.

Popular Customs and Beliefs . . . The customs which we shall discuss are not all of one kind, nor of the same origin. A great many of them are just details of the Jewish ritual. They grew out of Jewish religious life, and need no special introduction to the reader. They were, from the very outset, part and parcel of the Jewish ritual. But there were some spurious customs in Jewish life which Jews had observed in common with other peoples, and which, in the course of centuries, had been spiritualized and Judaized. Originally they were charms and safeguards based on ancient, primitive beliefs. They stemmed from pre-historic times, when the forebears of the Jews were still worshipping many gods; or they came to the Jews later by way of the heathen peoples among whom they lived, beginning with the Canaanites, the pre-Israelitic inhabitants of Palestine.

But the Jews evolved a religious faith based on ethical monotheism, on the belief in a universe ruled by one supreme ethical being. This religious faith demanded that its adherents lead a sanctified life. It was in sharp contrast to the nature worship and the way of life of all other polytheistic nations. It made of the Jews "a people that shall dwell alone and shall not be reckoned among the nations" (Num. 23:9).

A monotheistic religion, in which the one and only God is the sole cause of all phenomena in nature as well as in human life, is bound to be hostile to heathen superstition, and to frown upon all usages based on the belief in evil spirits and witchcraft. The teachers and preachers of the Jewish monotheistic religion were, therefore, battling vehemently against the customs which the Jews had in common with their heathen neighbors. The Mosaic Law exhorts the people against defilement by the ways of the heathens. "After the doings of the land of Egypt, where ye dwelt, shall ye not do; and after the doings of the land of Canaan, whither I bring you, shall ye not do; neither shall ye walk in their statutes . . . And ye shall not walk in the customs of the nation, which I am casting out before you; for they did all these things, and therefore I abhorred them . . . Turn ye not unto the ghosts, nor unto familiar spirits; seek them not out, to be defiled by them: I am the Lord your God" (Lev. 18:3; 19:31; 20:23).

But people seldom recognize the inconsistencies of their beliefs and religious practices. The masses of the Jewish people, notwithstanding their adherence to the God of Israel, clung tenaciously to the spurious customs so rooted in their life. This led to a struggle between the laws of the official Jewish religion and the customs of the people. In the long run the folk prevailed. The rabbis continued to yield to them, and to give sanction to customs which were originally not at all in the spirit of the Jewish monotheistic faith. However, this struggle became a historic process of mutual adaptation. The questionable customs were reinterpreted by the teachers of the Torah, and filled with Jewish content, so that they fitted into the colorful picture of Jewish life.

The attitude of the rabbis toward popular beliefs was not stable nor uniform. Some of the rabbis were more, some less amenable to them. Apparently the attitude of each rabbi depended in great measure upon the environment in which he had grown up, whether it was among the learned classes or among superstitious peasant folk. The attitude varied also in the different periods of Jewish history. In Biblical times the Jewish monotheistic religion was in danger of being submerged by the polytheistic and idolatrous nature cults of the heathen nations. The Jewish religious leaders in those times were therefore adamant in their refusal to accept anything that savored of heathenism. The Mosaic Law is replete with interdictions against the practicing of customs used in foreign cults. In post-Biblical times, however, the situation changed. The Jewish monotheistic faith had become strongly entrenched among all classes of the Jewish people and Jewish leaders were no longer so fearful of foreign usages. In those days many customs of heathen origin gained admittance among Jews, and were approved by the religious leaders. However, even then the gates were not wide open to all popular customs and beliefs. In the Talmud and the Midrash we have, on the one hand, lists of approved customs and, on the other, of forbidden customs which are designated by the special term for all heathen practices, *midarchei ho-Emori* (of the ways of the Amorites).[1]

The Amorites were not the only ones from whom the Jews had taken over numerous observances. A great many popular beliefs and folkways were derived from various other peoples in whose midst they lived: the Greco-Romans, the Babylonians, the Germans, and the Slavs. In the following chapters we shall meet with copious instances of these customs.

Many Jewish customs were, in time, incorporated into the Jewish ritual code, some as ritual laws obligatory on all Jews, and others not as binding laws, but merely as current usages. A great many customs were not even recorded in the ritual code. Certain superstitious practices and beliefs spread pro- fusely among Jews in the Middle Ages under the impact of the superstitious non-Jewish environment. Many religious authorities protested against the practicing of certain customs as *darchei ho-Emori*. But the protests of the rabbis were in vain. The folk would not discard any customs that appealed to the popular mind. In time the origin of these spurious customs faded from memory. People forgot that they were based on superstition. Not from magic powers but from the One and Only God in heaven did the Jew now expect aid and support in the critical moments of his life. So many ordinary customs, not religious in origin, were reinterpreted and elevated to serve spiritual ends. To the mind of the pious Jew all these customs were practiced "for the sake of heaven."

Epochs in Jewish Life . . . A few words must be said here regarding the epochs in Jewish history into which the chapters of this book are subdivided.

We begin in each case with Biblical times, referring fre- quently to various passages in Biblical books. The Bible is an extensive literature, reflecting all phases of Jewish life for nearly a thousand years. It is the source not only of Jewish religious ideals and Biblical history; but it is also our main source book for Jewish life in ancient days. Many of the cus- toms and traditions, many of the rites and folk-beliefs which regulate the life of the individual, from birth to death, may be studied in the Bible.

On leaving Biblical times we enter the epoch of the Second Temple, by which is meant the last 200–250 years of that epoch in Jewish history. Although the Second Temple was finished in the year 516 B.C.E. and was destroyed by the Ro- mans in the year 70 C.E., we know little of Jewish life in this era until the year 166 B.C.E., which marked the beginning of the Maccabean revolt. In these last two centuries of the Second

Temple many changes took place in Jewish life, owing to the contact with the Greco-Roman world. In this period, too, the foundations of the Talmud were laid, and it may therefore also be called the Early Talmudic period.

When we reach the beginning of the Common Era, the picture of Jewish life becomes more vivid and colorful, owing to the rich material available in the Talmud and kindred literature. From the third century on, the center of Jewish life was shifted from Palestine to Babylonia, and we have to deal, in that period, with Jewish life in two different environments. The Balylonian Talmud was concluded at the end of the fifth century. The post-Talmudic time, until the eleventh century, is called *G'onic*, after the religious authorities who ruled Jewish life in that epoch of Jewish history. The two heads of the two Talmudic academies in Babylonia, in Sura and in Pumbeditha, who were then recognized by all Jewish communities as the supreme judges and religious leaders, bore the title *Gaon* (pride, alluding probably to "the pride of Jacob" in Psalm 45:5).

From the eleventh century onward the hegemony of Jewish life was shifted from the Orient to the European continent. In the course of the following centuries, centers of Jewish life developed in many European lands. The dispersion of the Jews became more wide-spread in the Middle Ages, and local customs in the Jewish communities more varied. There was a great discrepancy in custom between the Ashk'nazim (German and Polish Jews) and the S'fardim (Spanish and Portuguese Jews). But there were numerous differences in rites and customs also within the communities of the Ashk'nazim.

In recent centuries the main center of Jewish life had shifted from Western to Eastern Europe. Until the Second World War, Eastern Europe continued to be the reservoir of Jewish life, Jewish traditions, Jewish learning, and all Jewish creative activities. It was there that the Jewish way of life with all its peculiarities, with all its rites, customs, and folkways, had reached its fullest growth. Owing to the extensive area of

Eastern Europe, Jewish customs and modes of life in its component parts were not identical. But the account in this book of Jewish life in Eastern Europe is, in general, descriptive of all the Jewish communities there.

These communities, alas, are gone. The Germans, with savage cruelty, exterminated the Jews of Eastern Europe in World War II. The Jewish life in an East European community, which the author describes from memories of childhood, is no more. It belongs to the past, to history.

PART ONE

𝔄 𝔍𝔢𝔴𝔦𝔰𝔥 ℭ𝔥𝔦𝔩𝔡 𝔍𝔰 𝔅𝔬𝔯𝔫

i

In Ancient Times

In the various books of the Bible there are many passages referring to the birth of a Jewish child. They give us the following picture.

The Birth of a Child . . . The woman in travail was probably placed on a birth-stool in a half-sitting, half-lying posture.[2] A few women, relatives and neighbors, stood near her. There was also a midwife present. Jewish women had a reputation for natural strength and vitality. For the most part they were delivered easily and quickly, like the Bedouin women, often "ere the midwife came unto them." [3]

However, the life of the woman was endangered, especially when her first child was delivered. At times, however, the delivery was so painful that the woman died in labor. The midwife and the other women tried to calm and encourage her by holding out the prospect of a son.[4] People believed that the pain of the delivery of a child was a curse from God. He had punished Eve by his decree that woman would bring forth children in pain.

As soon as the woman was delivered of a son, someone was sent quickly to bring the good tidings to the father: "A man-child is born unto you!" [5] The heart of the father was filled with joy, for "a heritage of the Lord are sons." It was a great misfortune not to have a son who could "raise his name upon his inheritance." But a woman was not happy with only one son. Even when she had borne four sons and she "left off bearing," she was unhappy. This unhappiness is described in the story of Leah. A large family was the greatest blessing. The ideal life was one in which "one eats the labor of his hands, his wife is a fruitful vine, and his children are like olive plants round about his table." [6]

The new-born babe was immediately bathed in warm water, rubbed with salt and wrapped in swaddling clothes.[7] It was then given to the mother to be nursed. Immediately, the news spread through the entire neighborhood. The women of the town carried the news from one to another, and soon a number of them gathered at the house of the confined woman to bless her in the name of God.[8]

Naming the Child . . . The child was given a name as soon as it was born. Sometimes the father chose the name, sometimes the mother; often a name was suggested by relatives and friends.[9]

The present accepted custom of naming children after deceased relatives, especially grandparents, did not exist among Jews prior to the Babylonian exile. There is no record of the same name repeated in the genealogy of a family, as in later epochs of Jewish history. In pre-Exilic times we have the genealogy of the dynasty of King David, with the names of twenty-one kings of Judah, none of whom bears the name of an ancestor. None is named after David, the founder of the dynasty. There is not the slightest suggestion of such a custom anywhere in the Biblical records of pre-Exilic days. Every Jew ardently desired to have his name remembered and firmly fixed in regard to his children and his property. The greatest curse was to have one's name "blotted out of Israel." But this did not imply that a man's descendants should be named after him. It only meant that he had to have a son who would inherit his property. In a levirate marriage, when a man died without issue and the brother had to marry the widow, the first-born of this marriage was recognized as the son of the deceased, but did not bear his name.[10]

In those days a child's name expressed a definite idea, as in Gen. 4:25, "And Adam . . . called his name Seth: 'for God hath appointed me another seed instead of Abel.' " Or it might have expressed a hope aroused by the birth of the child, as in Gen. 30:24, "And she called his name Joseph, saying: 'The Lord add to me another son.' " Sometimes the name was chosen because of an important event or a certain condition that prevailed at the time of birth, as in Gen. 10:25, "the name of the one was Peleg; for in his days was the earth divided." Often the name expressed devotion to God, and was compounded with *El*, the general name for God, as in Bezalel and Ezekiel; or with *Jah*, the name of the God of Israel, as in Isaiah and Jeremiah. Children were named also after animals and plants (Rachel—ewe, Jonah—dove, Shaphan—cony, Deborah—bee, Tamar—palm-tree). Whatever the origin of these names, in historical times it apparently expressed love for animals and plants or a desire that the child should have characteristics similar to those of the respective animal or plant such as strength, nimbleness or grace.

Circumcision . . . If the baby was a boy, he was circumcised on the eighth day after his birth. Usually the father performed the operation, but in an exigency it was also done by the mother. The operation was performed with a sharp knife of polished stone.[11]

Circumcision is not an exclusively Jewish rite. It was, and still is practiced also among peoples and tribes all over the world—in Asia, Africa, Australia, the islands of the Pacific Ocean, and, sporadically, among the Indian tribes of North, Central, and South America. Today, many European and American Christians practice circumcision for reasons of health. Roughly estimated, between two hundred and three hundred million people, one-seventh of the world's population, are practicing circumcision at present. In ancient times the Jews practiced it in common with many of their neighbors— the Egyptians, the Phoenicians, the Ammonites, the Moabites, the Edomites, and the Arabs. (The Philistines, the Syrians, and the Canaanites of Palestine were not circumcised.) However, it was only among Jews that circumcision became a wholly religious rite, a sign of a covenant between God and man.

The origin of circumcision, like the origins of many rites and customs, is obscure. A great many theories, widely divergent but all well grounded, have been advanced by scholars. Some have explained the custom on hygienic grounds. These scholars follow the Greek historian Herodotus (fifth century B.C.E.), according to whom the Egyptians practiced circumcision for reasons of health. In the time of Herodotus it might have been only the opinion of the Egyptians, for by that time the origin of the rite must have been completely forgotten. Present scientific authorities believe it unlikely that the sanitary motive played an important part in the origin of ancient rites which date back to the pre-historic period of the race.

Much more at present in favor in the scientific world are the theories that connect the origin of circumcision with certain religious ideas of primitive man. They are considered religious because, in primitive times, almost all ideas, including medicine and science, were in the domain of religion. One of these theories explains the origin of circumcision as a rite of initiation in the tribe. According to another theory, it was originally a rite observed at puberty as a preliminary to marriage. All of the theories cannot be enumerated and discussed here because they are not in the scope of this chapter, which deals with the history of circumcision as a Jewish rite. We may only say that the origin of circumcision among the various peoples and tribes must not be attributed exclusively to any single motive. Besides, it is not so much the origin of a rite or custom that concerns us, as the significance which it attained and the role which it played in life long after its origin had been forgotten.[12]

As a Jewish rite, circumcision dates back to the pre-historic period of Jewish life. The Jews began to settle in Palestine at the beginning of the Iron Age, but circumcision goes back to the Stone Age. This explains the fact that much later, in historic times, Jews performed the operation with a knife of stone. People are very conservative in performing religious rites and ceremonies. They are reluctant to change and to adopt the innovations of technical progress. In various ceremonies dim candles are still used in place of the brilliant electric bulb. The Sacred Scriptures and all passages of the Scriptures used in religious services must still be written on parchment with a quill or a reed. In the same manner, the knife of polished stone was employed in the rite of circumcision even in the Iron Age; and only in the course of time did the iron knife eventually replace one of stone.

Even as far back as the ancient days of the independent Jewish kingdom, the origin of circumcision as a Jewish rite had been forgotten, and legendary tales were told about it.

One story connects it with Moses and his Midianite wife, Zipporah. It is a short story, fragmentary, obscure, and puzzling to modern readers. Here is the full text:

And it came to pass on the way at the lodging-place, that the Lord met him, and sought to kill him. Then Zipporah took a flint and cut off the foreskin of her son, and cast it at his feet; and she said: "Surely, a bridegroom of blood art thou to me." So He let him alone. Then she said: "A bridegroom of blood in regard of the circumcision."—Exod. 4:24–26.

Many Biblical scholars interpret this story as ascribing the introduction of circumcision among the Jews to Zipporah, the Midianite. It was she who first performed the rite, in order to assuage the wrath of God. Other scholars interpret this story to mean that originally the Jews, like many other peoples, performed the rite of circumcision as a preliminary to marriage. Only later was the rite transferred to the early childhood, and this story attributes the transfer to Zipporah. Although these interpretations are plausible, they are mere hypotheses.[13]

Another legendary story in the Bible ascribes to Joshua the circumcising of all the children of Israel with knives of flint in order to "roll away the reproach of Egypt from off them" (chap. 5). That spot, according to this story, was therefore called "the hill of foreskins." The story implies that the Egyptians reproached and shamed those who were not circumcised. There is little support given to the theory of some scholars that the Jews adopted circumcision under the Egyptian influence. However, from the name, "hill of the foreskins," we may assume that it was highly probable that there was a time in ancient Jewish history when all the children of one approximate age were circumcised together at a certain spot. Later, however (in which period of ancient Jewish history we do not know), the eighth day after birth was fixed as the date for circumcising each male child, individually.[14]

At any rate, these older traditions, which link the beginning of circumcision among the Jews with the names of Moses and Joshua, clearly show the obscurity of the origin of this rite in the minds of the Jews, even in the ancient Biblical times when these stories were told.

In the Ten Commandments, as well as in the other codes of law in the Pentateuch, circumcision is not enjoined. Probably it was taken for granted as an ancient rite which must not be abandoned. It was the first prerequisite for inclusion in the community of Israel, as it is evident from the Biblical story of Dinah and Shechem. To be uncircumcised was synonymous with being unclean. The Israelites disdainfully called the Philistines "the uncircumcised." [15]

The four great prophets of the Assyrian epoch (Amos, Hosea, Isaiah, Micah) never mentioned circumcision. Jeremiah was the first great prophet to mention it. He saw a symbolical significance in circumcision, for to him the rite signified removing the coarseness of the heart. He, therefore, exhorts the people: "Circumcise yourself to the Lord and take away the foreskins of your heart." According to Jeremiah, a man with a rude heart retained, so to say, the foreskin of his heart, even though he was circumcised. Thus he said briefly and pointedly: "All the nations are uncircumcised, but all of the house of Israel are uncircumcised in the heart." We find this same

1. Palestinian Clay Lamp, *Roman Period*

2. Palestinian Bronze Lamp, *Roman Period*

3. Coin of the Second Revolt Under Simon Bar Kochba
LEFT: Vase. INSCRIPTION: First Year of the Redemption of Israel
RIGHT: Wreath. INSCRIPTION: Simon Nassi Israel

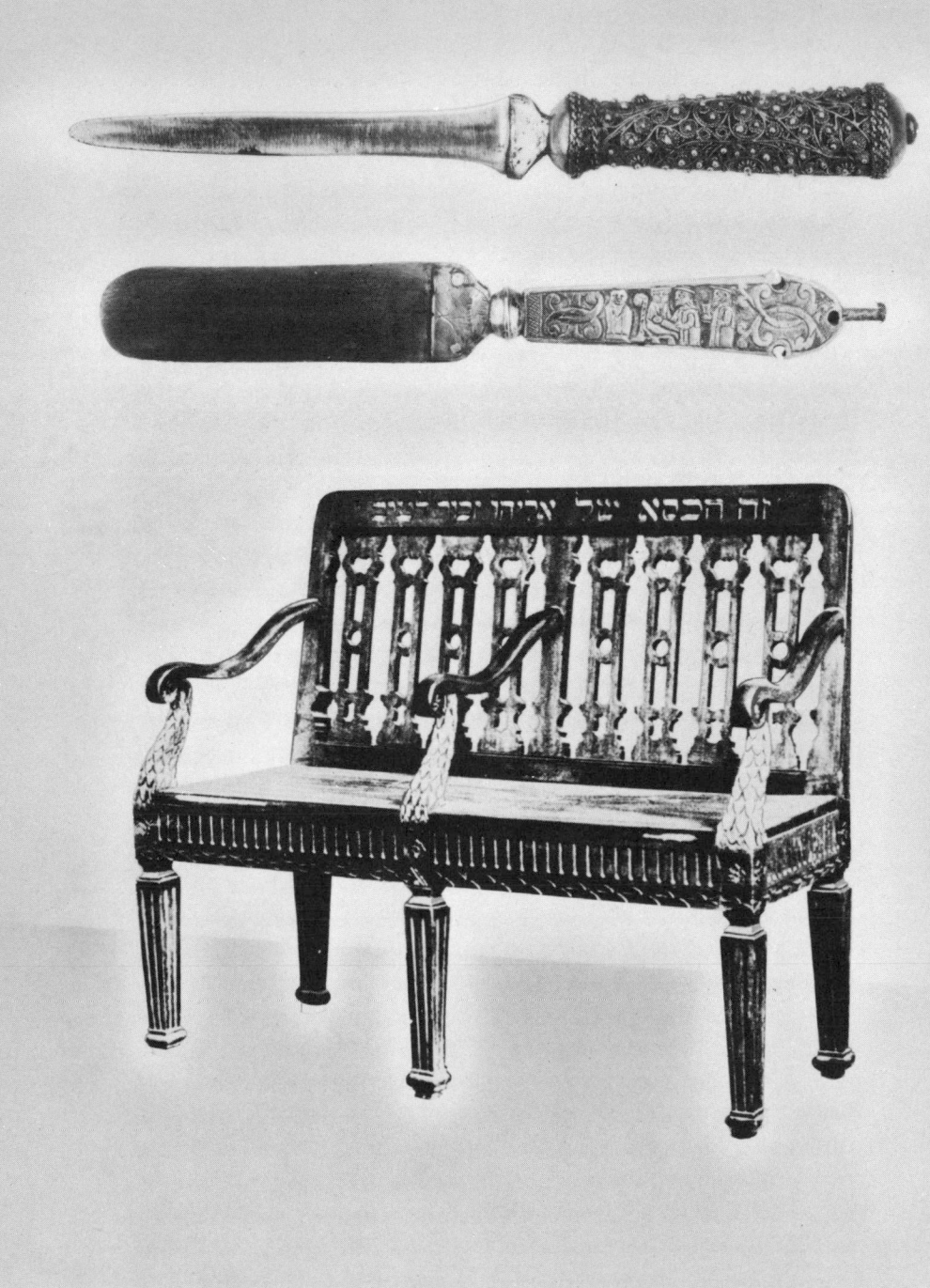

CircumcisionKnives—*Hebrew Union College Museum, Cincinnati*
Chair of Elijah used at Circumcision Ceremony

idea in some other places in the Bible, and therefore we cannot be sure whether or not Jeremiah originated it.[16]

This first phase of circumcision as a Jewish rite ended with the Babylonian exile. In Palestine, where the Jews practiced circumcision in common with several neighboring peoples, the practice could not attain any great significance as a particular Jewish rite. This situation changed during the Babylonian exile. The inhabitants of Mesopotamia did not know circumcision. Therefore it became there a mark that distinguished the Jews from their heathen neighbors. Ezekiel, the prophet who lived among the Babylonian exiles, spoke scornfully of the uncircumcised. According to Ezekiel, the distinction between circumcised and uncircumcised is continued even after death. In the description given by Ezekiel, there is no Valhalla (the abode of the dead) reserved in the nether world for heroes of war, but there are two separate divisions, one for the circumcised and one for the uncircumcised.[17]

Circumcision attained its greatest importance in the Priestly Writing which, according to modern critical study of the Bible, was one of the various sources or documents from which the Pentateuch was composed. The Priestly Writing is recognizable by its chronological precision, uniformity of style, and omission of all folk-tales and popular conceptions. It divides the history of the world into four periods: from Adam to Noah; from Noah to Abraham; from Abraham to Moses; and from Moses to the end of the world. In the first period, there was no covenant between God and man; therefore God destroyed the world in a flood. The second period was inaugurated by a covenant between God and Noah, the token of which was the rainbow in the sky. The third period was inaugurated by a covenant between God and Abraham, the token of which was the circumcision of all males. The fourth period was inaugurated by a covenant with Israel through Moses at Mount Sinai, the token of which was the observance of the Sabbath.[18]

Thus circumcision was declared to be the outward sign, in

the flesh, of a covenant which bound Abraham and his children to "walk before God Almighty and be whole-hearted." The circumcision of a child or a proselyte meant his reception into the community of the nation which separated itself from its heathen neighbors and consecrated itself to the one true God. This implied the observance of the divine commandments which were binding upon all the members of the community.

As the sign of the covenant of Abraham, circumcision assumed a deep spiritual meaning, and still is the outward mark of belonging to the Jewish community.

The Hebrew word for covenant is *b'ris*. Hence, circumcision is called, by Jews, *b'ris milo* (the covenant of circumcision) or, for short, b'ris.

We do not read anywhere in the Bible of anyone having celebrated the birth or the circumcision of a child. In Biblical times, it was neither the birth nor the circumcision, but the weaning of the child that was marked by a joyous feast.[19]

Pidyon ha-ben (Redemption of the First-Born) . . . If the boy was the first-born child of his mother, he had to be redeemed from the *kohen* (priest) for five shekels of silver. After he had become at least a month old and had thus proved his vitality, he was brought to the sanctuary, and there he was redeemed.[20]

An old Mosaic Law decreed that the first-born of the mother belonged to God, and the father must therefore redeem him.[21] But it must not be assumed that originally pidyon ha-ben had to do with human sacrifices. The sacredness of the first-born son of the mother never implied, among Jews, that he be offered to the deity on the altar, but that he had a priestly character and was to be a servant in the sanctuary. Hence he had to be redeemed from the priest in order that he might be relieved of priestly duties and lead an ordinary life.[22]

Rising from Childbed . . . The Mosaic Law prescribes that for seven days after giving birth to a son, the mother is ritually unclean, and for thirty-three days, excluded from the sanctuary. If the child is a daughter, the time of her defilement is double (fourteen and sixty-six days). Only after these days had passed and the mother of the new-born child had offered a burnt offering and a sin offering in the sanctuary, is she declared ritually clean, and allowed to participate in all sacred ceremonies.[23]

The notion that giving birth to a child defiles the mother was common to all nations of antiquity, and is prevalent today among many peoples and tribes. In certain regions it is still customary to completely isolate a woman in childbed for a certain number of days in a separate house or hut, in the belief that everything with which she comes in contact becomes unclean. The distinction made in the Pentateuchal law, which regulates the number of days that the mother is defiled according to the sex of the child, is also common to many peoples.

It is the opinion of modern scholars that this notion had its origin in the primitive conception that a woman, in giving birth to a child, is under the influence of certain demons, and must therefore be kept away from everything that is sacred. However, we shall see later how the demonic origin of the idea that a woman was defiled by childbed was forgotten in later times and new interpretations given to it.[24]

ii

In the First Centuries C.E.

The picture of the birth of a Jewish child becomes more detailed and colorful when, leaving behind Biblical times and proceeding onward in Jewish history, we arrive at the beginning of the common era, the age of the *Tannaim,* as the Talmudic sages of the first two centuries of the common era were called. The main source for the study of Jewish life in this period is the Talmud and cognate literature. In Talmudic literature we find, in connection with the birth of a child, many interesting facts of which we have no Biblical record. Some of these facts originated at this time because of the more advanced stage of Jewish civilization and the further development of religious and social institutions among Jews. Some may have been old customs and modes of life which have not been recorded in the writings of previous ages.

The Birth of a Child . . . In the period at which we have now arrived, we have definite knowledge that the woman in labor was placed on a birth-stool which was probably the property of the midwife. The latter was called *Chayo* (the one that brings life—a name which was applied also to a woman in childbed) and also *chachomo* (the wise or skillful one). She was paid for assisting in the delivery, for her skill had become a vocation transmitted usually from mother to daughter or to daughter-in-law. If no midwife was available in the locality, one of the many women who were present in the house made herself helpful. A physician was sent for in an emergency.[25]

As soon as the child was born, even before it was bathed, the women who were standing about seized it and held it in their arms, and hugged and kissed it, especially when the child was a boy. Then the midwife cleansed the babe, rubbed it with salt, and bathed it in warm water. Next, she anointed the child with warm oil and powdered it with powder made of pulverized leaves of myrtle. She then straightened the limbs of the babe and swaddled it from belly to feet. In regions infested by mosquitoes a mixture of unripened grapes was prepared and applied on the skull of the child in order to keep away gnats and mosquitoes.[26]

In this period the Jews, like their neighboring nations, surrounded the bed of the mother with various safeguards and charms to protect her and the child from evil spirits and witchcraft. The rabbis of the Talmud were hostile to these magic folk-practices. However, they had to accede to the popular demand and sanction some of them.[27]

A new feature in this period was the cradle. Among the poorer classes the kneading trough was used as a cradle. The same word, *arisoh*, is used for both. Among the richer classes, the cradle was an adorned carriage on wheels, with bells attached to it. The ringing of the bells lulled the child to sleep, and also acted as a charm to keep away evil spirits.[28]

Planting a Tree . . . As in Biblical times, the birth of a child was not celebrated with a feast. Among the Palestinian Jews, however, it was customary to plant a tree in the garden to commemorate the birth. For a son, a cedar was planted; for a daughter, a pine. At the wedding, the bridal chamber was built from the wood of the pine and the cedar trees which the parents had planted.

Planting of a tree at the birth of a child was believed to act as a charm to insure that he would grow and thrive like the tree. In the popular belief, there was a mysterious relation between the life of a person and the growth of a tree. The custom of planting a tree to celebrate the birth of a child was not original with the Jews, but was adopted from the Romans and other foreign nations, among whom they lived.[29]

The Jew among the Uncircumcised . . . When in the last
centuries of the Second Temple, Antiochus Epiphanes prohibited circumcision under penalty of death, the rite gained in
importance among Jews. They became martyrs for circumcising their new-born males. Mothers were executed with their
circumcised children. To the Jews, the blood of the martyrs
enhanced the religious importance of the "emblem in the flesh"
carried by the children of Abraham.[30]

Soon the political situation changed, and when it did, the
significance of circumcision underwent a temporary change.
Antiochus' persecution incited the Jews to revolt against the
Syrian oppression. The leaders of the rebellion, the Macca-
beans or Hasmoneans, were victorious in their protracted
struggle, and ultimately succeeded in founding a new, independent Jewish kingdom which comprised nearly the whole
of Palestine. The Hasmonean princes conquered many non-
Jewish regions of the land and Judaized their inhabitants. In
that period, circumcision became the physical means of Juda-
izing the new non-Jewish subjects of the Jewish theocratic
state. It became an outer mark of the subjection to the rule of
the Hasmoneans.

But Judaization as a means of political expansion did not last
long. Rome soon conquered Judea, and the independent state
of the Hasmoneans came to an end. However, the end of the
Jewish state did not halt the wide-spread diffusion of Judaism
in the pagan world. The problem of circumcision loomed
large in the religious propaganda of the Jews.

In that period of early imperial Rome, the Jews were dis-
persed over almost the entire civilized world, and they carried
on extensive propaganda for their faith, and made countless
proselytes. Hundreds of thousands in higher circles of pagan
society cherished a strong admiration for the Jewish religion
and the Jewish way of life.

However, it was no easy task for a pagan to completely embrace Judaism. This entailed the severance of all intimate relations with friends and relatives. For men especially, circum-

cision was a great obstacle to the adoption of the Jewish religion. There were, therefore, proselytes of various grades. Many were satisfied with only a minimum of Jewishness. They visited the synagogue occasionally on the Sabbath or on a Jewish festival, and observed this or that bit of Jewish religious life, but persisted in most of their pagan practices. On the other hand, some underwent circumcision, and became full-fledged Jews. Between these two extremes there were, of course, many intermediate stages of conversion to Judaism.[31]

In those days, not all Jewish missionaries who made proselytes insisted upon circumcision in every case. The following story is told by Josephus Flavius concerning the conversion to Judaism of the royal house of Adiabene, a kingdom in northern Mesopotamia.

A certain Jew by the name of Ananias succeeded in converting to the Jewish faith many women of the highest rank in the royal court, among them the queen, Helena. She became an ardent Jewess. The king, Monobazus, showed much sympathy for the Jewish religion, but he did not embrace it. But their son, Izates, heir to the throne, completely adopted the Jewish religion, with the exception of circumcision. This he was dissuaded from doing lest he estrange himself from his subjects, most of whom regarded the Jewish religion as peculiar. But when Izates ascended the throne, he resolved to complete his conversion by being circumcised. Ananias argued with Izates that he could be a Jew and worship God even though he omitted circumcision. But when another learned Galilean Jew convinced the king that one who is uncircumcised breaks the laws of Moses, the king carried out his determination to complete his conversion, and his act was emulated by many of the princes of the royal family.[32]

In Conflict with the Outside World . . . In the Greco-Roman world, circumcision was mistakenly regarded as an exclusively Jewish rite, and the Jews were ridiculed for being circumcised. The Greco-Roman writers had little understanding of the Jewish way of life, as glaringly shown by the fact that they derided the Jewish observance of the Sabbath. The Greco-Roman slave-holders regarded the institution of a weekly day of rest for all toilers as a manifestation of laziness on the part of the Jews.[33]

Circumcision separated the Jews from the Greco-Roman world and, later, from the Christians too, after the latter had repudiated the rite together with the entire ceremonial law of the Pentateuch.

But the sneers of the Greco-Roman world and the casuistic arguments of the Christian church against circumcision only intensified in the Jews their zeal for the "indelible covenant in the flesh" of the children of Abraham. This feeling was strengthened by the persecution of Hadrian, the Roman Emperor, who, like Antiochus, three hundred years before, prohibited circumcision as one of the fundamental practices of Judaism, under penalty of death. In those years of religious persecution, circumcision was performed secretly. It was not divulged in the neighborhood. Indirectly one discovered that a circumcision ceremony would take place the following day when, on the preceding evening, he noticed the preparations for the feast.

This persecution did not last long. Antoninus Pius, Hadrian's successor, rescinded the decrees against Judaism. Circumcision was again permitted, but only for born Jews, not for proselytes. Because the Jews had suffered for circumcision, it grew in importance. A generation after the persecution, Judah the Patriarch declared that circumcision was more important than all other precepts of the Jewish religion put together, possibly reflecting the thought that the unity of a people in exile must be maintained and strengthened.[34]

The Circumcision Ceremony . . . Circumcision had thus become a religious ceremony of great significance. It was attended by benedictions, and celebrated with joy and feasting. On the eve of the occasion, the house was full of activity—oil lamps were burning, the handmill was clattering, grinding wheat into flour, in preparation for the important and joyous ceremony. On the next day a large company gathered to witness the rite.

The operation was no longer performed by the father, but by a special *mohel* (one who performs the circumcision operation) who used an iron knife. The stone knife of Biblical times had been discarded. The version of the benedictions recited at the ceremony had already been fixed by this period. The mohel said: "Blessed be Thou, O Lord, our God, King of the Universe, who has sanctified us with His commandments and enjoined upon us the circumcision." The father followed with: "Blessed be Thou, O Lord, our God, King of the Universe, who sanctified us with His commandments and enjoined upon us to initiate our sons into the covenant of our father Abraham." The assembled people responded: "As he has entered the covenant, so shall he also enter into the study of the Torah, into the chupo and into good deeds." [35]

A Circumcision Feast in Jerusalem . . . In a Midrashic tale we have a vivid description of a circumcision feast in Jerusalem shortly before the second destruction of that city. The father of the child in this tale was Avuyo, one of the wealthy nobles of the Holy City. A son was born to him, who was named Elisha. All the celebrities of Jerusalem were invited to the joyous ceremony, among them the famous sages, Rabbi Eliezer and Rabbi Joshua, the two great disciples of Rabbon Jochanan ben Zakkai.

A description of the festive occasion in the house of this wealthy dignitary in Jerusalem follows:

First the circumcision is performed, followed by a sumptuous feast. There is eating and drinking in profusion. After the banquet, the guests amuse themselves in joy and merriment. In one room the people of high rank are gathering. They clap their hands and dance; they sing psalms and recite Greek acrostics. Rabbi Eliezer and Rabbi Joshua sit in another room, surrounded by pious and learned people, whose festive joy is more spiritual in character. Rabbi Eliezer and Rabbi Joshua begin to discourse on the Torah. They start with the Pentateuch and proceed to the Prophets; from the Prophets they proceed to the Writings. The words of the Torah are spoken by them with such clarity and brilliance that to the people listening it seems that not words but a stream of light fills the room. The father, Avuyo, stands nearby and listens. He notices the tremendous effect of their words on the listeners, and Avuyo makes a solemn vow that when little Elisha grows up he will devote his life to the study of the Torah.[36]

Avuyo fulfilled his vow. Elisha became one of the great Jewish sages of that epoch. Later, however, he deviated from the path of Jewish Orthodoxy, and was shunned by his colleagues and condemned by them as a heretic.

In general, the circumcision of a child in Jerusalem was a great festive occasion in which many people participated. Whether the father of the child was rich or poor, a large company assembled at the home whenever a circumcision ceremony was to take place. In Jerusalem there were special brotherhoods for the purpose of attending to important religious duties. There was a brotherhood to participate in circumcision ceremonies; a brotherhood to attend weddings; and a brotherhood to console mourners.[37]

A Circumcision Feast in Galilee . . . In another Midrashic tale we have a description of a circumcision feast which took place more than a hundred years later than the one just described. Catastrophic and far-reaching changes in Jewish life had occurred during these 150 years. Jerusalem and the Temple had been destoyed, and sixty-five years after that disaster came the revolt of Bar Kochba. In the bloody suppression of that revolt, Judea, the southern part of Palestine, had been entirely devastated, and the center of Jewish life and Jewish learning had shifted to Galilee, the northern part of the land. The greatest city in Galilee, and the center of the administration of the Jewish community, was Sepphoris. Here the leaders and representatives of the Jewish community resided, and it was in the house of one of the wealthy leaders of Sepphoris that the circumcision ceremony took place.

The father invited many people from neighboring towns and villages. Some guests came from En-Teenah, a small town near by. Among them was the famous Tanna, Rabbi Simeon ben Chalaphta, an older contemporary of Rabbi Judah the Patriarch, the compiler of the Mishnah. The wealthy father treated his guests with seven-year-old wine, and at the feast he said: "I pray the Lord in Heaven that I may give you from this same wine at the wedding of my son." After the father had spoken, the throng in the house responded in unison: "As you have initiated him into the covenant so you shall initiate him into the study of the Torah and into the chupo." We are told in the Midrashic tale that the feasting and banqueting lasted until midnight.[38]

Naming the Child . . . A girl was still named soon after birth, but the naming of a boy occurred at the circumcision ceremony.[30]

After the Babylonian exile, a great change took place in the naming of children. The custom of naming a son after his grandfather, which prevailed among the ancient Egyptians and Greeks, was now adopted by the Jews. We first hear of it in the fifth century (B.C.E.) among the Jews of Elephantine and Assuan, on the southern border of Egypt. The existence of a community of Jewish soldier colonists there, hundreds of years before the conquests of Alexander, is a newly discovered chapter in the history of the Jewish dispersion (see pp. 139–41). The archives of this Jewish community were unearthed at the threshold of our century. They contained many papyri written in Aramaic, among which we find the first records of Jewish children named after grandparents.

Later we find this custom also prevalent among the Palestinian Jews. In the high-priestly family we find the names of

Onias and Simon succeeding one another. In the Hasmonean dynasty, Hyrcanus II bears the name of his grandfather John Hyrcanus. Still later we find the genealogy of the famous Hillel with only a few names in it, mostly those of the grandfather.

Children were also named after the brothers of their father. Two sons of Simon the Hasmonean, Judah and John, bore the names of their father's brothers, apparently after the decease of the latter. Occasionally the child was named in honor of the living. A child might be named for his father or grandfather who was still alive.[40]

A more striking innovation was the use of foreign names, first found in the later books of the Bible. According to modern scholars, Sheshbazzar, Zerubbabel, Belteshazzar, Shenazzar, Mordecai, and Esther are Babylonian names. In Daniel-Belteshazzar and in Esther-Hadassah we have the first use of two names for one person, one Jewish and the other non-Jewish.

This tendency became more pronounced in the Greek period, when Greek or Grecianized names were favored. We find Greek names in the aristocratic circles sympathetic to Greek culture (the high priests and the Maccabean and Herodian princes and princesses). Great religious teachers of the Pharisees, the spiritual leaders of the people, bore the names Antigonus, Symachus, and Tarphon (Tryphon). Latin names also came into vogue. Jews called their children Marcus or Justus, and did not even hesitate to name them Titus. Double names, one Jewish and the other Grecian, became popular, as Judah-Aristobul, Salome-Alexandra, Simon-Peter, Saul-Paul. The purists among Palestinian Jews in the centuries following the second destruction of Jerusalem considered it meritorious to bear a genuinely Hebrew name. But outside of Palestine names were mostly non-Jewish.[41]

This was not the only innovation regarding names in the days of the Second Temple. The common pre-Exilic custom of compounding names with that of God was abandoned altogether, or so shortened that only one letter remained of His name. Thus Jehoiadah became Jaddua; Hananiah became Honi; and Mattathiah became Mattai.

The Biblical names, Abraham, Moses, Aaron, and David, were avoided in Talmudic times. Only in the post-Talmudic era did they become popular among all Jewish groups. Biblical names, unheard of in the days of the Second Temple and in subsequent Talmudic times, became popular in G'onic times. We find Jehiel, Joel, Jehoram, Enoch, Obadiah, and many others.

The first record of a form of prayer for naming a boy is found in G'onic times. It was written in Aramaic. This was later changed to Hebrew among European Jews, who did not speak Aramaic; and the Hebrew version is still used today.[42]

Pidyon ha-ben . . . At this period the original meaning of the redemption of the first-born had been almost forgotten, and it was observed merely as a symbol of devotion to God. Many kohanim, especially if they were rich, returned the money to the father. Such instances are mentioned as early as the end of the first century (c.e.). This practice of returning the five *shekels* became still more popular in later times.[43]

The observance of pidyon ha-ben had also begun to be marked in Talmudic times by the reciting of benedictions and by a feast. The father recited two benedictions: one "over the redemption of the first-born" and the other, the benediction "Shehecheyonu" ("Who has kept us in life and preserved us and permitted us to reach this season"—a benediction on the arrival of a new season or of any joyous event in one's life).[44]

Rising from Childbed . . . The belief that a woman was defiled by childbirth because she was under the influence of demons was forgotten, and new interpretations were given. It was explained that on arising from childbed, she must bring a sin-offering because she then breaks the vow made in labor, under the spontaneous reaction of pain, to be forever separated from her husband. Explanations were also given for the belief that a woman was unclean twice as long after the birth of a girl as in the case of a boy. One explanation refers to the story of creation, and says it is because Adam was brought by the angels into the Garden of Eden forty days after he was created, whereas Eve was brought eighty days after her creation.[45]

Arising from childbed was observed in Temple days by the offering of two sacrifices. The mother was not obliged to appear personally in the Temple. There was a special chest in the Second Temple for receiving money for these offerings, and it was arranged that the money for the two offerings be placed in this chest on a particular day. The two sacrifices were then offered on the altar, and the woman, wherever she lived, was ritually clean by evening.[46]

iii

In the Middle Ages

In the Middle Ages more and more of the festival occasions in the family were exalted by religious rites, mostly performed at the synagogue, with the participation of the whole community. Thus the Jew, with his religious devotion, created for himself in his community and his synagogue a haven of refuge in a surging sea of hatred and persecution. The abundance of his religious life compensated him for the meagerness and deficiency of material conditions in the ghetto. That this life was a powerful influence may be seen from the fact that it was able to overcome to some extent the superstitions of medieval days, and to modify them to the point where the Jew felt he was in the domain of religion.

Watching Mother and Child . . . From the moment of birth until the circumcision ceremony was over, mother and child were surrounded by various charms and talismans. They were to guard against Lilith, the female demon who, in the belief of the folk, sought to kill the child as well as the mother in childbed. On the walls of the room where the mother lay, there were amulets inscribed with conjurations against Lilith and her whole clique. It was a general custom in the Middle Ages, as it still is among the Jews of the Caucasus and Morocco, to close the windows of the room at night. The magic circle was also employed. As soon as the woman was delivered of the child, a circle was drawn with chalk or charcoal on the floor of the room. The circle was circumscribed with such weighty names as Lilith, Adam, and Eve, and three tongue-twisting names of angels who, in the popular belief, were feared and shunned by Lilith. The woman in childbed was prohibited from leaving the house before the fourth Sabbath after the birth of the child.[47]

The most efficacious means of exorcising demons was, of course, to recite the monotheistic credo of the Jewish religion, "Sh'ma Yisroel." The "reading of Sh'ma" (Hear, O Israel: The Lord Our God, the Lord is One), therefore, took place in the room of a woman in childbed every night, particularly on the eve of the b'ris. This was called "Watch Night" (Wachnacht) by the German Jews. Relatives and friends gathered in the house and studied Torah all night so that the child might not be "benumen" (bewitched), as the German Jews called it.

Watch Night . . . The observance of the eve of the b'ris was already mentioned by Jewish writers in the twelfth century. Scholars are of the opinion that its origin is not Jewish. It sprang up under foreign influences, and later adapted itself to the Jewish way of life. In the popular belief of the Jews, the b'ris ended the power of the evil spirits, and therefore the eve of circumcision was regarded as the most dangerous time of all, when the demons exerted themselves to the utmost to seize their last chance to injure the mother and the child. We find an exact duplication of this belief in the folk ideas of the Germans, except that, according to the German belief, it was baptism which ended the power of the evil spirits.

In the popular belief, evil spirits shunned the light. In the dark and gruesome hours of the night they spread their terror; hence the extremely dangerous character of the night preceding the b'ris, and the various magic precautions taken for the safety of the mother and the child: the numerous lighted candles, the iron knife which the mohel placed under the pillow of the mother, and the many other safeguards and charms employed.

The main feature of the night, from which its name was derived, was the vigil kept by the mother and the people who gathered in the house. To a person who might possibly be the prey of evil spirits, sleeping was regarded as very dangerous, because in the primitive belief, the soul remained outside of the body during sleep, and could easily be seized. In some parts of Germany it was customary among the Jews to keep vigil the whole night preceding circumcision.[48]

In the course of time, the observance of the eve of the b'ris was, to a great extent, divested of its original magic character, and invested with a Jewish religious garb. It was declared to be merely a prelude to the circumcision ceremony. For this purpose it was hermeneutically linked with certain passages of the Bible. Thus the joyous observance of this night of vigil was declared to be the joy of a mitsvo, of fulfilling a religious precept, and it was regarded as a religious act to partake of the feast. The main feature of the observance had become the reciting of a prayer, and the reading of certain portions of the Bible and the Talmud and Midrashim that dealt with the precept of circumcision. With its magic background nearly forgotten, the Watch Night or Night of Vigil persisted to our own day as a prelude to the b'ris.[49]

Circumcision . . . In following the circumcision ceremony through the ages, we notice that it continually gained in importance and, from a family affair, became a festival for the whole community. This process had already begun in the days of the Second Temple. However, it was not until the G'onic period (from the seventh to the eleventh centuries) that the b'ris became a festival for the community in the full sense of the word. It was then (about the ninth century) that the celebration of the ceremony was transferred from the home to the synagogue.

Long before that time it had been customary to perform the ceremony early in the morning, for a mitsvo, a religious act, must not be delayed. When the ceremony was transferred to the synagogue, it was performed immediately after the morning prayers. The entire congregation remained in the synagogue in order that each one might attain the religious merit attached to his presence at the ceremony.

As long as the circumcision ceremony was performed at home it had no connection with the services of the synagogue. Performance in the synagogue associated it with the services, and all the people assembled in the synagogue felt that it was a joyous day—a festival. Certain passages in the services, which are not recited at festival or semi-festival days, were also omitted on that day. On the other hand, certain passages in the morning prayers were recited with a special chant. In addition, the worshippers in the synagogue recited and chanted special poetic insertions which the *Paitonim*—the liturgical poets of the Middle Ages—had composed for the joyous occasion of a b'ris. At the meal of a b'ris, also, *z'miros* (liturgical table songs) appropriate to the occasion were sung. These z'miros described the Jews as surrounded with God's precepts as by a fortress. On their heads and arms they wore phylacteries. On the door-posts they placed *m'zuzos*. Their garments were hung with *tsitsis* (fringes), and their bodies bore the sign of the covenant.[50]

Other new features were added, which embellished and enriched the ceremony of the b'ris.

The Chair of Elijah . . . The most important feature added to the ceremonial of the b'ris in post-Talmudic times was the custom of placing a chair for the prophet Elijah. In the ninth century, when the b'ris was transferred from the home to the synagogue, the chair of Elijah is mentioned not as an innovation but as a well-established custom.

In order to explain the meaning of this custom, it was linked with certain passages of the Bible. In the First Book of Kings, it is related that Elijah complained to God that "the children of Israel have forsaken Thy covenant" (19:10, 14). The Jewish homiletical interpreters of the Scriptures in the Middle Ages explained this to mean that Elijah complained that the children of Israel had discarded circumcision. Therefore God said to Elijah: "Because of excessive zeal for Me you have brought charges against Israel that they have forsaken My covenant, therefore you shall have to be present at every circumcision ceremony." In addition, "the messenger of the covenant," who is spoken of in the Book of Malachi (3:1), was identified with the prophet Elijah, and it was only proper that this angel of the covenant should be present whenever a Jewish child entered the covenant of Abraham.[51]

As in all similar cases, the custom did not grow out of these citations. The citations were quoted later in order to explain an established custom. For this reason we must seek the origin of a custom, not in the interpretation and meaning later read into it, after the origin itself had been almost forgotten, but in the character of the rite, in the practice itself. We must compare it with similar rites and practices among Jews and also among other peoples.

The essential feature in the custom of using Elijah's chair was the placing of a seat of honor, a throne, for a guardian angel who was believed to guard and protect the child. First there was the belief in a guardian angel for the new-born child. It was only later that this guardian angel came to be identified with the prophet Elijah. We thus have to trace the origin and development of this belief.

As long ago as in Biblical times it was a popular Jewish custom to set up in the home a table, bedecked with food and drink, and dedicated to *Gad* and *M'ni*, two ancient Canaanitic deities of fortune, originally a god and a goddess. The prophet denounces those "that prepare a table for Gad and that offer mingled wine in full measure unto M'ni" (Isa. 65:11). We hear a great deal more of Gad in post-Biblical times. In the Talmud, "the bed of Gad" was a familiar piece of furniture in the Jewish household. It was called in Aramaic *arso d'gado*. No one was allowed to sleep or sit on this bed or in this chair. Some even invoked this deity of fate with the formula: "Be lucky, my Gad, and cease not!" The rabbis of the Talmud forbade this invocation as a heathenish practice.

They also prohibited the custom of leaving crumbs on the table after each meal as an offering to Gad. But notwithstanding the prohibition of the rabbis, leaving crumbs on the table for good luck was still a popular custom as late as the sixteenth century.[52]

In Talmudic times, the "table for Gad," originally meant for the luck of the household, had been brought into close relation to the birth of a child. As far back as the second century C.E., it was a popular custom among the Jews in Palestine to set a table with food before a woman in childbed. The sages of the Talmud considered it a heathenish practice. Yet it persisted in a certain form until modern times. In the sixteenth and seventeenth centuries, we hear of a table or bed set, on the eve of the b'ris, with all kinds of foods for the mazol (good luck) of the new-born child. For the origin of this particular custom we must look in another direction. Among the Romans it was customary at the birth of a child, to set a meal in the court of the house, dedicating it to the deity who was believed to protect children from sickness. Jews apparently accepted this belief that there was a guardian deity of the home and the child, for whom a table should be set with food. Among Jews, however, the belief was completely changed. The guardian deity was superseded by the prophet Elijah who, already in Talmudic times, was regarded as the guardian angel of the Jews. It was only natural to identify him as the guardian angel of the Jewish child. The story in the Bible which tells how Elijah revived the child of the widow may have been a factor. We also meet Elijah as the protector of the child in the legend inscribed on the amulets against Lilith which will be dealt with in a subsequent chapter.[53]

Since the role of the non-Jewish guardian deity of the child was given to the prophet Elijah, the bedecked table, too, should have been dedicated to him. In fact, there were Jews here and there in the Orient, even as late as the eighteenth century, who, on the eve of the b'ris, dedicated to Elijah a table with food. However, this custom had not become widespread. Among the Jews of Europe a table or bed was set with food on the eve of the b'ris for the mazol of the child, without associating it with the prophet Elijah. But this, too, smacked of "preparing a table to Gad," and the rabbis interdicted it.[54]

Eventually the custom lost all of its ancient heathen character. The table was decked with food on the Watch Night, not for the good luck of the child, but for the invited guests as a prelude to the feast of the b'ris. As for the prophet Elijah, only a chair on which he might sit, without any offering of food, was set apart for him at the b'ris. Thus the chair of Elijah proves the spiritual vitality of the Jewish religion in filling an originally non-Jewish rite with genuine Jewish content and transforming it into a highly religious symbol—the prophet Elijah as the "messenger of the covenant" and the guardian of the Jewish child.

In the later Middle Ages Elijah was thought of as omnipresent, and it was believed he attended such occasions in person. Legends were current about saintly rabbis who, holding the child on their knees, saw Elijah sitting on the chair dedicated to him. It was told of Rabbi Judah the Pious, the famous Jewish mystic who flourished at Regensburg in the twelfth century, that once, when he officiated as *sandek*, he delayed the circumcision because he did not see Elijah come in and sit on the chair which had been prepared for him. When people in the synagogue asked him the reason for the delay, he told them that Elijah stayed away because he foresaw that the child, in his maturity, would be inclined to abandon the faith of his ancestors.[55]

The Sandek . . . During the period when the b'ris was transferred to the synagogue, a new leading personage was introduced into the ceremonial. Before, there had been only two, the father and the mohel. Now a third was added—the assistant of the mohel, who held the child on his knees during the operation. He was named sandek, a title derived from a Greek word meaning godfather.

The people of the Orient use their knees as we use a table, and holding the child on the knees during the operation was taken as a matter of course, without any special religious significance. It was not until the ninth or tenth century that this assistance became a religious function. Since the name is derived from Greek, scholars attribute to a Byzantine influence the importance given to the sandek.

Great religious merit was attached to the function of the sandek. To begin with, the sandek had a share in causing a child to enter into the covenant of Abraham. In addition, the sandek had his seat right near the chair of Elijah, implying, in the belief and imagination of the people, that he sat by the side of the great prophet. The sandek, therefore, had to be a pious, God-fearing man, worthy to sit near the prophet Elijah. The sandek also shared, with the father and the mohel, the privilege of being called to the bimo, the central platform of the synagogue, to recite the benediction over the reading of the Torah, if the b'ris fell on a day on which the Torah was read. Moreover, the sandek was preferred to the mohel, and preceded him in being called up to the reading of the Torah. Besides, officiating as sandek was believed by the people to bring good fortune and wealth. Small wonder then that, in appreciation of the privilege accorded to him, it became the general custom for the sandek to defray the expenses of the feast.

Soon the function of assisting the mohel was divided between a man and a woman. It was usually the sandek's wife who brought the child from the mother's room to the entrance of the synagogue. Still later, the sandek was given two assistants, usually a man and wife, brother and sister, and so forth. In our own day, among East European Jews, these assistants of the sandek were called *kvater* and *kvaterin*, the equivalent of a medieval German word which, in modern German, is *Gevatter* (godfather).

In the Middle Ages it was customary among German Jews not to let the same sandek perform his duties for two brothers. Though various explanations were given for it, this custom has not persisted. In Eastern Europe the reverse became the accepted usage. Usually one man, the rabbi of the community, officiated as sandek at every circumcision ceremony. An explanation was even evolved that children grow to resemble the sandek, and of course all parents wish their sons to bear an intellectual and moral resemblance to the rabbi.[56]

A B'ris in Rome . . . It is Rome in the thirteenth century. A boy has been born into a Jewish family and on the eighth day the b'ris is announced in all the synagogues of the Jewish community. A box of spices is carried from synagogue to synagogue. When worshippers at the morning services recognize the odor, they know that in one of the synagogues a child is to enter the Covenant of Abraham. The synagogue where the circumcision takes place is brightly illuminated with many candles, one of which is extraordinarily large. A ribbon is hung on the door of the synagogue. Two richly adorned, covered chairs are placed near the door, one for the prophet Elijah and one for the sandek. A festive feeling pervades the worshippers during the morning services. They recite the prayers up to *Olenu*. Then the b'ris ceremony begins, and at its conclusion Olenu is recited.

Meanwhile the little boy has been bathed in warm water and dressed in a linen shirt and tunic, and a pretty little cap, and adorned like a bridegroom going to his wedding.

When the baby is carried with great pomp into the synagogue, the father calls loudly, "Blessed be they who are sitting here!" And the congregation responds, "Blessed be he who is coming here!" With his right hand the father delivers the child to the sandek. The sandek receives the child with his right hand and places him on his lap. The mohel stands near the father to indicate that he has been appointed his deputy to circumcise his son. All the people in the synagogue rise when the father hands the child to the sandek and remain standing during the ceremony.

After the operation, the mohel takes the child from the sandek and hands him to the father. The father in turn hands the baby to another man who assists the sandek by holding the child on his lap while the benedictions are recited antiphonally. The blesser says "So and so, the little fellow" and the assembled answer "may he grow big." The blesser says "May the child live" and the assembled answer "to bring joy to his father and mother." The blesser says "May he be a brother to seven" and the assembled answer "and father of eight." The blesser says "As he entered unto the covenant, so may he enter unto Torah, chupo and good deeds." [57]

A B'ris at Mayence . . . Marching on in time from the thirteenth to the fifteenth century, and traveling a little northward from Rome to the Rhineland, we arrive at Mayence. Mayence was worth visiting at that period, just to meet the greatest religious authority of his time, the famous Rabbi Jacob ben Moshe Halevi, known universally by his abbreviated name, *Maharil*. He was the rabbi of the community and also head of the *y'shivo*, the Talmudic academy at Mayence. Making a living from matchmaking, this great rabbi contributed his income from the rabbinate to the maintenance of the y'shivo.

Maharil himself did not write any books. However, an admirer and disciple of his, R. Zalmon of St. Goar, a small town on the Rhine, wrote a "Maharil Book" which consists mostly of ritual customs and ceremonial regulations according to the decisions and ritual practice of Maharil. But here and there R. Zalmon interrupts the ritual regulations and pious homilies of his great master to describe minutely and vividly a ceremony at which the latter officiated—a b'ris, a pidyon ha-ben, or a wedding. For us today the book is a veritable historic treasure, as it furnishes us a faithful picture of the life of the German Jews in the fifteenth century. We shall draw extensively upon this abundant source of information on Jewish life in the Middle Ages, and shall become acquainted with Maharil in his role as rabbi at various functions, beginning with the ceremonial of a b'ris.

When a b'ris occurred in Mayence, Maharil himself often served as the sandek. He prepared for this ceremony by first immersing himself in a *mikve* (ritual pool of purification).

In the synagogue where the b'ris took place, twelve candles were lighted to signify the twelve tribes of Israel. In addition, one large candle burned. A large chair, draped with a rich cover, was provided for the prophet Elijah. After the morning prayers had been recited as far as Olenu, the sandek's wife took the child from his mother and carried him as far as the door of the synagogue. She did not enter the men's section of the synagogue where the ceremony took place, for a woman might not mingle with men in a synagogue. Sometimes the sandek himself went to the mother's house to receive the child. Maharil frowned upon this. It was regarded as much a misdemeanor for a man to walk amidst women as for a woman to intrude among men.

In this source book we have a description of a b'ris for twin brothers in the synagogue of Mayence. There was only one ceremony but everything was done in duplicate. Instead of twelve smaller candles and one large candle, twenty-four smaller candles and two large ones illuminated the synagogue. The twin boys were carried into the synagogue together and two mohalim, assisted by two sandeks, performed the operations simultaneously. But the benedictions were recited only once. One mohel recited the benediction before the operation, and the second mohel responded "Amen" and performed the operation. The benediction which followed was recited by the second mohel and the Hebrew word "ha-yeled" (the child) was changed to "ha-y'lodim" (the children).

A B'ris in Worms . . . We proceed to another Jewish community in the Rhineland. It is the ghetto of Worms in the seventeenth century, two hundred years after the time of Maharil. We are again fortunate in having a rich source upon which to draw. It is a book about the customs of the Jews of Worms written by *Juspa Shamosh*, the secretary of the community and the *shamos* (sexton) of the synagogue at Worms. In some respects Juspa Shamosh is even superior as a writer to R. Zalmon, as he depicts life in general, the folkways of the people, as well as the hustle and bustle preceding and following religious ceremonies.

There were several mohalim in Worms, and as soon as a woman gave birth to a boy, one mohel after another paid a visit to the parents, offering his services. The wives of the mohalim also visited the mother, in order to have this honor accorded to their husbands. As they were not remunerated for their services, they competed for the privilege of performing a mitsvo.

On the Friday night following the birth of a boy, relatives and friends visited the parents, and were served with fruit and wine. This celebration was called *ben zochor* (a male child, a phrase from Jer. 20:15).

Three days before the b'ris, the beadle of the synagogue would stride through the streets of the ghetto, crying aloud: "Zu der yiddish kertz!" (to the circumcision candle, "kertz" for candle and "yiddish" for Yiddishen, i.e., to Judaize by circumcision). Thereupon the women gathered at the house of the parents to make the one large and the twelve small candles which were to burn in the synagogue at the b'ris.

During the days immediately before the b'ris, women friends visited the mother. They helped her bathe the child and before departing they left coins for the woman who took care of the mother during her childbed.

The b'ris took place at the synagogue if the weather permitted. The sandek's wife, accompanied by the most eminent women of the community, brought the child into the women's section of the synagogue. There was a special door there, made for the occasion of a b'ris. It was called "Yiddish Tir" (circumcision door). At the threshold of this door the sandek's wife delivered the child to her husband. After the b'ris the father invited all the people who witnessed the ceremony to partake of a festive meal at his house. On this occasion z'miros (table songs) were sung and a discourse on Torah was delivered. The wine for the meal was provided by the sandek.

On the third day following the b'ris, when the child could again be bathed, there was a little celebration in the home. It was a kind of a sequel to the b'ris, and in this the mother, too, participated.[58]

Naming the Child . . . A boy was named during the ceremony of the b'ris in the synagogue. A girl was named in the synagogue on the fourth Sabbath after birth, when the mother, rising from childbed, visited the synagogue. On this Sabbath, the father was called to the bimo to witness the reading from the scroll of the Torah. After the father had finished the benediction over the Torah, the *chazan* (cantor) named the girl in accordance with the prescribed Hebrew formula. In southern France, in some parts of Hungary, and in Belgium, it was customary to bring the baby girl into the synagogue on this occasion.[59]

In the later Middle Ages, the custom of naming children after their deceased ancestors gained in importance, and was observed with religious reverence. It was considered a prime duty toward the deceased. On the other hand, in that period, naming a child after a parent or grandparent who was still alive was prohibited, regarded as un-Jewish, and surrounded by superstitious fear.[60]

However, this notion prevailed only among the Ashk'nazim. The S'fardic Jews continued to name children after living grandparents. In rare cases, even the son and the father had the same name. Today, even among the Ashk'nazim, the custom of not naming a child after a living ancestor prevails only among Orthodox Jews. Among Reform Jews, the son often bears the father's name with the addition of junior, as among the Christians. Among the Jews of Yemen, in families where children had met untimely deaths, long life for the new-born child is supposedly safeguarded by calling him by the father's name.[61]

The tendency to give children names of non-Jewish neighbors, which began as far back as the time of the Babylonian exile, has continued through the Middle Ages to the present day. We have referred above to Jews bearing Babylonian and Greco-Roman names. Later they were called by Aramaic, Persian, and Arabic names; the Jews in Europe bearing Germanic, Romanic, and Slavic names. Hebrew names were absorbed into other languages (Baruch, the blessed, became Benedict), and foreign names were sometimes translated into Hebrew or Aramaic (Fabius-Phoebus was translated to *Shrago*, which is Aramaic and means light, and in Yiddish it became Feive or Feivel). But of all languages Jews have spoken, none has produced so many adaptations and transformations of Hebrew names as Yiddish.

Dual Names and Holekreisch (*also pronounced Holkrasch and Cholkreisch*) . . . Jews in the Orient were content with one name. They used a non-Jewish name even in religious ceremonials. Among European Jews, however, a child was given a second Hebrew name. For all religious affairs and Hebrew documents one had a special Jewish name of Biblical-Talmudic origin, which was given to the boy at the b'ris. The non-Jewish name, adopted from non-Jewish neighbors, was for civic life. This dualism in names among European Jews can be traced as far back as the thirteenth century and prevails to this day also in America. One's civic name, for instance, is Morris or Max, but he is called up to the reading of the Torah with the name Moshe or Mordecai; or his civic name is George, but he is called up to the reading of the Torah by the name Gedaliah.

Parents were not so interested in giving a daughter an additional Hebrew name, since a girl participated very little in religious ceremonies where a genuine Jewish name was more appropriate.

Among the German Jews, and partly also among the Polish Jews, a child was named twice. The Hebrew name was bestowed at the b'ris in the synagogue, and the ordinary name was given on the fourth Sabbath after birth, at the home of the parents. This giving of the civic name was marked by a strange ceremony which the German Jews called Holekreisch.

On this Sabbath there was a family festival. The mother, arising from childbed, visited the synagogue to attend the morning services. She was dressed in her best attire and was accompanied by the *rebitsin* (the wife of the rabbi) and a group of eminent women of the community. The father was called to witness the reading of the Torah. While he was standing on the bimo, a wrapper for the Torah scroll, with the name of the child embroidered on it, was handed to him. It was sent to him by the mother. He placed it on the table of the bimo near the Torah scroll, as the first gift of the child to the synagogue. The wrapper had been used as a swaddle at the b'ris, and was provided by the sandek. After the services, invited guests gathered in the home for the ceremony of Holekreisch. In Worms, in the seventeenth century, the ceremony took place after the noon meal, the beadle of the synagogue first striding through the narrow streets of the ghetto and calling loudly: "Zu der Holekreisch!"

First the guests were treated with delicacies. Thereupon they were arrayed in a circle around the cradle in which the child was lying. In the case of a boy, a Pentateuch and a praying-shawl were put in the cradle. The principal part was played by boys of pre-bar mitsvo age in the case of a boy, and by girls in the case of a girl. The children lifted the cradle containing the child three times, calling out loudly each time:

> Holekreisch, Holekreisch,
> Wie soll das Kindchen heissen?
> (What shall the little child be called?)

Each time they answered with the non-Jewish name which had been given to the child. Thus the ordinary name given to the child while lying in the cradle was called "the cradle name" (*shem ho-ariso*).

The origin of the custom of Holekreisch is very obscure. The etymology of its name had been lost as far back as the fourteenth century. The second half of the term, *Kreisch*, was easily recognized as the German word *Kreischen*, meaning to shriek or scream. Difficulty in derivation lay with the first half of the name, *Hole*, which became distorted into *Chole*. Some famous rabbis in the fourteenth and fifteenth centuries tried to trace it to the Hebrew word *Chol*, which means profane, not sacred. Consequently they interpreted Holekreisch to mean loudly calling out the every-day name of the child.

Modern Jewish scholars have discarded this far-fetched explanation of the term Holekreisch as untenable. They identify Hole with the old Teutonic goddess, Dame Holle or *Holda* who, in German mythology, played the roles of both Lilith and Venus. Accordingly, this strange ceremony of the Jews in medieval Germany might be traced to an ancient pre-Christian Teutonic custom. In pagan times, when naming a child, the Germans apparently performed the ceremony with shouting and noise to drive away Dame Lilith-Holle. This heathen practice was doomed to extinction among the Germans in Christian times, when the child was baptized in the church. Among Jews, this custom, derived from German neighbors in the early Middle Ages, was preserved throughout the ages because giving the child a secular name was not a religious observance associated with the synagogue, but merely a home celebration.

In time, Holekreisch assumed a Jewish significance when the chazan recited verses of the Bible before the cradle was lifted. In some communities the chazan, not the children lifted the cradle. In Worms, the children themselves, before lifting the cradle, recited in a chorus the verses of the Bible.

Holekreisch was not a generally accepted custom among the Jews of Germany and Poland. Regarding boys, the Holekreisch ceremony was confined to South Germany, where it still prevailed as late as the second half of the nineteenth century. In Austria, Bohemia, Moravia, and Poland, Holekreisch was not performed for boys at all, and rarely for girls.[62]

Double Names . . . The dualism in names was not the only reason for giving a child two names. In the late Middle Ages, it became customary to give a child two genuinely Jewish names. We first hear of this custom in the fifteenth century, but as late as the seventeenth century it was still rare to give two Jewish names to a child at the circumcision ceremonial. Later, the custom spread, and in modern times probably more double names than single names are given to Jewish children.[63]

The chief motive in giving children double names was the desire of the parents to do reverence to two deceased relatives, particularly when these relatives belonged to the two different lines of the families of both parents.

This desire of the father and mother to name the child after his or after her deceased relative quite often caused family quarrels, though a belief prevailed that quarreling over the name endangered the life of the child. In time, certain regulations settled the quarrels over the name. The name of the first child belonged to the father, that of the second child to the mother. Another compromise stipulated that one parent be permitted to give the child the sacred name, and the other parent the ordinary name. If this was not satisfactory, the child was called by two Jewish names derived from the two families. In this case, it was usually agreed that the name which belonged to the father came first.[64]

There was another reason for giving a child two Jewish names. If a child died, the next born to the family was named after him. But it was considered inauspicious to bear the name of a departed brother or sister unless it was preceded by another name. This added name was usually Chayim (life or the living ones, male plural) for a boy, and Chayo (the living one, female singular) for a girl.

There were also many cases in which a child was given a single name at the outset, and a second name later, as a charm against sickness. The added name was usually Chayim or Chayo. Another method of selecting a second name in the case of sickness was to open a Scroll of the Torah, and bestow the name of the first Biblical character that caught the eye.

All these reasons for giving a child a double name were needed only for one time. Once a double name appeared, the descendants perpetuated it in its entirety.

The Mutual Conversion of Male and Female Names . . . In naming children after dead relatives, great difficulties arose (and still do) when the dead relative, whose name was to be perpetuated, was a male, and the new-born child a female, or vice versa. In such cases the name had to be converted, if possible, from male into female, or from female into male. Often the change was made with little difficulty. There are certain names common to both sexes, like *Simchoh* or *Sishe*. Some names have two forms for male and female, as Chayim-Chayo, Moshe-Mashe. Others can easily be converted because of similarity in sound, like Dinah-Dan. When the situation arose, many devices were thought of to change the gender of a name. In a great many cases, ingenuity failed, making it impossible to do justice to the names of certain deceased relatives.[65]

Pidyon ha-ben . . . In the G'onic period, when new features were added to the ceremonial of the b'ris, the ceremony of pidyon ha-ben was made more impressive by the introduction of a dialogue between the father and the kohen. This is used to this day. The father presents his son to the kohen and introduces him as the first-born of the mother. The kohen asks the father whether he wishes to give him his son, or whether he prefers to redeem him for five shekels. The father replies that he chooses to redeem him and hands the money to the kohen.

PAPER AMULET to Ward Off Evil Spirits at Childbirth

PLATTER for the Redemption of the First-Born

1. SILVER FILIGREE AMULET   2. SILVER AMULET with Cover
Hebrew Union College Museum, Cincinnati

3. AMULET in the Form of a Hand in the Synagogue Eliyahu Ha-Navi

4. SILVER AMULET

The latter receives the money, and returns the child to the father who then recites the two benedictions mentioned previously: "over pidyon ha-ben" and "shehecheyonu" (see p. 29). The kohen thereupon bestows his blessing upon the father and the child.[66]

In instances where the father died or for any other reason neglected the duty of redeeming his son, it was customary, in the Middle Ages, to hang a medallion with the Hebrew letter H (which stands for five) around the son's neck. This was a reminder that it was incumbent upon him to redeem himself when he reached maturity. Later this proved to be impracticable, because, quite often, the medallion was lost. So the device of the medallion was discarded, and some relative or the community as a whole redeemed the child.[67]

In the late Middle Ages there were religious authorities who decreed that the kohanim return the money, because it was no longer possible for any kohen to prove his priestly descent from the children of Aaron.

As time passed, the valuation of the five Biblical shekels proved a complication for religious authorities. Usually the equivalent monetary unit of the country concerned was substituted for the shekel. Thus in Russia, the sum of five rubles; in Germany, five thalers, and in America, five dollars was given to the kohen. But nowadays it is taken for granted that the kohen will return the money. However, the father, according to the ritual law, has not fulfilled his duty if he has in mind that he will get the money back.

In the above mentioned "Maharil Book" we have a description of a celebration of a pidyon ha-ben in Mayence in the fifteenth century, which took place in the absence of the child. The father of the child was a resident of Erfurt. A month after the birth of his son he happened to be in Mayence. He performed the ceremony of pidyon ha-ben in the house of Maharil with his participation, and according to his instructions.

First of all, the father placed money in a silver dish and

asked Maharil if this really amounted to five shekels. Maharil told the father that according to his calculation more money must be added. The father did this, and then all guests seated themselves at the table.

All tasted a slice of bread, reciting the benediction over it. Thereupon the ceremony of pidyon ha-ben was performed by reciting the dialogue between the father and the kohen. After the ceremony was over, the kohen took a goblet of wine in his hand, blessing the "One who creates the fruit of the vine," drank a little from the cup, and passed it to the father to drink.

Then the people who had gathered in the house ate and drank and made merry.

Rising from Childbed . . . After the destruction of the Second Temple no substitute was advanced for the mother's offerings at the end of her defilement, and arising from childbed was not observed by any ritual. Only as late as the fifteenth century did the custom originate in which the mother visited the synagogue on the Sabbath after arising from childbed, and the father witnessed the reading of the Torah on the bimo on that Sabbath. This custom, mentioned previously in connection with the naming of a girl, still prevailed until recent days (see p. 43).

It is the opinion of modern scholars that this custom of the mother's visit to the synagogue after she arose from childbed sprang up in the fifteenth century under the influence of the Christian custom which decreed that the mother visit the church on this occasion. The Christian custom, however, developed under the influence of the Mosaic Law, as a substitute for the offerings in the Temple.

Thus, we have a custom that came from the Jews to the Christians, and reverted from the Christians to the Jews.[68]

iv

In Modern Times

Circumcision . . . Since the Babylonian exile, both circumcision and the Sabbath attained high significance as the two fundamentals of Judaism, representing the symbols of worship of the one and true God, and the acceptance of the Jewish faith. But while the strict observance of the Sabbath declined with the development of the new economic and cultural life of the Jews in nineteenth century Western Europe and America, the circumcision rite has remained fixed to our own day. Controversy raged over the custom among Reform Jews in Western Europe and America, but it weathered the storm. Among the Reform Jews in Western Europe, circumcision is universal. Among Reform Jews in America circumcision has been retained for the born Jew and discarded only for the proselyte.

Today even Jews who are indifferent to all religious rites practice circumcision without the traditional ceremony. At times the operation is performed by a surgeon and the blessings are recited by a rabbi.

The custom of performing the b'ris at the synagogue was still practiced here and there in the first half of the previous century. However, it was on the wane. The circumcision ceremony reverted then to its original quarters, the home. An exception was made when the b'ris came on Yom Kippur. In that case, the ceremony took place at the synagogue even as late as a generation ago.

Naming the Child . . . In later periods Jews were not always named after deceased relatives. Even in very recent times Jews occasionally named children for a special occasion occurring at the time of birth. When a boy was born on a Sabbath, or the circumcision fell on that day, he was sometimes called Shabbatai. If it occurred on a holiday, he was named Yomtov (Hebrew for holiday); if it happened on the ninth day of the Jewish month of Ov, the day of mourning over the destruction of the Temple and Jerusalem, he was called Menachem (comforter), one of the alleged names of the Messiah. Occasionally a girl born on Purim was named Esther. A boy born on Purim was called Mordecai. If born on Pesach, he was called Pesach. Sometimes a name was taken from the portion of the Pentateuch read during that week.

Among the *Chasidim*, the sect that arose in eighteenth century Poland and included nearly half of the Jewish people a century ago, it was customary to name the boy after a deceased *tsadik*, a Chasidic rabbi.

As to the date of naming a girl, it has become customary in recent times to do it on the first Sabbath after birth, or sooner; if possible on the Monday or Thursday following birth. On these two week-days a portion of the Pentateuch is read in the synagogue before the congregation, giving the father a chance to witness the reading of the Torah on the bimo, and to have the child named by the chazan or sexton.

After Biblical times, the creation of new Hebrew names had ceased. Only a limited number of the names recorded in the Bible were in vogue. In recent years, with the spread of the Zionist movement, the list of Biblical names has increased, and in the new State of Israel new Hebrew names are constantly devised; to mention only a few: Yigdal, Arnon, Raanan, Sharon, Amikam, for men; Aviva, Zahava, Sharona, Galila, for women.

There were times when Jews did not enjoy the right to choose names for their children. Some governments in Christian countries forbade them the use of non-Jewish names in every-day life, and forced them to bear Jewish names exclusively. In Prussia and Bohemia such restrictive measures were still in force in the first half of the previous century. In Russia a law to that effect was issued in the year 1893.

This medieval restriction in regard to Jewish names was revived by the Nazi Government in Germany together with the other medieval laws restricting and persecuting the Jews.

In Eastern Europe . . . We visit now a Jewish community in Eastern Europe in the last decades of the nineteenth century, at approximately the period when the mass emigration to America began.

A Jewish woman is in labor. The husband goes to call the midwife. If it is night, he does not go alone; an elderly woman usually accompanies him. Only the midwife and several elderly women are present at the delivery. The few who know that the woman is in labor keep the fact secret, for it is believed that the more the people who knew of the confinement, the harder the delivery.

As the pangs become severe, various charms are employed to ease the delivery. The woman is led around the table three times, making three complete encirclings. She may also be led over the threshold of her room three times. All chests, closets, and doors in the house are opened. All knots, ties, and buttons in the garments of the woman are undone. It is also a popular practice to chant before the woman, using the melody of the Haftoro, the first chapter of the First Book of Samuel. This chapter tells the story of Hannah, who had been barren for a long time until God hearkened to her prayer and gave her a son, and is read on the first day of Rosh Ha-shono. It is believed to be more effective for the woman in labor if the chapter is chanted by the man who was called up to witness the reading of this Haftoro on the preceding Rosh Ha-shono.

If these customs and charms are without effect, many more are practiced. The key of the synagogue is fetched and placed in the hand of the woman. She may be girded with the band of a Torah Scroll brought from the synagogue. Sometimes female relatives run to the synagogue where they put their heads in the Holy Ark where the Scrolls of the Torah are kept, wailing and praying for the suffering woman. Women relatives hurry to the cemetery to pray at the graves of pious dead of the family that they intercede in heaven on behalf of the expectant mother and her innocent child. Sometimes these women relatives "measure the field," which means spanning the ground of the cemetery with a ball of thread which they unroll. This thread is then taken to the candle-maker, who uses it for candle wicks which are donated to the synagogue. The shofor may be blown or the magic practice of *kaporos* performed in the room where the woman is in labor. If it is available, she is given a piece left over from the *afikomon* (the half matso hidden at the start of the seder on Pesach night and eaten at the end of it), or the blossom-end (pitum) of the esrog. She may chew, but not swallow this.

Mazol Tov! (good luck). The woman is over it! There is great joy over the increase in the family, particularly when it is a boy. No one wants a small family. "May God guard against having one child and one undershirt" is a proverb of the people; another, "One more child—one more loaf of bread" (i.e., the expense will be increased only by the cost of another loaf).

The babe is bathed soon after birth. The father and other relatives throw coins in the tub, as an omen that the child will be rich. This money, however, goes to the midwife. The tub must be an old one, usually a borrowed one in which children were bathed who grew up strong and healthy. The baby's first swaddles are made of an old shirt. It is not considered lucky for an expectant mother to prepare anything for the baby in advance. Some use swaddles made from old shirts for a whole year, as a charm to prevent the child from developing into a tearer of clothes.

If it is night, the midwife must not return home alone. The father of the child accompanies her, taking someone with him so that he will not have to return alone. Not only the mother and the child, but also the father and the midwife are guarded at night against evil spirits.

Let us look into the home on the next day.

The dwelling usually consists of two rooms. In the innermost corner of the back room the mother lies in a tent-bed, which resembles a canopy. Four poles at the corners support a spread over the top. Curtains are hung around the bed to isolate the mother and child as protection against evil spirits.

The mother, with a pale and contented face, lies dressed in a white bed-jacket and cap. At her feet lies the baby, swathed so tightly that it looks like a little living mummy.

The caretaker, a Jewish woman, hired to care for the mother during the weeks of her confinement and to do all the work in the house, moves about the room, pampering the woman in confinement. She continually gives her preserves, egg-nogs, and many other delicacies, but most of all, soup and meat of chicken. The bones of the chickens are put in a sieve, and kept. For it is believed that until the sieve is filled with bones, the woman in childbed has not recuperated.

The mother and the child are guarded against evil spirits by various charms and amulets. On the wall above the head of the bed, under the head pillow, over the door and windows, and over all the walls, printed amulets are pasted or hung on every available vacant space. The first and most important line of the amulet reads: "Adam and Eve barring Lilith." Written on it are the names of the three angels, Sannui, Sansannui and Samangaluf, whom Lilith dreads. There is also a legend on the amulet that tells how the prophet Elijah once met Lilith and her clique, how she told him that she was going to kill a woman in childbed and her new-born child. Elijah, wishing to transform her into stone on the spot, desisted only after she revealed to him the means by which she and her clique could be kept away from a woman in childbed: by hanging a sheet of paper on the wall on which all her seventeen names are enumerated. These various names of Lilith follow on the amulet, and at the very end there is the Song of Ascents, Psalm 121. These amulets are thus called *Shir Hamaalos* (Song of Ascents).

If the baby is a boy, a m'lamed (teacher in a primary Jewish school) with a quorum of ten pupils comes to the mother every evening to recite the Sh'ma (the declaration of the unity of God). This is a safeguard to keep demons from the room. After the recitation is over, the pupils receive raisins, nuts, apples, and cake. The m'lamed receives some money for his trouble when the week is over.

The first celebration of the birth of a boy takes place on the following Friday night. It is called *ben zochor* (see p. 42). At the synagogue the sexton stands on the bimo and, in behalf of the new father, invites the people to the ben zochor. After the Friday night meal, relatives and friends gather in the house to offer Mazol Tov (good luck) to the parents. The guests are treated to cider, beer, apples, cooked beans and peas. Among the visitors is also the chazan, who leads in the singing of z'miros.

There is another celebration on the next day, after the morning services. Relatives and friends again gather in the home of the parents to visit the new-born boy. B'rocho (benediction) is recited over wine and brandy, and various delicacies are served. This celebration is called *sholom zochor* (peace of the male child, an allusion to the Talmud which says that with the birth of a male child peace comes to the world [69]).

Watch Night is a festive occasion. Many candles glow throughout the house, and a great number of people participate in the ceremony. After a festive meal, prayers are recited and the Torah studied until after midnight. Among the guests is the mohel who leaves his circumcision knife under the mother's pillow over night. Before departing, all recite aloud *K'rias Sh'ma* near the mother.

The name for the child has already been decided upon, usually not one name, but two. The father has many deceased relatives in his family, and the mother has many in hers, and they desire to name their child for all of the deceased. A compromise is reached in most cases. The child is given two names, one for a deceased relative in the father's family and one for the mother's family.

The b'ris takes place in the parents' home immediately after the morning services. Preparations for bathing the child begin very early in the morning. Many elderly women take part in bathing the child. It is regarded as a *mitsvo*, a religious act, to help prepare the child for the b'ris. Every one of the women pours two handfuls of water on the child and everyone leaves a silver coin in the tub for the midwife.

At the synagogue, the people are still reciting the morning prayers, chanting in a special way certain parts of the prayers, and omitting certain prayers that are left out on semi-festival days. There is a general atmosphere of semi-festivity.

Between nine and ten the services are over, and people gather at the house. In the front room, where the b'ris takes place, two huge candles burn in silver or brass candlesticks. Numerous smaller candles light the room. On a special table are laid the ceremonial necessities for circumcision: a bottle of wine, a goblet, a plate of sand, a box of old, pulverized wood. Two large chairs are placed nearby, one for the sandek and another, covered with a white sheet, for the prophet Elijah. The honor of sandek is usually awarded to the rabbi of the town.

When all have gathered, the ceremonial begins. The mohel issues the order for wrapping the child, and this is done according to a fixed method, on the mother's bed. With a little cap on his head, the boy lies covered on a pillow, while the mother looks on with concern.

The midwife takes the boy from the mother and hands him to the oldest woman standing near the bed. She fondles and rocks him for a minute, then gives him over to the next woman, who does the same and then presents him to another woman.

The boy thus passes from hand to hand until he ultimately reaches the *kvaterin* (godmother) who carries him as far as the threshold of the front room. As soon as the child appears, the guests call out loudly: Boruch habo! (Blessed be the one who comes!) The *kvater* (godfather) takes the child and hands him to the mohel, who recites certain verses from the Bible. He or a member of the family who is honored thereby then places the child on Elijah's chair, announcing "This is the chair of the prophet Elijah, be he remembered for good!" and recites a prayer directed partly to God, partly to Elijah.

Now the actual circumcision begins. All people in the audience stand except the sandek. Wrapped in a large prayer-shawl, he sits in an armchair, with a footstool under his feet. The mohel stands near Elijah's chair with the father close behind him. The mohel or another who is assigned the honor of standing near the sandek (Yad ha-Sandek) then takes the child from Elijah's chair and places him on the knees of the sandek. The mohel then recites the benediction that precedes the operation. After the operation, the father recites the benediction over the "bringing the child into the covenant of Abraham, our father." The audience responds, "As he has entered into the covenant, so may he enter into the study of the Torah, into the chupo and into good deeds."

During a long benediction over a goblet of wine, the mohel names the child and moistens the boy's lips with the wine.

Meanwhile, men and women in the room hold and rock the whimpering child on the pillow. The child becomes a little calmer when the mohel wets his lips with the wine.

When the benedictions and prayers are over, all who have attended the ceremony wash their hands and seat themselves at the table to eat. Between courses, the chazan, in a sonorous voice, addresses greetings to the mother and the child on behalf of the guests, particularly the relatives. It is the conventional greeting in religious ceremonies, called after its first two words, *Mi Sheberach* (The one who blessed, etc.). Time after time the chazan repeats the Mi Sheberach. For each Mi Sheberach the sexton helps the chazan by whispering the name of one of the relatives in his ear. As a matter of course, each one gives the chazan a coin.

After the meal grace is recited, interspersed with special liturgical poems for a b'ris.

Then the sexton announces: "The *Ba-al-B'ris* (master of the circumcision, the father) begs the guests not to be displeased if the meal was not satisfactory. With God's will, at the bar mitsvo (or at the wedding) it will be greatly improved."

As the guests leave, they bless the father—and from afar, the mother—with the wish that they may bring up the child "to the study of the Torah, to the chupo and to good deeds."

After the b'ris, when the child has been circumcised and carries in his flesh the sign of the Holy Covenant, the amulets are removed from the room of childbed, for there is no longer any fear of Lilith and her demons.

When a girl is born, there are no ceremonials or feasts. On the first Sabbath the father is called to the bimo in the synagogue to witness the reading of a portion of the Pentateuch, and to pronounce the benediction over it. Following this, the chazan, or the sexton, pronounces the Mi Sheberach on behalf of the father, and names the girl.

The same afternoon, female relatives, neighbors, and friends visit the mother to wish her "Mazol Tov." They are served with cake, wine, and preserves. This is called "gehn oif kichlech" (to go and partake of cakes).

In the case of a girl, it is believed that there is no limit to the time during which Lilith and the evil spirits threaten mother and child. Accordingly, the amulets remain on the walls much longer, usually for about four weeks, until the mother has arisen from childbed.

On the Sabbath on which the mother arises from childbed, there is festivity in the house, whether the child is a boy or a girl. Women relatives and the midwife escort the mother from the home to the synagogue. Before leaving, the women are served with cake, pastries, and preserves. In the women's section of the synagogue all offer "Mazol Tov" to the mother, and in the men's section, the father is called to the bimo to witness the reading of a portion of the Torah. The chazan or the sexton, at the father's behest, pronounces the Mi Sheberach, blessing mother and child.

Among the Oriental Jews . . . The Karaites, the Jewish sect which came into existence in the eighth century, and gained new adherents through the eighth and ninth centuries, adopted the custom of performing the b'ris at the synagogue. As to the operation of circumcision it is forbidden among the Karaites to perform it with any type of knife, but to use instead a pair of scissors. They took literally the expression "knives of flint" (knives in plural) found in the Book of Joshua (chap. 5:2).

The Karaites abolished the ceremony of pidyon ha-ben altogether. They regarded it as one of the rewards accorded to the kohanim for their service in the Temple. Hence, after the destruction of the Temple, the kohanim were not entitled to it.

In Palestine, among S'fardim as well as among Ashk'nazim, circumcision, up to the present day, is performed in the synagogue or in the House of Study (Beis ha-Midrosh). Among the S'fardim in Palestine it is customary to distribute fragrant herbs among the assembled people, at the close of the circumcision ceremony. When the guests leave the synagogue with the child, the sexton sprinkles them with rose-water from a vessel pierced with little holes, made especially for this occasion.

The S'fardim also make the eve of the b'ris a special occasion. Unlike the Ashk'nazim, the S'fardim do not call it by the magic name "Watch Night," but by a genuinely Jewish name, *Midrash* (study). Guests are invited, and the following communal functionaries gather in the house: the chacham (rabbi), the Hebrew teacher, the cantor, and the sexton of the synagogue. The close relatives of the sandek bring an oil-burning menorah to the house where the woman is in childbed. The menorah is wreathed with flowers and fragrant leaves. Beating a drum, and singing joyously, the guests carry the menorah through the streets of the town until they reach the house. When all are present, the father calls on the chacham to deliver a discourse on the portion of the Pentateuch read that week. After the lecture, the chazan recites Kaddish and the guests are served with a preserve made of poppy-seed and honey, and small cups of coffee. The chacham receives money gifts from the guests at their departure.

Among the S'fardic Jews in the Orient, a girl is named only in the home. The parents invite guests to a meal and announce the name of their daughter.

The Jews of the Caucasus still perform the b'ris in the synagogue, but they do not observe the eve of the b'ris. This proves that in the early Middle Ages, when the ancestors of the present day Caucasian Jews adopted the Jewish faith, Watch Night was not yet observed.

The Oriental Jews of Asia and North Africa generally perform the circumcision rite in the synagogue. This is done in the morning, but the joyous feast is not held until evening. In the meantime, in the home of the parents, the women dance and sing to the accompaniment of musical instruments.[70]

In America . . . Many Jewish customs and folkways, inseparable from Jewish life through long epochs of Jewish history, assumed new forms, disintegrated, or were completely discarded by the Jews in America. The observances and practices in connection with the birth of a child which, for the most part, had been an integral part of the home atmosphere, fell prey to the new environment. Only in rare cases is a woman now confined in her home. As a rule she has the care of a modern physician and goes to a maternity hospital, provided with the latest medical equipment. Under such conditions, there is no opportunity to apply magic means to ease the delivery of the child, nor is the maternity hospital a fitting place to employ Lilith amulets to insure safety after the babe is born. The terror of Lilith, which withstood the vicissitudes of so many ages, has completely vanished in modern American life.

The observance of the Watch Night has also been discarded because the mother and the babe are no longer in the home. Here and there the ben zochor is still observed on the first Friday night, but only in rare cases.

The b'ris now performed in a special room in the hospital, reserved for the ceremony, lacks the home atmosphere of previous times. On the other hand, the pidyon ha-ben, observed in the home where both mother and child are, is quite a popular celebration, with all the atmosphere of a joyous family party. At the observance of this ceremony, the kohen receives five dollars which, as a rule, he either returns to the father or donates to charity.

Among Orthodox Jews in this country, if the child is a girl, it is still customary for the father to be called to the reading of the Torah on the first Sabbath when the chazan or sexton names the child.

The observance of arising from childbed has been discarded in America.

⬧

Beliefs Concerning Birth

Belief in Prenatal Existence . . . In Talmudic times (the first centuries of the Common Era) the belief was current among Jews that man's soul was independent of his body, existing eternally in the past and in the future. Only for a short, limited time is it placed in the body of a certain human being. All the souls of the world preexist in heaven in a kind of a spiritual reservoir, and at first have no desire to enter the human bodies on earth. They do it only by force. God decrees that a certain soul shall enter a certain body, and God also decrees the moment when the soul shall leave the body.

In this realm of belief, the vanishing mortal body plays an insignificant role in comparison with the pure and eternal soul. Accordingly, man attains the highest stage in his spiritual life not after the full growth of his body, but before he is projected in the form of a human being into the light of the world. In his prenatal existence in his mother's womb, a light burns over his head, and he sees from one end of the world to the other. He sees there much more than a human being is capable of seeing during the course of his entire life.

According to this belief, a special angel is appointed to supervise the souls. He receives an order from God to place a certain soul in a certain child at the time of its conception. At first the pure soul recoils from entering the foul body. It yields only to the force of God's decree. The angel brings the soul into the womb and joins it with the embryo. He places it under the good care of two angels who place the burning light over his head.

The next morning the supervising angel pays a visit to the

soul and takes it for a promenade through Paradise. There he shows it the saints in their full glory seated on golden thrones with crowns on their heads. He asks it: "Do you know to whom that soul belonged?" The soul answers, "No," and the angel says, "The saint whom you see in such glory was also created, like you, in his mother's womb. This is true of all the other saints whom you see here. They were pious and kept the commandments of God. If you will do the same, after your death you will share in this great glory. Otherwise, after death, you will descend to a place which I shall show you later."

In the evening, the angel takes the soul for a visit into the Gehenna to show it how the angels of destruction torment the wicked souls and flog them with whips of fire. The wicked ones groan and cry, "Ah!" and "Woe!" but no one sympathizes with them. The angel says to the soul: "Do you know that these were created like you, in their mothers' wombs, and came forth afterwards into the world? But they did not observe God's commandments. Therefore this terrible shame has come upon them. And now you should know, my son, that you are also destined to come forth into the world and to die afterward. Be not wicked, therefore, but righteous and you will have a share in the world to come."

Thus the prenatal man goes about under the guardianship and tutelage of the angel. In the morning he visits Paradise, in the evening, Gehenna, and in between, the angel shows him every nook and corner that his foot will tread, every place where he will dwell, the place where he will die, and the place where he will be buried. In the evening he brings him back into his mother's womb.

When the moment arrives for the child to leave the mother's womb, that same angel comes and tells him: "The time has arrived for you to emerge." But the child is not willing to go out into the world. He does it under compulsion, and starts to cry. In the moment of coming forth from the womb, the angel strikes the child on the upper lip just under the nose, making a dent on that spot. Thereby the angel extinguishes the light and causes the child to forget all that he has seen and learned in the womb of his mother. That which the child learns thereafter is merely a recollection of the knowledge acquired during his prenatal life.[71]

Some scholars think that this Jewish belief is an echo of the Platonic idea of man's soul knowing everything before birth. Others assume that both the Jewish belief and the Platonic ideas of the preexistence of man's soul are derived from a common source—the mythology of ancient Egypt. Another group thinks that the common source of the belief in the preexistence of the soul is to be found in the religion of the ancient Persians.[72]

Magic Means to Ease Delivery . . . Primitive man attributed every illness, every physical and mental disorder, to witchcraft and demons. He did not ascribe the difficulty of the delivery of a child to anatomic factors, but to the spell of sorcerers and the working of evil spirits. When a woman in labor suffered unbearable anguish and her life was imperiled, the explanation given was that she was bewitched by sorcerers or beset by demons.[73] Since very ancient times, Jews as well as other peoples employed various means and charms to ease the delivery.

There were three kinds of safeguards and charms which primitive people employed in the grave moments when it was considered imperative to combat the evil spirits. First, precautions were taken to shut them out, so that they could not harm anyone. Second, there were numerous means by which the demons could be frightened and put to flight. Third, the devils could be bribed by certain gifts, or be confounded by certain devices and tricks which induced them to leave voluntarily.

It is impossible to enumerate the huge variety of these practices, which were popularly supposed to have a magic effect. Nor do they lend themselves to a historical treatment which would follow their evolution from age to age. A great many of them are confined only to one land or to one period of Jewish history, and we know of them merely from books. Many of them were in vogue in various lands where Jews lived, and a considerable number of them persist, even to our own day.

One of the most popular means employed to keep the devils away was the circle, which is still known as the "magic ring." People believed the devil feared a closed circle, for if he entered a ring, he became entirely helpless. A magician, when he wanted to prove his power over the evil spirits, first drew a circle about himself and sat in it. Inside the magic ring, he was as safe as in a fortress, because the spirits could not reach him, and he could do with them as he pleased. This explains the custom of leading the woman in labor around a table. It also explains the practice of kaporos, swinging a hen in circles around the head of the woman. There were two additional motives for this latter practice. The hen was sacrificed in expiation of the sins of the suffering woman. Besides, a rooster or a hen was believed not only to placate the evil spirits, but also to frighten them. According to the popular belief, evil spirits shunned the light, and the rooster frightened them away when he crowed in the morning to announce the first light of day. As the rooster had magic power, this was also, as a matter of course, transferred to the hen.

In like manner, and in spite of the later interpretations attached to the custom, the shofor, the ritual horn of the ram, was blown in the room of the woman in labor. The primitive idea of frightening away demons with a loud noise gave the origin to this custom.[74]

Among a great number of peoples in olden times, the threshold, like the door-posts, was a sacred spot in the home. Many curious beliefs centered around it, both in ancient and in modern times. No wonder, therefore, that the woman in labor was led to and fro over the threshold as a means to ease delivery.[75]

Sympathetic or imitative magic has played a great role in these practices, for in the primitive belief every activity called forth its counterpart. Everything that opened was a magic means of easing the delivery of the child. We meet this wide-spread practice among the Jews of Eastern Europe as well as among the Jews of the Caucasus. In Lithuania, one who entered a house and found the chests and drawers open, would usually ask jestingly, "Is anyone in labor here?" [76]

A great many of these ancient magic practices persisted throughout the ages. They adapted themselves more or less to the higher religious beliefs, and then new means and practices of a different aspect associated with the higher spheres of religion evolved in the course of time, and mingled with them. Certain psalms were recited, and the Holy Ark with its Scroll of the Torah was drawn into this domain. A custom arose at which the Scroll itself was brought to the woman in labor. This practice was frowned upon by the rabbis, and did not become popular. Usually, only the band which girded the Scroll was brought to the woman and was bound about her. It was also customary to spin a long thread from the Holy Ark in the synagogue to the bed of the woman. In like manner, a mysterious power was believed to reside in the key of the synagogue, because the key was an opener, and suggested the opening of the womb and the easing of the delivery. The key also opened a sacred place, the synagogue, and that, the people believed, enhanced its efficacy. In accordance with the Talmud, there is a "key of birth" which is held in the hands of the Almighty Himself.

The custom of chanting aloud passages from the Holy Scriptures about a barren woman whom God remembered and gave a child was also colored with religious meaning.

Also associated with the realm of religion was the custom of giving the woman a piece left over from the afikomon and the blossom-end of the esrog to chew. In this, as in the above mentioned practices connected with the synagogue, it is obviously the direct touch with things essential in religious ceremonials which was expected to arouse divine assistance.

In Terror of Lilith . . . In the folk-belief, the woman in childbed and her new-born babe, even more than the woman in labor, were exposed to the dangers of witchcraft and evil spirits. Primitive man saw countless young mothers die of fever in childbed. He heard babies crying bitterly without any obvious reason, saw them wasting away and dying an untimely death. People stood helpless against this vast destruction of human life. They explained it according to their outlook on the world and on nature, regarding it as the work of sorcerers and demons. They imagined hosts of evil spirits prowling around in their effort to destroy the mother and the child.

Primitive man personified all forces of nature, the good as well as the evil, and he personified this destructive force, about which he created a horrible myth. In his vivid imagination he saw a particular female demon whose function was to steal, to bewitch, to change into freaks, and to kill the child as well as the mother in childbed. This most dangerous and most popular of all demons was called Lilith. She is known among many nations under various names. She is known among Jews under different names, but for the most part by the name of Lilith. For several thousand years mankind has lived in fear of Lilith, and the fear has not yet vanished. Here is the best example of a primitive superstition persisting in our own days.

Origin of the Lilith Myth . . . The Lilith myth is not of Jewish origin, but originated in ancient Babylonia. Long before Lilith entered the realm of Jewish folk-belief, she played a prominent role among the demons of Babylonia and Assyria. Excavations in southern Mesopotamia prove that the Jews of Mesopotamia, the homeland of the Lilith myth, were devout worshippers of Lilith as late as the Middle Ages.

The religion of ancient Babylonia developed into triads of gods, and Lilith also became one of a triad of demons. In the popular beliefs of the ancient Babylonians and Assyrians is found a male demon named Lilu, a female demon Lilith, and also a maid Ardat Lili. However, it was one Lilith, one female demon who, in the frightened imagination of the people, personified horror for all times.

It is certain that the belief in Lilith came down to the Jews from the ancient Babylonians. We are not certain about the original etymology of the name Lilith. Many great authorities on this subject assert that Lilith had originally no relation to the word *layil*, night. Originally, it is maintained by these scholars, Lilith signified the demon of the storm, and only later, through a false etymology of the people (who derived it from layil), the name was interpreted and conceived as meaning the demon of the night. It would appear that the Lilith myth was a fusion of three different motifs. At first Lilith personified the storm, the hot wind that blows over the desert and brings heat and drought in its wake. As such, it also personified the internal heat of the body, a fever that kills women in childbed. Subsequently, when Lilith was thought of as the night demon, she became, in addition, the personification of the nightmare, the ghostly paramour of unmarried men, who aroused their passions without gratifying them. As a demon who killed women in childbed and exasperated men in their sleep, Lilith, as a matter of course, could not help hating children. It was only natural then to identify her with *Labartu*, a female demon of the Babylonians and Assyrians, whose special function was the killing of children.

The Lilith myth, which passed through these three phases before it reached the folk-belief of the Jews, had become a threefold monster in the morbid phantasy of the people: the personification of the cause of fever; the nightmare; and the untimely death of children.

Among the ancient nations of the East, Lilith played the role counterpart to *Ishtar* (called by the ancient Canaanites *Astarte*, in the Bible: *Ashtoroth* and *Ashtoreth*). The ancient Babylonians and many other peoples of the ancient East originally had two goddesses in their mythology, who counteracted one another—one good and benign, the other evil and malicious. The good goddess was Ishtar and the malicious and destructive goddess was Lilith, who in time was degraded to a demon. Ishtar was the goddess of love and fertility and, in the belief of the people, she protected and assisted women in labor and childbed. Lilith, on the contrary, sought to kill the mothers and their new-born babes. In the mythology of the Ancient East, Ishtar, the Great Mother, the Queen of Heaven, represented the good woman, who is a good wife and a good mother. Lilith typified the neurotic woman, without a husband, who detests men and hates the offspring of human wedlock.[77]

It may be worth while to remark that ultimately Ishtar suffered the same fate as Lilith—degradation to a demon. After she was identified for thousands of years with the Venus Planet and worshipped as the Great Mother and Great Goddess, she was, in the Christian belief of the Middle Ages, finally degraded to the status of a demon and witch who dwelt in the hill of Venus and seduced pious knights. The well-known Teutonic legend of Tannhäuser tells this tale.

Lilith in Jewish Folklore . . . In the Bible, Lilith is mentioned only once (Isaiah 34). She is described as a demon who, like all the evil spirits, is found in desolate and unclean places. There she dwells in the company of the *S'irim*, the satyrs, demons in the shape of goats. *Azazel*, to whom the scapegoat, loaded with all the sins of the children of Israel, was sent on the Day of Atonement, obviously belonged to this company. We do not know the Jewish concept of Lilith in Biblical times.

We hear a great deal more about Lilith in post-Biblical times. In Talmudic literature she is represented in the likeness of a woman with long hair and wings. This is quite understandable, for as the nightmare, the ghostly paramour of men, she should have the likeness of a pretty woman, and as a demon of the wind she was furnished with wings. When a man slept alone in a house, he was in danger of being seized by Lilith. According to the Jewish folk-belief in those times a woman could even bear a child in the likeness of Lilith. The Jews in Babylonia lived under Persian domination, and the

Lilith myth took on some additional traits of the Persian religion. Lilith was thought of as the mother of *Ahriman*, who, in the religion of the ancient Persians, was the chief of the devils, the king of evil, darkness, and death. Lilith was thus regarded as the queen of the female demons, just as *Ashmedai* was regarded as the king of the male demons.[78]

In medieval Jewish lore the Lilith myth spread far and wide. It was interwoven with the Biblical tale of Adam and Eve, and Lilith became, in the fantastic folklore, the demoniac first wife of Adam. She was called the First Eve, a name which she still retains on the amulets of the present day.

The Lilith myth fitted in very nicely with the story of Adam and Eve. Since Lilith sought to kill Eve's daughters and their human offspring, it was proper to explain that her desire was motivated by jealousy and rivalry. Lilith hated the daughters of Eve because she hated Eve, and she hated Eve as the woman who superseded her as Adam's wife. Besides, from the point of view of Biblical interpretation, the Lilith myth was a good supplement to the story of Adam and Eve. How God created the first man and wife is told twice and in two divergent versions in the Bible. The first chapter of Genesis tells how God created a male and a female simultaneously. In the second chapter God first created man, and later created woman from man's rib. Therefore, this could be interpreted to mean that God created a wife for Adam twice, because the first one was a failure. It substantiated and amplified the exclamation of Adam, in the second chapter of Genesis, that here at last was bone of his bones and flesh of his flesh. This passage invited the amplification that Adam formerly had a first Eve who was not a good mate.

This motif of rivalry and hatred between Lilith and Eve was elaborated in various versions. The most popular of them is the following:

When God created Adam, he also created a wife for him out of the earth. This first woman was Lilith. However, they were not a happy couple. Because they were both of the same origin, she considered herself his equal and refused to obey him. They quarreled with one another until in a moment of rage, with the help of the ineffable name of God which she uttered, she flew away from Adam and vanished into the air. Adam complained to God that the wife He had given him had deserted him. God sent three angels to bring her back. The angels found her in the Red Sea, in the spot where the Jews later passed in the Exodus from Egypt. They tried to make her return by holding over her the dire threat that if she would not return, hundreds of her demon children would die daily. Lilith preferred this punishment to returning to Adam. They then threatened to drown her in the sea. She implored them to spare her, and in return she granted them a concession. She told them that she was made for the purpose of injuring babies, boys until the eighth day, and girls until the twentieth day, and she swore that wherever she saw the names of these three angels written in a home, she would keep away from the child and the mother, and would not injure them.

The story ends with the three angels releasing Lilith after she had taken that oath. For this reason the names of these three angels are written on amulets and hung upon the walls of the room where a woman lies in childbed.

According to another version, the prophet Elijah encountered Lilith, and she swore that she would keep away from every woman in childbed if a sheet of paper was hung on the wall with all her seventeen names written on it (see p. 55).

In Mohammedan lore, Lilith bears the name Karina, and the role of the three angels or the prophet Elijah who struggle with her is played by King Solomon. In the European-Christian legends, the role of the benevolent actor is played by the Holy Mother Mary, by the archangel Michael, or by a certain saint whose name is similar to the names of the three dreaded angels in Jewish legends.

The Lilith myth grew and spread in Jewish lore throughout the ages, assuming its greatest proportion in the later Middle Ages. Its growth was partly an amplification of older traditions and beliefs, and partly due to the general spread of the belief in demons and witchcraft in Europe at that time. Superstitious beliefs pass from generation to generation, from race to race, and from land to land. In the Jewish popular belief of those times, Lilith, the Queen of Sheba, Venus in her degraded state as a seductive witch, and the German goddess Dame Holle, in her dark and dreaded aspect as an ugly old woman, were all fused together.[79]

Charms against Lilith . . . The fear of Lilith and her demoniac troop was very old among Jews, but the application of inscribed amulets as a protection against Lilith appeared later. In general, written amulets represent a later development than oral conjurations. First the words were uttered, and later these words were written down. First the conjuror orally narrated the story of the encounter between the three dreaded angels and Lilith, or between the prophet Elijah and Lilith, and it was believed that this spoken account drove away the evil spirits. Later, the spoken recital was put into writing, and became an amulet. People evidently considered the written amulet just as effective as the spoken words of the conjuror.[80] Authoritative knowledge of the use of written amulets against Lilith goes back only as far as post-Talmudic times. But we may assume that oral conjurations against demoniac powers in the room of a woman in childbed were employed in much earlier times.

The amulet was not the only safeguard employed against Lilith. There were many more, e.g., the magic circle and the shutting of the windows which have already been described. Two more of these safeguards need special explanations. On the eve of the b'ris, the mohel's knife was placed under the mother's head-pillow. Among many peoples, iron was a popular and wide-spread safeguard against demons. The belief in demons stems from the Stone Age, which explains why the new metal was hateful to them, and kept them out. At the celebration of the ben zochor on the Friday night preceding the b'ris and also on the Watch Night, cooked beans and peas were eaten. Legumes were considered by Jews as well as by many other peoples as a sort of an offering to appease the demons.[81]

The Magic Power of Names . . . In the primitive stage of culture, names played an important part in the magic beliefs and practices of the people. A name, according to popular belief, could be used as a charm. It could be used as a remedy in the case of sickness or as a safeguard to ward off illness and death.

To begin with, it was believed that there was a charm in keeping the name secret for some time. It was a popular practice, even in recent times, not to disclose the name of a boy before the b'ris. As we have previously pointed out, people believed that the days preceding the b'ris were critical, because the danger of Lilith and her clique of evil spirits hovered over the child. If they could not identify the babe by name, they might be defeated in their purpose.

It was not unusual to permanently conceal the name of the child, and to call it instead by a special charm-name. This was a popular practice in families which had lost children by untimely death. The parents, worried lest the same fate overtake the new-born child, gave it a charm-name to ward off the Angel of Death. Calling a child by a special name was believed to confound and delude the *ministering* angels as well as the evil spirits.

The simplest way was not to name the child at all or to keep the name completely secret. But it was not easy to rear a child without calling him by a given name. A scheme was devised whereby the true name given to the child was not pronounced by anyone. Instead, the child was called by a substitute name throughout his life. There was a certain trick even in regard to the substitute name. The child was nicknamed *Alter,* or if a girl, the feminine, *Alte* (old one). A boy was called *Zeidl*

(Little Grandfather) and a girl *Babke* or *Babtche* (Little Grandmother). The Angel of Death, receiving a decree in heaven to take the life of a child with this or that (real) name, would be entirely confused and unable to identify his would-be victim.

However, there are some genuine names which served as a safeguard to insure the life of a child. One is the name mentioned heretofore, Chayim or Chayo, a name which means life. Another safeguard against death is the name *Ben-Zion.* It is the only Hebrew name that begins with *ben* as a separate word. (In *Benjamin*, ben is merely a syllable, not a word.) Ben means son in Hebrew. The Angel of Death, who supposedly takes names literally, is thus confused in identifying the child. To him Ben-Zion was not the name of the child, merely implying that the name of the father was *Zion*, and the child was the son of Zion.

In case it might have been the sin of the mother that caused her children's death, another stratagem was devised which could be used only if there was a grandmother in the house. The grandmother was called "Mama" and the mother by her given name. This, however, did not take into consideration the father. Perhaps the sins of both parents caused the death of their children. In that case, more drastic measures were taken. A mock sale was staged in which the child was formally sold to other parents. Sometimes the child was not sold but given away as a gift. Of course, the new parents who were selected were chosen because they had reared many healthy children.

All these practices were safeguards to forestall sickness and death. Sometimes a name was used as a therapeutic measure. In the case of a severe illness a new special name was added to the old one. This custom has previously been described (p. 48). A more drastic measure was to discard the old name altogether. This practice of changing the name of a person as a charm against demoniac powers was wide-spread among all peoples, and in the Middle Ages it became popular among Jews also.

The instances in the Bible where a person's name is changed have no relation to the belief in the magic power of names. This kind of change is based on the ancient belief in the identity of the person with the name he bears. When a change took place in the fortune of an individual, and his name no longer suited his new station, the name had to be changed.

In Talmudic times a custom prevailed among Palestinian Jews for husband and wife to exchange their names at night, he calling himself by her name and she by his name. It was considered an effective protection against demons. The rabbis of the Talmud forbade it as a heathenish practice. On the other hand, the belief gained favor among Jews in those times that a change in name, like a change in place, rendered void the evil decree issued in heaven against a person.[82] However, it is not recorded in the Talmud that this theoretical belief was ever put into practice in a case of sickness. In post-Talmudic times, this practice of changing the name as a remedy in the case of a sickness became popular among the Franco-German Jews and, in time, became a universal Jewish custom. Even a special ritual was evolved for effecting the change of the name.

A ritual quorum of ten assembled in the synagogue or the house of study. The Holy Ark, containing the Scrolls of the Torah, was opened. One man, who sometimes held in his hand a Scroll of the Torah, recited a special prayer in which he emphatically notified the heavenly authorities of the change in the name of the person who was ill and requested them to no longer identify the person bearing the old name with the person bearing the new name. Everyone present gave something to charity in behalf of the sick person because "charity delivereth from death."[83]

PART TWO

The Child Grows

vi

Beginnings

In the Jewish family every stage in the child's life was an important event and observed as a joyous occasion with symbolic rites and religious ceremonies.

"Cradling" the Child . . . After the b'ris, the first event in the life of the child was the occasion on which he was placed in the cradle for the first time. Mention of the cradle is first made in Talmudic sources (see p. 21). We hear more about it in the Middle Ages.

In that period, the first "cradling" of a boy after the b'ris was a religious ceremony attended by a ritual quorum of ten men. The little boy was placed in the cradle, dressed in the fine clothes he wore on the day of his circumcision. Then a copy of the Five Books of Moses was placed on him, and the people standing about said: "May this child fulfill what is written in this book!" In addition, the quill of a goose, used as a pen, and an ink bottle, were placed in his hand as an omen that when he grew up he should be worthy of being a scribe and writing a Scroll of God's Torah with his own hand. The people who were gathered in the house then recited certain excerpts from the Bible, beginning with "So God give thee of the dew of heaven, and of the fat places of the earth, and plenty of corn and wine" (Gen. 27:28).[84]

This attractive observance has been discontinued, and today there remain only some magic practices connected with "cradling" a child. In Eastern Europe, it was customary to throw dainties—sugar, raisins, cake, and also coins into the cradle before the child was placed in it, as omens for a sweet and abundant life. This practice is still observed in America. Sometimes a living creature was rocked in the cradle before the child was placed in it. In the case of a boy, a little rooster was rocked; in the case of a girl, a little hen. Occasionally, a cat or a dog also served this purpose. It was believed that if the cradle held any mishap for the child, the danger would be transferred to the animal or fowl.

Jews as well as other peoples believed that a cradle should not be rocked when empty.[85]

Lullabies . . . No Jewish cradle songs of ancient or medieval times have been preserved, nor are they quoted in the Jewish literature of those periods. In the Middle Ages, some religious authorities disapproved of lulling a Jewish child to sleep with non-Jewish lullabies.[86] But this does not prove that genuinely Jewish lullabies did not exist in those times. Recently, many of them, popular in Eastern Europe, have been published in Yiddish. The motif of the most popular Jewish cradle song was Jewish piety and the love of the Torah. The song told of a little white kid who stood behind the cradle. The little goat went out to trade in raisins and almonds, but the child would go forth to learn Torah and would be a faithful and pious Jew throughout his entire life.[87]

Weighing the Child . . . In Talmudic times there was a very interesting Jewish custom in connection with the growth of a child. Jewish mothers weighed their children and donated the equivalent in money of the increase in weight to charity. Mention is made in the Talmud of a certain mother who weighed her only son every day and donated gold proportionate to the increase in weight to the Temple.[88]

This custom prevailed until recent days in certain forms. In some regions of Eastern Europe, it was customary to weigh the child every year on his birthday, and give the equivalent of his weight in bread to the poor. There was also a custom (to be described in detail in a subsequent chapter) of giving

1 and 2. SPICE-BOXES—*The Jewish Museum, New York*

3. KIDDUSH CUP—*Hebrew Union College Museum, Cincinnati*

Bimo of the Wooden Synagogue at Gwodziecz

the equivalent of the weight of the child's hair to the poor. When a child was sick, one of the popular remedies was giving the equivalent of his weight in bread to the poor. After the birth of a child, some Jewish mothers vowed to give an extra loaf of the white Sabbath bread to the poor; and every Friday morning when the Sabbath loaves were taken from the oven, the promised loaf was sent to a poor family. In the case of a boy, the vow was kept until his bar-mitsvo; in the case of a girl, until her wedding.

Weaning the Child . . . In Biblical and Talmudic times, the child was nursed at the breast for from two to three years, and this practice still persists among the Arab peasants of Palestine.[89]

In Biblical times, though the circumcision was not marked by a feast, weaning the child was the occasion for a joyous feasting. Later, however, this was reversed, and the celebration of weaning the child was discarded.[90]

Among the Jews in Eastern Europe, weaning a child was marked by certain symbolic acts. The first food that the child received after weaning was not the mother's, but was usually procured from a neighbor. When the child took the food from the other woman, the mother announced that it would be the last time that the boy or girl would be supported by others. A second parallel custom placed a tiny bag around the child's neck, into which coins might be dropped. This also signified that the child had received donations for the last time in his or her life.

The First Steps . . . Among the Jews in Eastern Europe, there were some curious customs and beliefs connected with aiding a child to walk. The child was placed on the threshold and a knife was drawn three times under the soles of his feet. The knife was supposed to cut the fetter which prevented the child from walking. Some made a cut with the knife on the spot where the child stood.

If the child stumbled and fell, water was immediately poured on that spot and the spot was perforated with a knife. Believing that the earth drew the child toward itself, certain means were employed to counteract that effect. There was a saying among women that if children fall and are not hurt, they fall on invisible pillows that angels place under them.

The First Hair-Cut . . . Primitive people believed that the hair of a man was permeated with a living force, containing his strength and vitality. Small wonder, therefore, that the first hair-cut of a child was linked with many primitive notions, and was an occasion for impressive ceremonies among various peoples all over the world.[91]

It was not permitted to cut the hair of the child before he reached a certain age, because his health would be impaired if he lost the living force which the hair was believed to contain. The age differed among various peoples. The Jews of Eastern Europe did not cut the hair of a child until the child was able to speak; otherwise he might remain dumb. The Jews shared this notion with the Poles from whom they apparently learned it.

Among the Jews of Eastern Europe, usually a boy was three years old before he had his hair cut for the first time. In some regions, guests were invited to a feast on this occasion. The honor of cutting off the first lock was awarded to the oldest guest. The ceremony was enhanced if this oldest guest happened to be a kohen. The hair was weighed, and its equivalent given in metal coins to the poor.

Even more impressive is the observance of the first hair-cutting among the Jews in Israel. The ceremonial is performed when the boy is four years old, usually taking place on the day of Lag Bo-omer, the semi-festival on the eighteenth day of Iyor. On Lag Bo-omer the Jews of Safed and Tiberias perform the ceremony of the first hair-cutting in the court-yard around the grave of Rabbi Simeon ben Yochai (second century c.e.), at the nearby village of Meron. This famous

Jewish sage, a disciple of Rabbi Akiba, became the legendary father of Jewish mysticism, and on Lag Bo-omer a fire cele, bration (hadlakah) is held annually in his honor at Meron.

It is a strange festival of tumultuous joy and religious fervor. The court of the sacred grave is packed with thousands of people, old and young, men, women and children, coming from all parts of Palestine and Syria to the grave of the holy disciple of Rabbi Akiba. They dance sacred dances and, in religious songs, they hail the Son of Yochai and work themselves up to the highest pitch of exaltation.

The ecstatic crowd is surrounded by the intense light of a huge blazing flame continuously fed by rags and oil. An old S'fardic Jew, with an iron rod in his hand, is busy feeding the flames with the fuel handed to him by the pilgrims. One pilgrim hands him a coat, the other a dress, the third a kerchief. One woman gives him a white silk dress for fuel and the other hands him a bottle full of oil.

In the midst of this ecstatic throng, carrying flags, swords and Scrolls of the Torah, and playing flutes and harps and beating drums, many fathers assemble, carrying their little sons in their arms. The three-year-old boys are dressed in their best clothes. On their heads they wear round caps adorned with gilded brims. From under each cap a thatch of unkempt hair and ear-locks protrude. The parents distribute wine and delicacies to all who pass by. One of the *gabo-im* (men in charge), with a pair of scissors in his hand, approaches a boy and, speaking conciliatory words, begins shearing off the ends of the ear-locks. The little boy, astonished and frightened, bursts out crying, but the hair of his ear-locks is already scattered on the ground.

The performance goes on, ear-lock after ear-lock dropping to the ground. The regular barber, who finishes the haircutting afterwards, blesses each father, expressing the hope that God may help his son to grow up a worthy and God-fearing Jew.

Only the Jews of Safed and Tiberias perform the ceremony

of the first hair-cutting at the grave of Rabbi Simeon ben Yochai. In other parts of the land on Lag Bo-omer, the ceremony is performed in the home of the parents. Relatives and friends are invited and each receives the honor of snipping off a few hairs until all of the hair except the ear-locks is cut. The ear-locks, they are forbidden to cut.[92] The guests then partake of a light meal. Many S'fardic Jews in Palestine perform the ceremony of the first hair-cutting at the synagogue during the semi-festival days of Pesach (Passover). It is considered more meritorious to have the hair cut by a poor Jewish barber. In the synagogue this observance is accompanied by great joy and merriment.[93]

The Belief in the Evil Eye

In primitive days, men regarded death and sickness as unnatural, believing that they were caused by supernatural hostile forces. In a later, higher stage of culture and religion, the wrath of God or the gods was believed to be the cause of all calamities. But in pre-historic times, before men evolved the belief in individual gods, they attributed death and sickness to witchcraft and evil spirits. This primitive belief in magic persists today even among peoples in the most advanced stage of culture.

According to the primitive belief in magic there were two ways of bewitching, one deliberate, the other unintentional. People believed in the existence of sorcerers and witches who had both the power and malice to do harm by means of their witchcraft. They also believed that certain persons were endowed with an evil eye, which enabled them to injure another merely by looking at him with envy or admiration. A person endowed with this evil power unconsciously could harm or bewitch another. Everything was subject to the evil eye—people, animals, plants, fruits, and even lifeless objects. But more than all these, children were in great danger of being injured by the evil eye, because they were frail and often suffered from sickness or accident. When a naked child slumbered in a cradle, he was in most imminent danger. A boy was believed to be more vulnerable to the evil eye than a girl.

There were two ways to bewitch unintentionally with the evil eye—by a tacit glance, or by a look coupled with a word in praise of beauty, health, strength or any other desirable quality. This type of bewitchment was called "spellbound by being called" (barufn) or "spellbound by being shouted at" (baschrien).

Since ancient times, belief in the evil eye has existed among almost all of the peoples of the world, persisting to the present day. It was, and still is, particularly prevalent in the Orient, the ancient home of all magic.[94]

The Evil Eye among Jews . . . The evil eye, in its magic sense, is not mentioned in the Bible. The term was used in Biblical reference to signify envy or covetousness and did not refer to the magic power; for example, in the Book of Proverbs: "He that hath an evil eye hasteneth after riches, and knoweth not that want shall come upon him" (28:22). Nor is the magic belief in the evil eye mentioned in the Mishnah, which is a product of the second century (c.e.). We may assume that the Palestinian Jews who had the hegemony in Jewish life to the third century frowned upon this magic belief, which they regarded as incompatible with the Jewish religion. They shunned all references to it.

From the third century on, especially in Babylonia, the belief in the magic power of the eye played an important part in Jewish literature. Rab (Abba Aricha) who died about the middle of the third century (c.e.), one of the greatest religious authorities among the Babylonian Jews, asserted that ninety-nine deaths out of a hundred were caused by an evil eye.[95] The spread of the belief in the evil eye might have been due to the influence of the environment, for at that time the center of Jewish life shifted to Babylonia, a land of magic and superstition.

In the Middle Ages, the center of Jewish life shifted to the European countries where witchcraft, credulity, and crass superstition held sway. There the belief in the evil eye increased among the Jews, and with it there was an increase in the variety of magic safeguards against it. Among the Jews of Eastern Europe, and even more among the Jews of the Orient, the belief in the evil eye still prevails.[96]

Safeguards against an Evil Eye . . . Since ancient times, among Jews as well as among other peoples, two kinds of magic were used as a protection against an evil eye. One consisted of preventives, the other of cures. According to popular belief there were numerous ways of preventing the evil eye from doing harm and there were also numerous forms of magic to cure the harm already inflicted.

Here are a few of the preventives:

In Talmudic times, a child was not taken to weddings and feasts in order to escape exposure to an evil eye.[97]

In the Middle Ages, in the time of Rashi, parents called a comely child "blackie." [98]

In Eastern Europe, parents were reluctant to show their handsome children to a person who had never before seen them.

In Eastern Europe one who saw a good-looking child for the first time exclaimed: "Without an evil eye" or "An evil eye shall not injure him" (or her) or "umbarufn" or "umbaschrien." Some even regarded the utterance of the words "an evil eye" as dangerous. They said instead "a good eye shall not injure him" (or her). In addition, the person who spoke expectorated three times.

The Use of Amulets . . . Among the preventives against an evil eye the amulet played the most prominent part.

Amulets were in vogue among Jews even in Biblical times. A great number of amulets dating back to those times was excavated recently in the mounds of Palestine. Small perforated pieces of stone, blue pearls, small hands made of silver, and many more ornaments were extracted from the ancient mounds in the Holy Land. Scholars have agreed that these ornaments were amulets worn as a protection against the evil eye. Ornaments in general were originally a protection against an evil eye because their glitter attracted the gaze of the onlooker and distracted it from the person who wore them. The Orientals who were addicted to the belief in the evil eye were therefore extravagant in their use of glittering ornaments.

Jewish children wore amulets in Talmudic times, and throughout the Middle Ages. They still wore them in recent days in some locales in Eastern Europe and even more often in the Orient. The amulets served as a "safeguard" not only against an evil eye, but against witchcraft and demons in general.

Jewish children wore various types of amulets. In Talmudic times they wore little bells and threads with knots. In Egypt in the twelfth century, they wore around their necks little tablets of silver and gold, containing certain inscriptions. Among the German Jews in the Middle Ages, they wore red or blue beads and pearls. In Eastern Europe and the Orient, Jewish children wore a little "hand" made of gold or silver, or a red ribbon or a string of red beads as amulets against witchcraft. They also wore a piece of quicksilver, or amber, or a piece of garlic or a little bag containing salt. Garlic was the most popular of all these safeguards. A mother, worried about the welfare of her handsome or distinguished child, placed a piece of garlic in his pocket. Sometimes a piece of the afikomon was placed there, too, or in a pocket of the ritual four-cornered garment to which the show-fringes are attached (Eastern Europe.) [99]

Treatment for an Evil Eye . . . There were very many symptoms of injury by an evil eye, e.g., pallor, fever, emaciation, and excessive yawning. If a child yawned more than usual when there was no other indication of any ailment, he or she had evidently been stricken by an evil eye. The first aid given was fumigation. A piece of the garment of the person suspected of having employed witchcraft was put on glowing coals with a piece of incense or devil's dung and a little dirt gathered from the four corners of the room. This was placed under the cradle around which a large sheet was hung so that the smoke blew into the child's face.

This charm, popular among Jews in Eastern Europe a generation ago, is easily understood in the light of the belief in magic of the peoples of the world. From ancient times, fumigation had been employed as a magic means for the expulsion of evil spirits because demons were supposed to be unable to stand the smoke of acrid incense. In order to choke the demons with the smoke, they had to be caught, and they could best be reached in the heaps of dirt gathered in the corners of the room. According to the popular belief, dirt-heaps were favor·ite abodes of the evil spirits. Fumigating with the dirt of the room mixed with incense and a piece of the garment of the one suspected of bewitching the child was thus regarded as an effective charm against the harm caused by an evil eye.

The most efficacious remedy for injuries caused by an evil eye was the whispered charm. A generation ago, in every Jewish community in Eastern Europe, there was one man or woman or several who knew how to "whisper off an evil eye." When a child was not feeling well and was believed "eaten up by an evil eye," someone in the house took a small kerchief or a baby cap to the conjuror who whispered the conjuration on the kerchief or the cap, holding it close to his or her mouth. The kerchief was then wrapped around the neck of the child or the cap placed on its head. In carrying the kerchief from the conjuror to the child, the messenger had to keep his mouth tightly closed and not utter a word to anyone until the kerchief was placed on the child's neck; otherwise, the whispered charm lost its power. This practice was repeated three times on three successive days.

Perils to the Child . . . The evil eye was not the only danger to which a child was exposed. In Eastern Europe there were many other perils, of which we shall mention only a few.

Before an infant cut his first tooth, he or she could not be exposed to moonlight. Even the swaddles drying in the outside air were brought back into the house before the moon was visible. Many people believed the moon was the cause of illness.[100]

Nor could a child be carried through a window without danger. If this was done by mistake, the child had to be carried back through the same window; otherwise he would not grow. To step over a child was dangerous, and if anyone did it, the same person had to step back in the opposite direction (if he stepped from east to west, he had to step from west to east).

Remedies of Jewish Popular Medicine . . . As antidote to the superstitious belief in certain dangers to the child, we find the cures and remedies of Jewish popular medicine. A few East European examples will be given here.

At the time of an epidemic, children wore red ribbons on the wrist or neck.

At the end of every month, mothers gave their children worm-herbs or worm-cakes, because every child's illness was believed to be caused by worms, if not symptomatic of an evil eye.

Various remedies in Jewish popular medicine were employed for a child who had been frightened, most popular of which was the whispering charm. The "fright" was "whispered off."

When a child was seriously ill, he or she was measured with a thread. The thread was taken to the candle-maker who used it in making wicks for candles which were donated to the synagogue.

The number of years of the age of the sick child was multiplied by eighteen and given in money to charity (eighteen is the numerical value of the two Hebrew letters *Ches* and *Yud* which together form a word meaning "living").

Some customs practiced in the case of a sickness have already been described—the custom of weighing a sick child and giving the equivalent of the weight in bread or money to the poor; the custom of selling the sick child in a mock sale to other parents, and the custom of adding one more special name or of discarding the old name altogether (see pp. 74–76 and 81).

viii

The Child in Home and Synagogue

Throughout the ages of Jewish history, the home has always been the main citadel of Jewish faith and piety. There, in the intimate atmosphere of Jewish family life, the child received his first impressions of the Jewish way of life.

The child sensed the flavor of the sacred Sabbath rest and the festive spirit of the Jewish holidays even before he realized their real significance. Together with the mother and the other adults in the house, he listened with pious attention when the father recited *kiddush* and *havdolo* on the Sabbath and festivals, and ardently responded with "Amen." He looked wonderingly at the candles burning in the Chanuko lamp, he observed the seder, the ceremony on Pesach night, and little by little he absorbed the spirit of piety permeating the home.

Nor were these impressions confined for long to the home. Soon he began to visit the synagogue and a new horizon opened for him.

Even before the child began to attend the cheder (elementary Hebrew school) he was taken by his father to the synagogue. Although he was not yet able to read in the siddur, nevertheless he enjoyed carrying father's siddur from the home to the synagogue or the beis ha-midrosh.

In the Middle Ages, among the S'fardim, it was customary for the father who took his son for the first time to the synagogue, to bring a waxen candle as a donation to the synagogue.[101]

Among the German Jews, the custom of bringing a boy to the synagogue on the Sabbath at the end of the first year of his life prevailed until our own day. In his hands he held a wimpel, a new girdle for the Scroll of the Torah, with his name and date of birth on it. His father was called up as the last of the seven to witness the reading of the Torah. Then he guided the hands of his little son in placing the new girdle on the Scroll of the Torah. The chazan or sexton recited the Mi Sheberach, blessing the child to enter into the study of the Torah, into the chupo and into good deeds. This custom prevailed only among German Jews. In other regions the child was not brought to the synagogue until he was a few years old and could walk to the holy dwelling with his father.

In the synagogue, the little boy learned to respond with a loud and fervent "Amen" to the benedictions pronounced by the precentor. When the precentor carried the Scroll of the Torah from his praying desk near the Holy Ark to the bimo, the reading-dais in the center of the synagogue, the father lifted up his little son to give him the same opportunity as the adults have to kiss the Scroll of the Torah. On the eve of the Sabbath and the holidays, and on their departure, when the precentor recited, respectively, kiddush and havdolo over a cup of wine, the little boys gathered around him and each one was treated with a sip of wine, a custom prevailing to this day. At the conclusion of the services they received the blessing of the rabbi of the congregation.

There were many ceremonies in the synagogue in which the little boy participated, although he could not yet recite the prayers. On Purim during the public reading of the Book of Esther, he joined the big lads in "beating" Haman whenever his name was mentioned. On Simchas Torah, the last day of the Sukos festival, he took part in the procession in which the Torah Scrolls were carried seven times around the bimo. Mounted on the shoulder of his father or his older brother, he marched around the bimo, carrying a flag with a Hebrew inscription in his hand, amidst the exuberant joy and merriment of the whole assemblage. He also ascended the bimo on Simchas Torah morning to witness the reading of the Torah when "all the lads" were called up.

Visiting the synagogue at this tender age was a great asset to the religious upbringing of children, but from the point of view of silence and order during the services, children were a great liability and embarrassment. The Jews in Spain solved this problem by segregating the youngsters in a separate corner, where they were sternly restrained and silenced by an overseer especially appointed for this purpose.[102]

Beginning Torah in the Home . . . In his tender childhood, before school age, the Jewish child received in the home not only his first impressions of Jewish religious life but also his first lessons in Jewish lore. As far back as early Talmudic times, the child began to be taught as soon as he could speak. His father taught him to recite the Sh'ma, the declaration of his faith; also the Biblical verse, "Moses commanded us a law, an inheritance of the congregation of Jacob" (Deut. 33:4), and other verses of this type. The child learned to sing some of the sacred songs sung not only in the temple, but also in the synagogues and in the homes. He was told Biblical stories, and learned of the lives of the great Jews of olden times in vivid and colorful tales. He was surrounded by various religious symbols and sacred rites. He noticed the three most important outward signs of adherence to the precepts of the Torah; the *m'zuzo* on the door-post, the phylacteries on the head and the arm, and the *tsitsis* on the corners of the garment. He was curious to know why one thread of the tsitsis was blue (as it was in olden times) and his father explained that it was a sign to remember the commandments of God in order that one should not go stray "after his own heart and after his own eyes" (Num. 15:39).[103]

This intensely religious atmosphere of the Jewish home persisted to our own days in Eastern Europe, in certain parts of Central Europe, in the Orient, and even here and there in America.

As soon as the little boy was able to speak, at approximately the age of three, his mother made the ritual four-cornered garment with "show-fringes" for him. He was taught to recite the benediction over the fringes, to kiss them immediately after the benediction. He wore the four-cornered garment and also *peos,* ear-locks of his hair on the temples. He already knew that these two adornments were religious commandments and that they applied only to boys.

The child was taught that as soon as he opened his eyes in the morning, he should recite from memory the short prayer: "I thank Thee, O Living and eternal King, that Thou hast graciously restored my soul to me; great is Thy faithfulness." Then the added words: "Moses commanded us a law, an inheritance of the congregation of Jacob." These verses were carefully chosen so as not to include divine names, because they were recited with hands unwashed.

After he arose, he poured water alternately three times over his hands. If he was unable to do this for himself, he held out his hands and someone else poured the water over them. He washed his face, too, but this was done voluntarily, whereas washing the hands in the morning was a precept, called "finger-nails water." Many beliefs involved the hair and the nails, the extraneous parts of the human body. According to popular belief, the evil spirits, who held their natural sway at night, clung to the nails even in the light of the morning, and did not depart until water was applied to them. Jews, as well as many other peoples, regarded water as a charm for protection against evil spirits.[104]

These morning precepts which the child learned applied to girls as well as to boys.

At this tender age the child was also taught to recite from memory the several benedictions prescribed for various kinds of foods and beverages. Of course, the little boy or girl did not yet know which benediction applied to this or that food. An adult usually recited slowly the Hebrew words of the benediction, and the child repeated them, word for word.

ix

Going to School

The Elementary Jewish School . . . In the Bible, no mention is made of schools. The father was commanded diligently to teach the words of the Torah to his own children. From all that we know of life and letters in Israel in Biblical times, we gather that, even prior to the Babylonian exile, there were some schools for children. In the Biblical writings stemming from the days of the kings and prophets, we hear of men who could read and even write. There flourished in ancient Israel a written literature of which the books of the Bible are a mere remnant. Certainly not all the writers and readers of this literature learned to read and to write from their fathers' home instruction.[105]

However, those schools were not the concern of the community and did not deal with popular education. Apparently they were the concern only of certain individuals. Probably these schools were attached to the large sanctuaries, and the priests were the teachers, for in ancient days the priests were the learned men and spiritual leaders of the community.

In the centuries following the Babylonian exile and the rebuilding of the new community in Jerusalem under the leadership of Ezra, Nehemiah and their associates, this situation changed. The Torah, the will of God embodied in the Five Books of Moses, then became the main content of Jewish religious life. Piety expressed itself primarily in observing, in all minute details, the precepts of the Torah. Since a knowledge of the Torah was the first prerequisite, popular education became an urgent necessity. It was the beginning of the age of the scribes, the rabbis, the learned men, the teachers of the

Torah, who superseded the kings and the prophets as the leaders and guides of the people.

To meet the needs of the time, new institutions developed, whose purpose it was to spread the knowledge and understanding of the Torah among the people.

The first new religious institution we find in this period was the synagogue (*beis ha-kneses*, house of assembly or of the community), which probably sprang up in the Babylonian exile. Originally it was not so much a house of worship as a house where the people assembled on certain days, especially on the Sabbath and the festivals, to receive religious instruction, to hear the Torah and the Prophets read and expounded. Somewhat later, we find a second institution for fostering the knowledge of the Torah: the beis ha-midrosh (house of study, of interpretation), the higher academy of Jewish learning. Both institutions were for adults, the beis ha-kneses for the masses of the people and the beis ha-midrash for the circles of higher learning; but neither provided adequately for popular education. The small children depended exclusively on the instruction of their fathers in the home. Hence the beis ha-midrash was later followed by the establishment of the *beis ha-sefer* (the house of the Book), as the elementary Jewish school has been called.[106]

According to Talmudic tradition of the third century (c.e.), the spread of popular education among Jews was a long process which passed through many stages. In ancient days every Jewish father taught his own son. The fatherless child or the child of an ignorant father received no instruction. Later, schools were established in Jerusalem to which boys were sent from all over the country. When these proved inadequate, schools for youths of sixteen or seventeen were opened in the largest town of every district. Because it proved difficult to discipline these adolescent youths, schools were finally established in every community for children of six or seven. These schools were called botei sefer where children learned the Sacred Writings.[107]

In the last years preceding, and in the first few centuries following the destruction of the Second Temple, the network of elementary Jewish schools for male children spread until it became universal in Palestine as well as in Babylonia. No Jewish community, however small, was without a primary school for children. The community cared for its upkeep. All the fathers in the locale who sent their children to the school contributed to the maintenance of the teacher. Even bachelors generously contributed to the upkeep of the school. Not all schools were communal institutions. There were also many private schools, and some well-to-do families engaged private teachers in their homes.[108]

Thus, by sheer moral force without any state authority, the Jews succeeded in establishing a system of universal popular education in the early centuries of the Common Era. In ancient times Jews could not conceive of a Jewish child growing up without learning Torah. According to the Talmud, God himself taught Torah to children who died before reaching school age.[109]

The Early Jewish Primary School . . . The child began to go to the beis ha-sefer at the age of six. Some attended at the age of five. The school was usually attached to the synagogue. If a special teacher was not available, the chazan taught the children. In that period, the chazan was the sexton of the synagogue, not the cantor, as the term is used today. There were also many private schools held at the residence of private teachers.

The Jews, like the Greeks, did not send girls to school. Schools were for boys only, and all teachers were married men. An unmarried man was not allowed to teach in a primary school. One teacher was allowed only twenty-five students in his class. If the number exceeded twenty-five, he was obliged to keep an assistant. If the number of the children reached fifty, they were divided into two separate classes under two teachers.[110]

Let us make a tour of a few primary schools in Palestine in that period and observe their appearance and methods.

As soon as we approach the school, even before we enter, we are met by a chorus of resounding children's voices repeating and rehearsing the words and passages of the Bible which the teacher recites to them. The teacher makes the children repeat everything at the top of their voices. The advantage of learning aloud was valued highly, first, because it was advantageous for the memory, and secondly, a kind of mystic power was ascribed to the words of the Torah distinctly pronounced by the mouths of the innocent children. The verse of the Bible, "The voice is the voice of Jacob, but the hands are the hands of Esau," was interpreted to mean that as long as Jewish children learned to loudly recite Torah, the hands of the enemies of the Jews would not have power over them. The noise emanating from a schoolroom was not an asset for the neighborhood. Sometimes neighbors sought judicial means to keep a teacher from establishing himself in their vicinity.[111]

Some schools were completely unfurnished. The schoolroom was almost empty and the walls were bare. The pupils put their coats on the floor and sat on them. In some schools, the children sat on a matting of reeds which covered the floor; some were furnished with benches arranged in rows. The benches had bases provided with holes to hold the feet. The teacher's seat depended upon the furnishings of the school. In schools provided with good seats for the pupils, the teacher might be seated on a soft armchair. The schools were provided with a writing tablet on which the teacher wrote the letters of the alphabet, which the children learned to copy. A copy of the Torah was a requisite of all schools.[112]

The pupils were seated in rows, apparently in a semi-circle, looking straight into the teacher's face. The teacher emphasized the fact that his pupils must remember correctly every word, and even every letter of the Torah. In order to accomplish this feat, the children repeated and rehearsed countless times.

The beginners' curriculum consisted of only one subject, learning to read and write Hebrew, the language of the Holy Writings. This was not easy, for Hebrew was still an unvocalized language, consisting exclusively of consonants. Nor was Hebrew the spoken language of most of the pupils. The broad masses of the people spoke Aramaic. Hebrew as a spoken language was confined only to the higher circles of learned men, making it difficult for the children to learn to read an unvocalized Hebrew Bible.

In teaching the children to write, certain pedagogical devices were applied. First, they learned to write the simple letters, the *yud* and the *vov* (the tenth and sixth letters of the alphabet); afterwards, the more difficult letters. The teacher drew the letter on a tablet of wax or a piece of papyrus. The pupil then retraced it, the teacher holding the pupil's hand and guiding it over the tablet or the papyrus. The requisites needed for writing were on sale in the market among all other merchandise and the children brought them from their homes to the schoolroom. Among the school requisites were small parchment rolls for the special use of children. These "readers" contained only certain portions of the Holy Writings which were studied by the children, as the Sh'ma, the Hallel Psalms, and the Ten Commandments.[113]

The teacher, in order to keep his attention, pointed with a stylus to the copy which the child read. In the beginning, the teacher cared little whether the pupil was capable of grasping the subject matter. First, the pupil had to be "fed" with the lesson to know it exactly. Only later, when the pupil had memorized the text, did the teacher try to explain it. The teacher was eager to provoke the pupils to ask questions. Clever pupils asked clever questions. If a pupil was dull and did not know how to ask questions, the teacher "opened his mouth," i.e., he put the question in his mouth.

The pupils were rated according to their abilities, and were thus divided into four categories: those who were quick to understand and quick to forget, those who were slow to un-

derstand and slow to forget, those who were quick to understand and slow to forget, and those who were slow to understand and quick to forget.

Teaching the Holy Writings began with Leviticus, the
third of the Five Books of the Torah. In the course of the
years, the children learned all the books of the Bible. The main
subject which engrossed their attention was the Pentateuch,
the first section of the Bible, containing the laws of the
Torah.[114]

The children went to school very early in the morning.
With great love and care the mother washed her child and
dressed him neatly. Sometimes a father led his son to school
before he (the father) had breakfasted or even before he had
finished his toilet. In the hot summer months, the children
began their schooling at six o'clock in the morning, and at ten,
they returned home. In the other seasons of the year, the
school hours were longer. In the evening, the children returned to school for two hours of study. No occasion was
considered sufficiently important to disturb the child's learning
of the Torah. The school season lasted throughout the entire
year. Even on Friday night the children went to school to
review the lessons which they learned during the week. Only
on holidays, on the days preceding the holidays, and on fast
days, no school was held.

The teacher stood in very high esteem. He ranked higher
than the father. If the pupil had tasks to do for both of them
and could not do these tasks simultaneously, he attended first
to the demands of his teacher and afterwards to his father's,
because it was said: his father brought him merely into the
physical life of this world whereas his teacher brought him
into the eternal life of the world to come.

The teacher was forbidden to hit a child with a rod. He
punished bad children with a leather strap. There were
naughty children who were punished with the strap nearly
every day.[115]

The pupil usually attended the *beis sefer*, the Bible School, until he was thirteen years of age and had reached the age of majority. When he left the beis sefer, he had an adequate knowledge of the religion, the history, the sacred language and the literary heritage of his people. At that age the boy began to undertake practical work and become a farmer, a craftsman, or a merchant.[116]

But not all boys were content with the knowledge of the Sacred Writings which they acquired in the primary school. After finishing the beis sefer many of them continued studying. They went to the beis midrosh where they delved into Jewish traditional learning and became versed in its various branches. Some of these boys attained a high proficiency in Jewish lore, and in their later years belonged to the *chacho-mim*, wise and learned men, the masters in the knowledge of the Torah, the legitimate leaders of the Jewish people.

In the Middle Ages . . . In the Middle Ages, the elementary Jewish school was an old established institution behind which was a history and tradition of over a thousand years. Every boy began school at the age of five or a little later, depending on the health of the child. Among the Franco-German Jews, the day on which the boy began school was celebrated as a great event in his life.

The little boy was washed and dressed in his best clothes. Three eggs were cooked for him, and three honey cakes were baked, the dough kneaded by an innocent virgin. Apples and other fruits were brought to him. In some communities school began on the New Moon of the month of Nison. In other communities this great event took place on Shovuos.

The festival of the giving of the Torah was selected as the day when the child should begin his study of the Torah.

At daybreak, the child was taken to the synagogue or to the house of the *m'lamed*, the teacher, by a pious and learned man of the community, who hid him under the skirts of his coat in order that an evil eye should not injure him. The teacher who was in charge of his instruction handed him a slate on which the Hebrew alphabet was written forward, from *aleph* to *tov*, and backward from *tov* to *aleph*. The following verses were also written on the slate: "The law which Moses commanded us is the inheritance of the congregation of Jacob." "The Torah will be my occupation." "And the Lord called unto Moses and spoke unto him out of the tent of meeting, saying." As the teacher read the words and letters on the slate, the little pupil repeated them after him. Then a little honey was spread on the slate, which the child licked off. The custom was based upon the verse in Ezekiel in which the prophet states he felt God's words in his mouth "as honey for sweetness." Next, a honey cake was brought, on which were inscribed several sentences of the Prophets and the Psalms, the import of which was the praise of God's words and His precepts. The teacher read, and the little boy repeated after him each word of these verses. Following the cake, a cooked egg was brought, on the shell of which was inscribed the verses: "From all my teachers have I learned wisdom," and "How sweet are Thy words unto my palate! Yea, sweeter than honey to my mouth!" [117] These verses were also read by the teacher and repeated by the child.

The lesson was now finished and the child was given the cake, the egg and the fruit to eat. Then he was led back home again, concealed under the skirts of the coat of an adult.

That night, at home, the parents of the boy entertained many guests at a festive meal in honor of the occasion.[118] It was the custom for everyone participating in the celebration to bless the child with the words "May God enlighten thine eyes with His Torah."

In the earlier Middle Ages, names of angels were inscribed upon the honey cakes, and amulets attached to them, but this custom was later discarded.[119]

The Cheder in Eastern Europe . . . A generation or two ago, there was little modern secularism in the Jewish life of the small towns in Eastern Europe. The cheder remained a continuation of the cheder of the Middle Ages, and was not a special house used only as a school. A special house, called *Talmud Torah*, a communal free Hebrew school, was attended only by the poorest children of the community. The cheder was a private school in the home of the m'lamed, the Hebrew teacher. There were several schools of this kind in every community, and there was strong competition among the m'lamdim, especially at the beginning of the term, in spring and in autumn.

The little house of the m'lamed which accommodated the cheder usually consisted of two or three rooms. One or two rooms constituted the private residence of the m'lamed and his family, where the *rebitsin*, the m'lamed's wife, was in charge. (The m'lamed was addressed by the title *rebe* [rabbi] and his wife was called rebitsin. These were the same terms that applied to the rabbi of the community and his wife.) The school consisted of one room, usually the front room, which was equipped with one or two tables with a long bench on each side of the table. The only other school equipment was the *taitl*, the pointer, used by the m'lamed to point to the letter or the passage in the siddur where a beginner was reading. There was no blackboard in the room because writing was not a part of the cheder curriculum. For writing there was a special teacher in town, who was an expert in penmanship. To him children went for an hour or two each day, a few days a week, for two or three years, to learn writing and arithmetic. Without exception all children attended cheder, but not all of them went to the teacher to learn writing. One could do without writing, for someone else could be asked to read or write a letter if the exigency arose.

The children in the cheder were divided into groups, called by the Talmudic term, *kitos*. There was a kito for reading in the prayer book, the siddur. The next higher kito was for the Chumosh, the Five Books of Moses. Still higher was the kito that studied the books of the Bible which follow the Pentateuch. The highest kito studied the Talmud. Each of these kitos was divided into grades or sub-kitos. At the same time that the m'lamed taught a higher kito at one table, the *behelfer*, the assistant, taught the little boys "reading" at the other table. When all of the children recited aloud some passage in the siddur or in the Bible, there was general tumult and confusion.

There were communities in which children of the aforementioned various grades did not attend one and the same cheder but a special cheder for each grade. A certain m'lamed held a cheder for beginners in reading only. When a child graduated from that cheder, he was promoted to a cheder of Chumosh (Pentateuch) and then to the cheder of Talmud.

The behelfer, usually a young unmarried lad, was a well-known figure in the life of the Jewish communities in Poland. He called for the little children, the beginners, at their homes, and brought them back home after cheder was over. The little boys, who had just begun to attend cheder, he carried to and from school on his back, sometimes several of them at one time. During the lunch hour, he procured a basket of lunch from each mother for her child. This was a complicated task, because the behelfer had to see to it that each child received the particular snack which his mother provided. One of the duties of the behelfer was to provide the children with entertainment and recreation. He carved bows and arrows for Lag Bo-omer, wooden swords for Tisho B'Ov, manufactured flags for Simchas Torah, tops for Chanuko and noise-makers for Purim. The behelfer was paid by the m'lamed, who was paid by the parents of the children.

The children spent the whole day in the cheder, from early morning until sunset. In the short winter days, the children went back to the cheder after *ma-ariv* (evening services). With lanterns in their hands, the little ones, accompanied by the behelfer, made their way to the cheder for another two or three hours of study. Even on the Sabbath, the children went to the cheder for one or two hours to review the lessons of the week, or to learn some special Sabbath lesson. This was done, not on Friday night, as in Talmudic times, but on Saturday afternoon. Saturday was also the time when the father tested the son to see how much he knew of the lessons he had learned during the week. In some locales it was customary to test the son on the Sabbath in the presence of the m'lamed, who went to the homes of the parents for this purpose. If the father was a man of learning, he did the testing himself. Otherwise, he brought the child to an uncle or to one of his friends who was well versed in the Torah. Only on holidays and the days preceding the holidays was the cheder closed. On many semi-holidays, the children attended cheder for only half a day. On Friday, too, the cheder was open for only half of the day, and most of the time was devoted to chanting the section of the Pentateuch and the portion of the Prophets for that Sabbath.

The children did not study their lessons all day long. There were many intermissions. When the m'lamed was teaching one kito, the children of the other kitos played games in the yard. On cold and rainy days they played their games in the rebe's private room where their freedom of action depended largely upon the good will and forbearance of the rebitsin. There were many games which engaged the children's leisure in cheder. Among the most popular were those played with buttons. Almost the whole year round there was heavy traffic in buttons. Mischievous boys, in their enthusiasm for the game, tore good buttons from their clothes, and were punished by their sharp-eyed mothers. There was also some seasonal trading in the cheder. A couple of weeks before Tisho B'Ov, the children traded the "burrs" which they threw at each other in the synagogue. In the weeks preceding Pesach, nuts were the popular merchandise bartered in the cheder.

For centuries the cheder was the home of the Jewish child. Here he spent most of his time, from the age of five or six until several years after his bar mitsvo. It was in the cheder that every Jew spent the days of his childhood and his adolescence; there he acquired his knowledge of the world as conceived by the child of the ghetto; there his intellect developed and his phantasy unfolded.

The rebe, as the m'lamed was called, was not content with translating the Bible. The literal meaning of the words was not of major importance. The rebe had to amplify and interpret the words according to the explanations of the Agada of the Talmud and the Midrashim. He discussed with the children the legendary and historical figures of the Bible as if he had known them personally. He described in minute detail every incident of the Biblical narratives as if he were recounting his personal recollections.

Occasionally, the rebe told the children various stories and fabulous tales not directly connected with the Bible and the Talmud. Many a rebe was a veritable treasure trove of stories about saints and miracle men, of fables about ghosts and demons, goblins and evil spirits. He depicted *Gan Eden* (Paradise), where the saints, seated on golden thrones, enjoyed the Divine Glory. He also depicted the blazing fire of Gehenna, and the frightful tortures which afflicted the sinful for the transgressions they had committed during their earthly lives.

The rebe was not the only story-teller in the cheder. Sometimes during hours when the children were at leisure, the rebitsin also told them stories of ghosts and goblins which she had heard from her mother, who had heard them from her grandmother, and so on. Some of the children of the higher grades were proficient in telling wonderful stories which they had heard from their fathers and older brothers, stories of the prophet Elijah, of Solomon and the Queen of Sheba, of Alexander the Great, of Napoleon, and others.

Every subject studied in the cheder was recited with its peculiar melody. There was a particular tune for reading in the prayer book, another tune for reading the Pentateuch and the Early Prophets, another for reading the Later Prophets, a special chant for the M'gilos (Scrolls), and still another tune for the Talmud. The peculiar melodies, the fantastic tales, and the age-old curriculum blended into a special harmony which remained a part of the child of the ghetto throughout the days of his life.

All of this applied to boys only. Girls were taught by a special m'lamed, a man or a woman. Usually, the m'lamed for the girls went to their homes to teach them for a little while every day. There was a special curriculum for the girls. They all learned to read in the siddur, but few of them were taught to translate the Bible. Instead, they read religious books in Yiddish. A rich religious ethical literature in Yiddish, intended for women, and for the less learned folk in general, flourished in the later Middle Ages. This literature was still very popular among mothers of the present generation of East European Jews, and almost every girl was taught to read it.

Beginning Chumosh . . . The beautiful ceremonial that was observed in the Middle Ages on the day the child entered the cheder has been discarded. Only some features still persisted a generation ago. In some regions of Eastern Europe, it was customary, when bringing the child to the cheder for the first time, to wrap him in a praying-shawl. The father carried the child and the mother accompanied them, carrying cake and brandy. In some communities a honey cake was still given to the child on this occasion. When the child entered the cheder, the rebe usually stretched his arm high above the child's head, dropping a penny on the table and saying, "Here, the angel threw down a penny for you for learning well."

Until a short time ago, an elaborate family celebration was held on the occasion of beginning the study of the Chumosh, which was characterized by a ceremony studied and rehearsed by two actors. One actor was the boy who was to begin to study the Chumosh, and who had to answer a long series of questions on this occasion, the other was a boy of the higher grades, selected to play the role of the questioner. For several weeks in advance, the rebe rehearsed the two boys in their parts. In some communities, the rebe himself questioned the boy. In others, instead of one older boy who acted as questioner, three boys were selected as "blessers." Each boy blessed the child with a different blessing, all three of them being under the cover of one praying-shawl, which was spread over their heads.

The great celebration took place on a Sabbath in the home of the parents. The rebe sat at a table set with cake, nuts, brandy, and various other delicacies. The father sat on his right side, and the guests were seated around the table. The women and the mother of the lad stood a little apart from the men, glowing with inner contentment and joy.

On a table or a chair in the midst of all the people stood the hero of the day, dressed in his best holiday clothes and adorned with a golden watch and chain, and other pieces of jewelry borrowed for the occasion. He was ready to perform his role, which consisted of answering questions and, in some communities, of delivering a discourse on a topic of the Torah.

Here are some specimens of the Midrashic discourse delivered by a Chumosh candidate:

"Why does the Torah begin with a beis (B'reshis), the second letter of the alphabet, and not with aleph, the first letter?" "Because God blessed the world when He created it and *beis* is the first letter of the word *boruch* (blessed), whereas aleph is the first letter of the word *orur* (cursed)."

"Why did God give the Torah to Moses and not to Abraham?" "Because if God had given the Torah to Abraham, the Jews would have forgotten it during the time they were slaves in Egypt."

The following is one version of a dialogue that took place between the questioner and the boy.

"What is your name, nice child?"

"I am not a child any more. I am a big boy who, in a lucky hour, is going to begin to study Chumosh."

"What does Chumosh mean?"

"Five."

"Five buns for a penny?"

"No, the Five Books of the Torah which God gave to Moses."

"What are their names?"

"*B'reshis* is one, *Sh'mos* is two, *Vayikro* is three, *Bamidbor* is four, *D'vorim* is five."

"And which of these will you now begin to learn?"

"I will begin with the third book, *Vayikro.*"

"What does *Vayikro* mean?"

"And he called."

"Who called? The beadle into the synagogue?"

"No, God called Moses, and told him the laws concerning sacrifices."

"And why do you have to learn the laws of the sacrifices?"

"Because the sacrifices were pure, and I am a pure Jewish child."

"And why is the *aleph* in the word *Vayikro* small?"

"Because the translation of *aleph* is 'to learn,' and one who is learned must consider himself small and not pride himself on his learning."

"So why are you proud?"

"Oh, no, I am not proud."

"Then why are you standing on the table?"

"I'll obey you and come down."

The boy would then climb off the table, and read and translate, word for word, the first verses of Leviticus, repeating each word after the "rebe." Then he received gifts from his parents and relatives, and all the people in the house ate and drank with great joy and merriment.

It was to observe an old custom that the boy learned from the book of Leviticus that day. On the following day he joined the Chumosh-class and learned the weekly portion of the Pentateuch. Each week he studied another section. At first, he learned only to translate each word separately. Later, he was promoted to a higher kito where he learned Chumosh with the amplifications and interpretations of the Midrash, found, for the most part, in the popular commentary, Rashi.[120]

The Cheder in Recent Years . . . The cheder, with its age-old curriculum, its characteristic atmosphere, and its numerous physical and pedagogical shortcomings, remained almost unchanged in Eastern Europe to the very threshold of this century. The *Haskalah*, the movement of enlightenment, which did not bring emancipation to the East European Jews, touched only the upper circles, influencing very slightly the masses of the people. The cheder withstood all the attacks made upon it by the spokesman of the Haskalah who, in an exaggerated manner, repeatedly exposed its unpleasant features.

Only with the growth of the new nationalistic movement among Jews at the end of the past century did modernization and secularization of the elementary Jewish school begin to make progress. In many communities the cheder, under the new name Cheder M'sukon (improved cheder), became modernized and secularized in many respects. The emphasis on Jewish subjects shifted from teaching of the Talmud to teaching of the Bible, Jewish history, Hebrew as a spoken language, and modern Hebrew literature. Amidst the working class, which followed the socialist movement, the process of secularizing the Jewish primary school reached its extreme. A new type of Jewish elementary school was established, completely secular in character, with Yiddish and modern Yiddish literature as its main subjects.

In Western Europe and America . . . In Western Europe, where the Haskalah movement went hand in hand with a gradual emancipation of the Jews, the old forms of Jewish life were shaken to their very foundations. With the advent of the nineteenth century, the cheder was gradually discontinued. Modern Jewish schools began to be established here and there. When the German school became universal and compulsory, the results were disastrous for Jewish education.

Here in America, where Jewish education is merely supplementary to the public school, its status is nevertheless better than in Western Europe. On the whole, because of the new adjustment of immigrants to a new environment and new conditions of life, Jewish education in this country is still in a state of flux. Several types of Jewish schools have assumed definite tendencies. There are Orthodox, Reform, and Conservative schools where emphasis is laid upon the religious aspect of Jewish education. There are schools of the Zionist circles where the main emphasis is laid upon teaching of Hebrew as a living language. There are also a few types of secular Yiddish schools, where the Yiddish language and literature are taught as the main subjects in national Jewish culture. There are week-day schools where the children are taught in the afternoon hours, as well as Sabbath and Sunday schools, congregational and non-congregational schools. East European immigrants have established private Hebrew schools, and numerous private teachers teach the children in their homes. There are also some Jewish parochial schools. But many Jewish children in this country do not even have a smattering of Jewish education, a thing unheard of since the days when the Jewish primary school became universal.

X

Bar Mitsvo

The Name . . . Bar Mitsvo (son of commandment, man of duty) is a Hebrew-Aramaic term, signifying a person who is obliged to observe the precepts of the Jewish religion. In this general sense bar mitsvo is an old term in Jewish literature. We find it in the Talmud where a minor and a non-Jewish slave in the household of a Jew were described as not being bar mitsvo, since they were not obliged to fulfill the commandments of the Torah.[121]

In its present application to the attainment of religious majority at the age of thirteen, the term "bar mitsvo" has been used only since the late Middle Ages. Previously, other designations were applied to a boy's coming of age. He was called *godol* (big, adult, of age) or *bar onshin* (punishable, responsible), but he was not called bar mitsvo. In present day Jewish life bar mitsvo has a twofold meaning. It is used to designate both the boy, who reaching the age of thirteen, has attained his religious majority, and the ceremony marking that occasion.

In its present sense, the term "bar mitsvo" is only about seven hundred years old. The observances marking the occasion when a boy becomes bar mitsvo are more recent. However, the age of thirteen as the actual age of majority is an old institution in Jewish life which we shall follow from its very inception.

In Ancient Times . . . In the Bible, a man attained his majority at the age of twenty. In Biblical times, from twenty years and upward, one was able "to go out to war in Israel," and at the same age, every man was obliged to pay an annual tax of half a shekel for the sanctuary.[122]

A Difficult Passage by Isidor Kaufmann.
This painting shows clearly the talis koton.

EXAMINATION IN HEBREW by Moritz Oppenheim

At about the beginning of the Common Era, attainment of majority was fixed at thirteen years for a boy, and twelve for a girl.[123] We must not assume that the outside influences of the post-Biblical period were responsible for the transfer of majority from the age of manhood to the age of adolescence. On the contrary, in primitive society, a child attained his social majority immediately upon reaching adolescence. This enabled him to participate in the ritual and social activities of the group, but in a more advanced society, with a mature legal system, the child was considered a minor until he reached manhood.

The age of twenty, stated in the Bible as the age of majority in military and financial matters, apparently represents a later development, when a more advanced legal system was in force among the Jews. This advanced stage was presumably preceded by an older and more primitive stage of social life in which a boy was initiated into his social and religious duties at the age of transition from childhood to adolescence, between twelve and fourteen years. The initiation into the tribe at this age was, and still is, celebrated among primitive peoples with an elaborate ceremonial which sometimes exceeds in pomp and grandeur the celebration of a wedding. Among Jews, too, in the ancient past, a celebration of this kind probably took place when a boy was initiated into the tribe at the age of thirteen. Apparently the age of thirteen was fixed for the attainment of majority because thirteen was a sacred number among the Jews in ancient times.[124]

In Talmudic and Early Medieval Times . . . The age of thirteen years for the attainment of religious majority was thus not an innovation of post-Biblical times, but the preservation or revival of an old social custom. In the highly developed religious life of the Jews in post-Biblical times, the custom was entirely divested of its primitive character, and invested with a religious and moral significance. The boy was now initiated into a religious community which was animated by sublime religious ideas and a lofty moral standard. The attainment of majority had become a religious experience.

We have stated in a previous chapter that a great educational movement was developing in the Jewish life of those days. At five years of age, the normal child began to read the Bible, at ten years he was expected to begin the study of the oral laws and traditions; and "at thirteen years, he was bound to the commandments" and became a responsible member of the community.[125] Until he reached the age of thirteen, his father was under obligation to personally teach him Torah, or to send him to the beis sefer, the primary school. After thirteen years, his father was no longer responsible for his religious education. He could, of his own volition, continue his studies at the beis midrash, the higher academy. The father, on the occasion of his son's attainment of religious majority, pronounced a benediction in which he praised God for relieving him of responsibility for his son's conduct.[126]

In the Jewish literature of that time we do not read of any celebration marking the attainment of religious majority. However, it seems that on this day the boy was presented to the oldest men of the community who blessed him and prayed that he should acquire the merit of learning Torah and doing good deeds.[127]

No ceremonial to celebrate the attainment of majority could have evolved in Talmudic and early medieval times because, according to the Talmud, a minor was permitted to participate in all religious observances as soon as he was considered mentally fit. He was called up to witness the reading of the Torah on the bimo and was supposed to wear t'filin, phylacteries. The minor was even inured to fast on Yom Kippur. Two years before he attained his majority, a child fasted until noon, and a year before his majority, he fasted the whole day.[128] The distinction between a minor and one who had obtained his majority was theoretical. The latter did as a religious duty what a minor did optionally. The majority was not distinguished by additional religious duties and privileges, and therefore the attainment of majority could not be marked by any special observances. Until late in the Middle Ages, the attainment of majority was an uneventful date in the life of the Jew.

At the Threshold of Modern Times . . . Gradually, during the later Middle Ages, this situation underwent a change. The religious rights which the Talmud accorded to the minor were now restricted. He was deprived of the right to be "called up" to the reading of the Torah. He was no longer permitted to wear t'filin. The attainment of majority gained new importance as an attainment of new religious rights and the ground was prepared for a ceremonial around the bar mitsvo, as a boy thirteen years old was beginning to be called.

A demand to restrict the right of minors to don t'filin was made by one religious authority as far back as the twelfth century, but it did not meet with approval. In the fourteenth century, notwithstanding the objections of some religious authorities, a minor was still usually taught by his father to put on t'filin as soon as he knew how to take care of them. However, the objections grew, and in the sixteenth century, among the Jews of Germany and Poland, it was the accepted custom that a boy could not begin to wear t'filin before the day following his thirteenth birthday. This custom was modified in the seventeenth century. The boy began wearing t'filin two or three months before he became bar mitsvo, so that by the time he reached his majority he was well acquainted with the practice and rules of laying t'filin.[129]

The right of a minor to be called up to the bimo for the reading of the Torah underwent a similar development among the Ashk'nazim (German and Polish Jews). As far back as the thirteenth century, among the Franco-German Jews, the privilege of being called up for the reading of the Torah was withdrawn from minors. Only on Simchas Torah, the last day of the Sukos festival, could minors enjoy this right. The attainment of religious majority signified the attainment of the right to witness the reading of the Torah on the bimo and to recite the benedictions over it.

These two religious rights, laying t'filin and being called up to the Torah, became the most essential features of the bar mitsvo observance. In the sixteenth century it was obligatory to call up the bar mitsvo lad to the reading of the Torah on the Sabbath coinciding with or following his thirteenth birthday. In very cautious, pious circles the elders watched lest the bar mitsvo lad be called up to the reading of the Torah before he had attained the full age of thirteen years. This might be the case if the boy's thirteenth birthday fell on the Sabbath.[130] For safety's sake, the custom arose which still prevails today, that even on the bar mitsvo Sabbath, the boy was not among the seven men called on every Sabbath to the reading of the Torah, but after them. He was called to the reading of the last paragraph of the portion of the Pentateuch read on the Sabbath, and of the Haftoro, the portion of the Prophets which is read after the week's portion of the Pentateuch. In regard to the Haftoro, the right of the minor was never restricted except on a few special Sabbaths.

The bar mitsvo ceremonial was not confined to the synagogue. New features were added which shifted the center of the celebration from the synagogue to the home of the parents, such as the bar mitsvo feast and the bar mitsvo *drosho* (discourse). The party held on the bar mitsvo Sabbath was regarded as a religious feast. The religious aspect of the bar mitsvo feast was enhanced in Poland where the drosho was introduced. In Poland, the center of Talmudic learning in the sixteenth and seventeenth centuries, there were precocious and highly gifted boys of bar mitsvo age, who were capable of delivering an original casuistic discourse in Talmudic law. Naturally, these boys were the exceptions, but there were many others who could with the assistance of their teacher accomplish this feat of learning. It was a test and display of Talmudic knowledge. In many cases, the teacher prepared the drosho and the boy learned it by rote, and then delivered it.[131]

In Germany as well as in Poland, the bar mitsvo was celebrated with great pomp, both at the synagogue and in the home. Source material gives many interesting details about bar mitsvo celebrations in the seventeenth century among the German Jews in Worms.

The lad was dressed in new clothes bought especially for this occasion. On the Sabbath of his bar mitsvo he chanted the entire portion of the Pentateuch from the Scroll of the Torah at the synagogue. If he happened to have a pleasant voice, he also recited all the prayers before the congregation. Some lads who were not so well versed in Hebrew recited only one of the prayers—the evening prayer, the morning prayer, or the additional Sabbath prayer (Musof). There were boys who were not able to recite even the week's portion of the Pentateuch, but every bar mitsvo boy was called up to the reading of the Torah, and vowed to give a pound of wax for candles to illuminate the synagogue.

The bar mitsvo feast was served in the afternoon, as the third meal of the Sabbath. An hour before *Mincho* (afternoon prayer), the bar mitsvo lad, dressed in his new clothes, went to the homes of the guests to invite them to the third meal. At the meal, the lad delivered a drosho on the customs of bar mitsvo, and acted as the leader in reciting the grace after the meal.[132]

The bar mitsvo celebration never succeeded in deeply rooting itself in Jewish life as a synagogue observance or as a home festival. The institution was of too recent origin and was not surrounded by an atmosphere of religious reverence. The bar mitsvo feast never attained the religious significance of the circumcision feast. The drosho certainly did not contribute to the earnest solemnity of the occasion, but proved rather a detriment to the bar mitsvo celebration.

At the Present Time . . . There is, in modern times, no uniformity in the bar mitsvo celebration. There are communities in the Orient, and there were some in recent days in Germany,

where the boy reads the entire week's portion of the Pentateuch from the Scroll of the Torah. In some communities, the
boy chants only the last paragraph of the portion of the Torah
and concludes with the chanting of the Haftoro. In Eastern
Europe, the bar mitsvo boy chanted only the Haftoro, and
even this was not obligatory. Some boys, especially those who
were proficient in Talmudic learning and capable of delivering a discourse with casuistic involvements on a Talmudic
topic, did not chant at all. They merely recited the benedictions over the Torah and the Prophets. There is also a diver-
gence in the custom regarding the *talis*, or prayer-shawl. In
some communities a boy donned a talis on the Sabbath of his
bar mitsvo; in others, he did not put it on until he was married.
The Ashk'nazic Jews always present gifts to the boy in honor
of his "bar mitsvo."

In America, the bar mitsvo celebration plays an important
role in Jewish life. When a boy becomes bar mitsvo, his family
usually celebrates the great event with a sumptuous banquet
in the parents' home, or in a large rented hall. The American
bar mitsvo celebration has lost almost all of its original content. Contrary to the original idea that the father was obliged
to provide for his son's religious education until he reached
religious majority and then relieved thereof, many parents hire
a Hebrew teacher only a short time before the thirteenth
birthday of their son, in order to prepare him for the bar
mitsvo celebration. The lad chants the Haftoro to the great
delight of his parents and his relatives who gather at the synagogue to witness the performance. After the services the people attending the synagogue are served with cake and wine or
brandy. On Saturday night or Sunday, the bar mitsvo feast
takes place. The lad then delivers his "speech" and receives
gifts from the invited guests.

Bar Mitsvo among the Jews in the Orient . . . Unlike the
Ashk'nazim, the S'fardim do not restrict the rights of the
minor. The S'fardim still adhere to the Talmudic law, which

allowed a minor to put on t'filin and to be called up to the reading of the Torah, and they celebrate bar mitsvo in their own peculiar way.

Primarily, the S'fardim celebrate the first laying of t'filin which takes place exactly a year before attaining majority. If the boy is an orphan, it takes place two years before attaining majority. (Among the Ashk'nazim, too, an orphan begins laying t'filin a year earlier than a boy whose parents are living.) On that day, the parents hold a sumptuous feast for all their relatives and friends, and the boy, if capable, delivers a drosho on a topic pertaining to the occasion. Only the rich hold a second celebration a year later, when the boy reaches his majority.[133]

Among the Jews of Morocco, too, the main emphasis in the bar mitsvo celebration is placed upon the first laying of t'filin. This takes place on the Thursday after the twelfth birthday. The feast is held at the home of the parents on the preceding day, Wednesday. On Thursday, the morning services are held in the home of the boy where all the worshippers gather and take part in the ceremony. The rabbi of the community binds the phylactery upon his head. A choir accompanies the ceremony with a hymn. The boy is then called up to the reading of the Torah as the third participant after the Kohen and the Levite (on Thursday and Monday only a small portion of the Torah is read, for which only three are called).

At the end of the services the boy delivers his discourse. Then he proceeds with his t'filin bag among the men and the women present, and everyone throws silver coins into the bag. The boy presents this gift money to the teacher. The guests partake of a breakfast and, in the evening, they again gather in the house.

On the following Sabbath, the boy is called up to the reading of the Haftoro. This is accompanied by a *piyut*, a liturgical poem, composed for this occasion. The Jews of Morocco alone produced synagogual poetry as recently as modern times, when the bar mitsvo celebration came into vogue.[134]

Confirmation . . . In the nineteenth century, when Reform
Judaism in Western Europe and America discarded as obso-
lete many of the religious ceremonies and forms of synagogue
worship, hardly anything remained to mark the bar mitsvo
celebration. The t'filin, the talis, and the calling up to the
reading of the Torah were discarded. The Talmud, which
comprised the subject matter for the bar mitsvo *drosho*, was
eliminated from the curriculum of the elementary Jewish
school. All the bar mitsvo observances were thus discontinued,
and the bar mitsvo ceremonial was superseded by confirmation, which was then introduced into Jewish life.

The word confirmation, as well as some of its outward
forms were taken over from the Lutheran Protestant Church.
These borrowed forms were adapted to Jewish life and filled
with Jewish content.

Germany was the cradle of confirmation as a Jewish institution. Its beginnings in the first decades of the nineteenth century coincided in general with the beginnings of Reform
Judaism.

Instituting confirmation as a Jewish ceremonial was a slow
and gradual process. At first, confirmation took place in the
Jewish religious school for boys only. Later, it was extended
to girls, and transferred to the synagogue. At first, it had no
fixed date, and was performed on a special Sabbath, such as
the Sabbath of Pesach week or the Sabbath of Chanuko week.
Gradually, Shovuos became the day of confirmation. The
festival of the giving of the Torah, which was the day of
beginning school for Jewish children in the Middle Ages, was
suitably selected as the day for initiating the child into the
Jewish faith.

The age of confirmation was advanced a year or more beyond the traditional bar mitsvo age. The children are confirmed in a group after they have finished their course in the
religious school, and have passed an examination in the main
principles of the Jewish faith. At the confirmation ceremony,
which is accompanied by impressive music, the children, with

awe and devotion, in an atmosphere of earnest solemnity, receive the priestly blessing from the rabbi, and obligate themselves to remain faithful to Judaism. This newly instituted ceremonial of confirmation is not yet uniform, and its details vary in different congregations.

In America, confirmation was first introduced in Temple Emanu-El, New York, in the year 1847, and has become an integral part of the synagogue services in Reform congregations.

Confirmation had many opponents, but became popular because of its solemn character and its impressiveness. Proof of this fact is the adoption of its chief features by the Conservative (Progressive Orthodox) and even by Orthodox congregations, who restrict it to girls only.

The bar mitsvo ceremonial, as it was and still is performed in various countries by various groups of Jews, constitutes an interesting chapter in the history of Jewish life and folkways in recent centuries.

PART THREE

Courtship and Marriage

xi

In Biblical Times

Negotiating a Match . . . In Biblical times it was the prime duty of parents to marry off their children. Their most cherished hope was to see their children's children, especially the sons of their sons, according to the words of the Psalmist and the sayings of Proverbs. People were married in early youth, and marriages were usually contracted within the narrow circle of the clan and the family. It was undesirable to marry a woman from a foreign clan, lest she introduce foreign beliefs and practices. Abraham was content only after his servant swore to him that he would take a wife for Isaac from among Abraham's own kindred. The most popular marriages were those of cousins, as described in the stories of Genesis.[135]

In those days, girls in the Palestinian towns enjoyed no social life. Most of their leisure hours were spent with their mothers in the house. "I would lead thee and bring thee into my mother's house," says the girl to her beloved in the Song of Songs. Women appeared in the streets and squares only when something extraordinary happened, such as an important parade, or a great panic. When a hero returned in triumph from war, the women, singing and dancing and playing timbrels and stringed instruments, led the parade to greet him. In a panic in Jerusalem just before the uprising of the Maccabees, "the women," we are told, "thronged the streets and the virgins that were kept inward ran together, some to the gates, others to the walls, and some looked out through the windows." [136]

Notwithstanding woman's retirement in ancient Israel, there was not the separation of sexes found in the Mohammedan

East. There were many opportunities for young people to meet and to see one another. Sometimes a young man met a shepherdess as she led her flock to the well. Sometimes he met her at dusk as, her pitcher on her shoulder, she walked to a nearby well to draw water. Often these strong youths offered assistance to the girls who were watering their flocks; and the help was gladly accepted. Boys and girls at work in the fields met and chatted with one another, especially in the seasons of the year when the grain was harvested and the fruit of the trees was gathered. They sang and danced in the fields and vineyards, and were merry and happy.

However, these chance meetings and casual acquaintances seldom resulted in marriage. As a rule the parents, or more precisely, the fathers, arranged the match. The girl was consulted, but the "calling of the damsel and inquiring at her mouth" after the conclusion of all negotiations was merely a matter of formality. The girl certainly could not help giving her consent after her father and her whole family had agreed to the match (Gen. 24).

As already remarked in a previous chapter, Jews as well as all peoples in Biblical times welcomed the birth of a son far more than that of a daughter. Yet in those days a father was more concerned about the marriage of his sons than about the marriage of his daughters. No expense was involved in marrying off a daughter. The father received a dowry for his daughter whereas he had to give a dowry to the prospective father-in-law of his son when marrying him off. This ancient Biblical custom still prevails among the Jews of Yemen and in the Arab villages of Palestine.[137]

The price paid by the father of the groom to the father of the bride was called *mohar*, and is still so called by the Arab peasants. Scholars disagree on the etymology of this word. The English Bible translates it "dowry." For the sake of accuracy we prefer not to translate the word. In the stories of Genesis, Shechem said to Dinah's father and her brothers: "Let me find favor in your eyes, and what ye shall say unto me I will give. Ask me never so much *mohar* and *matton*, and I will give according as ye shall say unto me; but give me the damsel to wife." Here "matton" was the counterpart of "mohar," the Hebrew word for the gifts given by the groom to the bride, besides the price paid by his father to her father. From this story, we infer that the father sometimes set an extraordinarily high mohar for his daughter in order to discourage the groom. The ordinary mohar seems to have been fifty shekels of silver.[138]

The mohar was not always paid in cash. Sometimes it was paid in kind, or in service. The book of Genesis relates the story of the servant of Abraham, who, after his request for Rebekah was granted, "brought forth jewels of silver, and jewels of gold, and raiment, and gave them to Rebekah; he gave also to her brother and to her mother precious things." The servant thus gave matton to Rebekah, and mohar to her brother and mother. He paid the mohar with precious things to her brother and mother, because according to the original version of the story, Rebekah had no father but only a brother and a mother. Jacob, as a poor wanderer who possessed nothing but the staff with which he had passed over the Jordan, could pay the mohar to Laban only by rendering service. King Saul scorned to receive money as mohar for his daughter, Michal. Instead of money, Saul demanded valiant deeds from David in an attack on the king's enemies, the Philistines. A similar case is told in the story of Caleb and Othniel, the son of Kenaz. Othniel received Caleb's daughter Achsah for his wife in reward for smiting and conquering Kiriath-Sepher.[139]

The Bible does not specify what was to be done with the mohar in case the marriage agreement was broken by either of the two parties. The Code of Hammurabi made provision for it. Hammurabi was the great king and lawgiver of ancient Babylon, called in the Bible "Amraphel king of Shinar" (Gen. 14:1). He lived many centuries before Moses. And his code of laws, which was discovered by excavators at the very beginning of the twentieth century, provided as follows: If the groom changed his mind, the mohar and the matton were both forfeited. If the girl's father broke the agreement, he returned double of everything given by the groom to him and to his daughter.[140] Very likely these laws of Hammurabi concerning the mohar and the matton prevailed among all the peoples of the ancient East, including the Jews.

Mohar as Purchase and Gift . . . The mohar was originally the purchase price of the bride, and it is therefore understandable why it was paid by the father of the groom to the father of the bride. In ancient days, marriage was not an agreement between two individuals, but between two families. The newly married man usually did not found a new home for himself, but occupied a nook in his father's house. The family of the groom gained, and the family of the bride lost, a valuable member who helped tend the flock, draw water from the well, grind flour, bake bread, and assist with all the household tasks. It was reasonable, therefore, that the father of the groom should pay the father of the bride the equivalent of her value as a useful member of the family.

Yet in the course of time the mohar lost its original meaning as a purchase price paid to the father for his daughter, and assumed the significance of a gift to the near relatives of the bride. As far back as in early Biblical times, it was customary for a good father to give the whole of the mohar or at least a large part of it to his daughter. A father who appropriated the whole mohar for himself was considered unkind and harsh, and the daughter long remembered how badly he had treated her. This situation is clearly described in Genesis, in the stories of Jacob and Laban. Rachel and Leah tell Jacob concerning their father: "Is there yet any portion or inheritance for us in our father's house? Are we not accounted by him strangers, for he hath sold us and had also quite devoured our price."

The portion of the mohar which the bride received from her father, and the matton, the gifts which the groom presented to her, were not the only possessions she brought to matrimony.

A rich father sometimes gave his daughter a field or other landed property, as we are told in the story of Job, and in the previously mentioned story of Achsah, the daughter of Caleb. We hear also of maids, female slaves, which the daughter received from her father as a personal possession. She received also her share in the estate of the family, "an inheritance among her brethren," as it is called in the Bible (Job 42:15).

Notwithstanding the outward form of paying a purchase price for the bride, even in ancient Biblical times, the Jewish woman enjoyed the right of possessing private property of which she alone could dispose.

The transformation of the mohar from a purchase price to a gift was the first phase in its evolution. An account of its later development will be given in subsequent chapters.

Betrothal . . . Nowadays there is only one ceremony in connection with marriage—the wedding. Until the wedding is performed, either the bride or the groom may have a change of heart. Until late in the Middle Ages, marriage consisted of two ceremonies which were marked by celebrations at two separate times, with an interval between. First came the betrothal; then, later, the wedding. At the betrothal the woman was legally married, although she still remained in her father's house. She could not belong to another man unless she was divorced from her betrothed. The wedding meant only that the betrothed woman, accompanied by a colorful procession, was brought from her father's house to the house of her groom, and the legal tie with him was consummated.[141]

This division of marriage into two separate events originated in very ancient times when marriage was a purchase, both in its outward form and in its inner meaning. Woman was not recognized as a person but was bought in marriage, like a chattel. The process of purchase consisted of two acts. First the price was paid and an agreement reached on the conditions of sale. Sometime later the purchaser took possession of the object. The same procedure was followed in marrying a woman. The mohar was paid and a detailed agreement reached between the families of the bride and groom. This betrothal was followed by the wedding, when the bride was brought into the home of the groom, who took actual possession of her.

In those days the betrothal was the more important of these two events and maintained its importance as long as marriage was actually based upon a purchase. But as women assumed more importance as individuals, and marriage ceased to be a purchase, and attained moral significance, the actual wedding became more important than the betrothal. Finally, in the Middle Ages, the betrothal was entirely absorbed by the wedding, and became identical with it, as will be described later.

There is no information concerning the procedure of a betrothal celebration. From various passages in the Bible, we find that, besides the payment of the mohar, a solemn agreement was made between the groom and the bride. We are told that "he swore unto her, and entered into a covenant with her and spread the skirt of his garment over her" (Ezek. 16:8). In time this agreement apparently was expressed in a fixed formula. In the presence of the assembled guests, the groom declared to the father: "I came to thy house for thee to give me thy daughter So-and-so to wife; she is my wife and I am her husband from this day and forever." The assembled people apparently responded with a blessing in the name of God.[142]

Among the Arab peasants in Palestine today, as also among the Jews of Yemen, betrothed couples are not permitted under any circumstances to see one another from the moment of betrothal, even if they are cousins, live in close proximity and have been playing with one another since their early childhood. Apparently this custom prevailed also among the Jews in Biblical times. In the stories of Genesis, Rebekah took her veil and covered herself when she met Isaac in the field, because she was then only betrothed and not yet married to him. According to modern anthropologists, the original motive of this inhibition was not delicacy or shyness, but the primitive belief that the bride and the groom had an evil eye for one another.[143]

The Wedding . . . The wedding days were a time of great joy among the ancient Jews. A wedding lasted not less than seven days and was celebrated by dancing, singing and the playing of various games—always accompanied by tumultuous merriment and unconfined joy.

Usually weddings took place in the beautiful month of Ador, when "the winter is past, the rain is over and gone; the flowers appear on the earth; the time of singing is come, and the voice of the turtle is heard in our land" (Song of Songs 2:11–12). Weddings occurred in autumn also, when the corn and fruit were gathered on threshing floors and in the wine presses, and the work of the year was over. In the warm nights, by the light of the moon, the mountains of Judah and Ephraim echoed with sounds of wedding merriment. To the prophet Jeremiah, the most distinct feature of desolation in the land was the absence of "the voice of mirth and the voice of gladness, the voice of the bridegroom and the voice of the bride" (7:34; 25:10; 33:11).

Many relatives and friends, and often a whole village or town, were invited to the wedding. At Laban's daughter's wedding, he gathered all the men of the place for a feast. The groom, or rather his father, provided for the wedding. Only in exceptional cases, as for example, Jacob, who was far away from his native land, did the wedding take place at the home of the bride's parents. Another exceptional case is found in the story of Samson and the Philistine woman of Timnah. Marriages between sons of Israel and daughters of the Philistines, as with women of other foreign nations, were interdicted and did not constitute a legal marriage. The Philistine woman of Timnah was not Samson's legal wife, but merely his concubine, and was supposed to remain with her father.[144] Barring exceptional situations, if the bride lived in another village, the groom did not go to the bride, but she came to him. The whole significance of the wedding then consisted in the bride's passing from the domain of her father to that of her husband.

Among the Arab peasants today, when the bride is from another village, it is customary for her to arrive in the groom's village accompanied only by women relatives and friends. They are invited as guests into the first house which they approach. When the bride has arrived safely at a place in the bridegroom's village, messengers are sent for her father, male relatives and friends. Possibly, the same custom also prevailed in ancient Israel.

Bride and groom were arrayed in their most festive attire, the bride heavily veiled until after she emerged from the *chupo*, the bridal canopy (or pavilion). Both wore crowns on their heads. The Prophets often used the attire of bride and bridegroom as a basis for comparison of a worthy example. "Zion will adorn herself with her newly returned children, as a bride with her ornaments," says the great anonymous prophet in the second part of Isaiah (49:18; 61:10). "Can a maid forget her ornaments or a bride her attire? Yet My people have forgotten Me days without number," says Jeremiah (2:32).

The groom was surrounded by a group of young men. The main role was played by the groom's most intimate friend who supervised all the arrangements for the wedding. The bride's relatives and intimate friends hovered about her.[145]

In reconstructing a Jewish wedding in Biblical times, we glean from the Song of Songs. As far back as the beginning of the second century the Song of Songs was no longer taken literally, but was interpreted allegorically as a dialogue between God and Israel. The Fathers of the Church followed suit, and interpreted the Song of Songs as extolling the love of Jesus for the Church. In recent centuries the allegorical interpretation has been abandoned and the beauty of the book as secular poetry recognized and appreciated. As to the literary form, for some time the theory prevailed that the Song of

Songs is a drama with King Solomon and the shepherdess, Shulammite, as its main characters. Towards the end of the nineteenth century the dramatic interpretation was discarded. Most scholars now agree that the Song of Songs is not a homogeneous composition, but a collection of odes sung at Jewish weddings in ancient times. This became unmistakably clear when scholars closely observed the wedding customs of the Arab peasants in Palestine and Syria. Scholars have long since recognized a similarity in many customs and modes of life between the Arab peasants of today, who are still untouched by Western influences, and the Jews of Biblical times.

Among the Arab peasants, various ceremonies are performed with great pomp on the day before the wedding. The most important are the sword dance of the bride, and the feast. The wedding celebration takes place not indoors, but under the open sky, on the threshing floor of the village, which, in March, is overgrown with flowers and suitable for the occasion. To the threshing floor, in a solemn procession, come the groom, his intimates and guests. In the evening the bride arrives, with great pomp, to perform the sword dance.

The Arabs call the seven days of the wedding the "royal week." Bride and groom play the part of king and queen, and are treated as such by the wedding guests. Among the Jews of ancient times, as clearly seen in the Song of Songs, bride and groom were also treated like a king and queen and, for that reason, wore crowns. But the Jews did not designate the couple king and queen, but named the groom after the most magnificent Jewish king, Solomon, and the bride, Shulammite, or Shunammite, after the beautiful Abishag, the Shunammite, beloved by Solomon's brother, Adonijah, for whom he forfeited his life.

Apparently the Jews in Biblical times also celebrated the wedding under the open sky. The Jewish daughters of Judah and Ephraim would dance on the threshing floor of the village with sword in hand "on the day of the gladness of their heart." Some of the songs sung on these occasions are preserved in the

Song of Songs. One song gives this vivid picture of the great procession in which the bride is led, either to the threshing floor, or to the groom's house.

Night is falling. In the distance is seen a long, merry procession of men, women and children, all in festive array. Leading them are the torch bearers who illuminate the way. After the torch bearers come the men, then the women, and finally the bride, veiled, and with a sword bound to her side. According to the Oriental custom, the bride is lavishly perfumed. With great pomp she is borne in a litter resplendent with exquisite draperies. The groom has sent her this beautiful litter called, "The litter of Solomon." Surrounding the bride is a military escort, young men equipped with weapons of war. From afar the procession looks like a caravan emerging from the desert, winding its way toward distant lands. Occasionally the procession stops. Young and old leap, dance, and sing:

> Who is this that cometh up out of the wilderness
>   like pillars of smoke,
> Perfumed with myrrh and frankincense,
> With all powders of the merchant?
> Behold, it is the litter of Solomon;
> Threescore mighty men are about it.
> Of mighty men of Israel.
> They all handle the sword,
> And are expert in war;
> Every man hath his sword upon his thigh,
> Because of dread in the night, etc.[146]

Everyone respected a wedding procession and stood aside while it passed. Even King Agrippa laid aside his royal dignity and allowed a wedding procession to overtake him and then precede him.[147] It is doubtful, however, whether this was done by the Jewish kings in Biblical times.

Arriving at the threshing floor, the assemblage at an Arab wedding forms a circle about the bride, consisting of one half men and the other half women. The bride stands in the center, brandishes her sword and dances according to the rhythm of an ode sung by a leader. The ode extols her rich attire and physical charms. Those surrounding the bride accompany her motions by swaying the upper part of their bodies and softly clapping their hands. The whole scene is illumined by flaming torches.

In the Song of Songs we have an ode on the sword dance. The bride, designated queen, bears the name of the beautiful Shunammite. The ode begins:

> Turn around, turn around, Shulammite!
> Turn around, turn around, that we may look upon thee.
> What will ye see in the Shulammite?
> As it were a dance of two companies.—7:1.

An ode in praise of the bride follows, as among the Arabs today.

When the sword dance is over and all are tired and hungry, the great feast follows. The guests eat, drink and make merry (5:1).

The Chupo . . . Nowadays the dance, feast, giving of presents, and many other features of the wedding take place after the chupo. In ancient times, as among the Arabs of today, the chupo was the final phase of the wedding. When the bride was led into the chupo-chamber, the most important feature of the wedding ended. In the course of the procession to the chupo-chamber, the relatives of the bride blessed her:

> Our sister, be thou the mother
> Of thousands of ten thousands,
> And thy seed possess the gate
> Of those that hate them.—Gen. 24:60.

The chupo in those times was entirely different from the chupo as we have it today. Then, the chupo was a wedding tent or chamber, especially arranged and decorated by the groom. By entering the chupo-chamber the bride passed from her father's authority to that of her husband.

In the Bible, the chupo is mentioned only twice. The Psalmist pictures the sun rising in the morning "as a bridegroom coming out of his chupo" (19:6). The prophet Joel describes a general fast when all gather to pray in the Temple; even "the bridegroom goes forth from his chamber and the bride out of her chupo " (2:16).

The "Seven Days of the Feast" . . . The merrymaking of the wedding lasted through the following week. These days of merriment were called "the seven days of the feast," a name which still clings to the week following the wedding in present day Jewish life.[148]

The Arabian wedding night is followed by the "royal week," when bride and groom are royally treated by all. It is the most joyful week of their lives. The groom is the king; his intimate attendant is a grand vizier. On the day after the wedding night when the bride and groom awake, they array themselves in the same garments worn on the previous day, and receive the grand vizier who brings in breakfast. Shortly after, the groom's friends arrive and as soon as they learn that the grand vizier has been received with favor by his Majesty the King, they proceed immediately to prepare the throne of the royal pair. As chairs and sofas are not available in the village, they resort to a peasant's device—the threshing-board.

The threshing-board is a communal piece of furniture which serves various purposes: for threshing grain; as a funeral bier; and as a throne for the bride and groom at the wedding festivities. A scaffold about two yards high is set upon the threshing floor, on which is placed the threshing-board, and over the board, a large varicolored carpet. Two pillows embroidered with golden thread and stuffed with ostrich feathers are placed upon the carpet, completing the magnificent throne for the royal pair.

Bride and groom sit on the throne. The merriment begins with a dance in honor of the young pair. The newly wedded pair are the theme of the ode then sung. The main content of the ode concerns their physical perfections and their attire, but it praises the queen in more restrained terms than those used on the previous day at the sword dance. Since she is now a married woman, her overt rather than her covert charms are lauded. The guests play games which last a whole week. On the first day they start in the morning; on the following days they begin shortly before noon and continue late into the night. Only on the last day before sunset does the merriment end. The king and queen on their throne are for the most part mere spectators. Sometimes they descend from the throne to participate in the games. Originally, the odes sung on this occasion were improvisations, but in the course of time, their text became fixed.

Among the Jews in Biblical times, festivities were carried on in a similar manner during the "seven days of the feast." Many of the odes in the Song of Songs were composed to honor and entertain the bride and groom who sat on their royal throne. Riddles were also a part of the wedding entertainment. One riddle often used on this occasion is preserved in the Bible: "What is sweeter than honey and what is stronger than a lion?" The answer was well known—"Love." [149]

We cannot tell whether Jews in ancient times used the threshing-board as a throne in "the seven days of the feast." Probably in the days of the kings and the prophets, the bride and groom sat on a sofa, or chairs, pieces of furniture which belonged to the households of well-to-do peasants. [150]

xii

In Late Biblical and Post-Biblical Times

A New Attitude towards Women . . . During Biblical times, even before the Babylonian exile, Jewish life was not stationary, but evolved and changed in manifold aspects, including the attitude toward women. In the course of time, women came to be regarded as endowed with personalities just as were men.

Even as far back as early Biblical times, we find traces of a new moral attitude towards women. True, a man was legally allowed to marry more than one wife but, barring kings and princes, very few used this right. As a rule, the ordinary Jew lived in monogamous marriage. "A man leaves his father and mother and cleaves unto his wife, and they become one flesh" (Gen. 2:24). In the concept of married life, the woman was not regarded as a purchased object. Husband and wife belonged to one another. Man was not whole until a woman was constantly with him to aid him (Gen. 2:18). Such a wife was not a mere purchase. The mohar paid to her father was a gift rather than a purchase price.

This new moral attitude towards women becomes still more conspicuous when we compare the various codes of law in the Pentateuch which originated in different periods of Biblical history. In the oldest Biblical code, the so-called Book of the Covenant (Exod. 21–23), only the man-servant was freed after six years of service, not the maid-servant who had been sold by her father into servitude. She was not free because she had never been free. She belonged either to her father, to her husband or to the master to whom she was sold. However, according to the Deuteronomic code, which reflects a later phase of Jewish civilization, the maid-servant like the man-servant was freed in the seventh year. A new attitude was evolved towards the daughter, who was now regarded as a personality.[151]

We shall soon see how, with the new attitude towards women, marriage among Jews (the mohar, betrothal, and wedding) assumed new forms.

An Ancient Marriage Record . . . At the beginning of this century, an actual marriage record of a Jewish family during the period of the return from the Babylonian exile was discovered giving real names and facts, the oldest marriage contract in Jewish history.

The marriage did not take place in Palestine or among the exiles in Babylon, but among the Jews of Elephantine and Assuan, at the southern border of Egypt, by the first cataract of the Nile (see p. 27).

Jews came to that remote part of Egypt as soldiers hired into foreign service. They were organized as a military colony among mercenaries of many other nations. Most of the soldiers in the garrison apparently were Jews. It seems that they were originally hired and brought over by the Egyptian kings from poor homes in Palestine in the latter days of the First Temple, when Egypt had regained her independence. Later, when Egypt was conquered by the Persian Empire, these Jewish mercenaries continued in military service under the Persian government. All of the records unearthed at Elephantine and Assuan belong to the time of the Persian domination. They are papyri inscribed in Aramaic, the universal language of the Persian Empire west of the Euphrates.

The Jews of Elephantine and Assuan were professional soldiers, obliged to go to war to defend the southern frontier of Egypt. This vocation was transmitted from father to son. They were soldiers and also colonists who owned property. They married, had families and had ample leisure for peaceful occupations. Some soldiers even engaged in trade with the people with whom they lived.

As soldiers, the Jews of Elephantine and Assuan were an integral part of the military organization. They were called officially "Jewish army" and were divided into groups, each of which had a flag of its own. As Jews, they had autonomy, their own religious community, their own Jewish court, and a temple in which sacrifices were offered to the God of Israel.

Most of the business documents which were unearthed in Elephantine and Assuan belonged to the family of a well-to-do Jewish soldier named Machseiah, the son of Yedaniah. In the documents, his daughter, Mibtachiah, married and received a valuable piece of property as dowry from her father. Her first husband died and she remarried, this time a non-Jew, an Egyptian by the name of As-Hor, who was called "the architect of the king." In the documents of his sons, As-Hor bears the Jewish name Nathan. Apparently he became a proselyte to the Jewish faith, and his sons bore Jewish names.

We are concerned with the marriage contract of Mibtachiah and As-Hor. It began with a declaration of marriage by As-Hor to Mibtachiah's father. "I came to thy house for thee to give me thy daughter, Mibtachiah, to wife; she is my wife and I am her husband from this day and forever" (see p. 130). Following this declaration of betrothal, all terms of the marriage contract were written in detail. As-Hor paid Machseiah, the father, five shekels, Persian standard, as a mohar for his daughter. Besides, Mibtachiah received a gift of 65½ shekels from As-Hor. From this we gather that the mohar which fathers received for their daughters was then merely a nominal payment, the formality of a lingering custom of olden times.

Of the 65½ shekels that Mibtachiah received from As-Hor, twelve shekels were in cash, the remainder in clothing and utensils. A complete list of the gifts Mibtachiah received is given and fully described, in regard to quality, size, and value: one garment of wool, dyed new, embroidered, on both sides, 8 by 5 cubits; one closely woven shawl, new, 7 by 5; another garment of spun wool, 6 by 3; one mirror, one tray, two cups, and one bowl, all of bronze. Each one of these items is also appraised in cash. According to the marriage contract, Mibta-chiah had equal rights with her husband. She had her own property which she could bequeath as she pleased, and she had the right to pronounce a sentence of divorce against As-Hor, even as he had the right to pronounce it against her. All she had to do was to appear before the court of the community and declare that she had developed an aversion to As-Hor. We do not know to what degree the equality of rights enjoyed by Jewish women of Elephantine was due to Jewish or to Persian-Babylonian law.

Mibtachiah impresses us as a very active woman. She was energetic and enterprising, had property of her own and was on an equal footing with her husband. She was also very particular about the cosmetics with which she beautified herself. Among the articles which she received from her father was mentioned a new ivory cosmetic box.

At the conclusion of Mibtachiah's marriage contract, the name of the scribe appeared. He was Nathan, the son of Ananiah, who had written the deed at the dictation of As-Hor. The names of three witnesses appeared on this remarkable document, which was written about the time Nehemiah was rebuilding the walls of Jerusalem.

The betrothal of Mibtachiah to the Egyptian architect As-Hor presumably took place at the house of Machseiah, son of Yedaniah. Imagine the house crowded with Jews as well as Egyptians, the relatives and friends of both the Jewish bride, Mibtachiah, and the Egyptian groom, As-Hor. After paying the mohar and delivering the gifts to Mibtachiah, the robust and simple folk of this military colony partook of a festive meal amid boisterous joy and merriment. [152]

The K'subo . . . This newly disinterred papyrus of a marriage deed or *k'subo*, as it has been called in Aramaic since the days of the Second Temple, is the first document of its kind found in Jewish history. In many points of content and form, Mibtachiah's marriage contract resembles the version of the k'subo, still in vogue in modern Jewish life. Yet we must not assume that the k'subo originated at that time (5th century B.C.E.). It was rather a well-established institution in the Persian period of Jewish history. In any references to marriage throughout the Bible, the mohar was paid and gifts presented, but a written contract was never mentioned. However, the Book of Deuteronomy specifically states that if a man dislikes his wife, "he writes her a bill of divorcement and gives it in her hand" (24:3). Modern critics of the Bible have agreed that on the whole, the Deuteronomic law is a product of the century preceding the Babylonian exile. If a written document was employed at that period in dissolving a marriage, we have to assume that it was also employed in contracting a marriage. In purchasing realty, written contracts were employed in Judah in the years preceding the first destruction of Jerusalem.[153] Scholars assume that the written contract was introduced into Jewish life in the Assyro-Babylonian period, under Assyro-Babylonian influences. Most tablets unearthed from the ancient mounds of Babylonia and Assyria were contract tablets. In Babylonia, marriage contracts were mentioned in the ancient Code of Hammurabi.[154] At the time when the Elephantine papyri were written, the marriage deed in Jewish life was an established institution of at least two hundred years' standing.

A Divorce Penalty . . . But it was the change in the main provision of the marriage contract, the paying of the mohar, rather than the introducing of the written marriage contract, that altered the character of marriage among Jews. The mohar institution was entirely transformed during late-Biblical and post-Biblical times. From a bridal price it finally became a lien to be paid by the husband in case of divorce, or by his heirs in case of his death.

The change in the mohar institution was a direct result of the basic changes which took place in the material conditions of life. In the simple conditions of early Biblical days, all sons and daughters married young. No one stayed single. We hear of only one exceptional case shortly before the first destruction of Jerusalem. The prophet Jeremiah remained a celibate, explaining his unique position as a divine command. In a prophetic vision he heard the command of God that he should not take a wife nor have sons or daughters, because a devastating catastrophe would soon overtake the commonwealth of Judah, and the sons and daughters born in that place would die grievous deaths, together with their mothers and fathers, without being lamented or buried (Jer. 16).

The Book of Proverbs, the oldest in the wisdom literature of the Jews, contains no exhortations regarding the advisability of marrying at an early age, nor the evils of unmarried life. There was no need of exhorting people on that score. The Book of Proverbs states that not all men are happy in their matrimonial life. A man married a prudent woman, a woman of valour, and was happy; another married an evil and contentious woman and was very unhappy.[155] Obviously no one was deterred from marriage on that account.

The situation changes, however, when we turn from Proverbs to the wisdom book of Ben-Sira (Ecclesiasticus). The author, Joshua Ben-Sira (Jesus the son of Sirach), flourished in Jerusalem not long before the uprising of the Maccabees. In his wise sayings he admonishes the young men of his days against the evils of remaining single:

> Without a hedge a vineyard is laid waste,
> And without a wife a man is a wanderer and homeless.

Apparently bachelorship, common among Jews in Talmudic times, had its beginnings in pre-Maccabean days. Economic conditions were such that men hesitated to shoulder the responsibility of matrimony. It was not unusual for women to support the men they married. Ben-Sira rebuked these men who married women solely for a rich dowry:

> Hard slavery and a disgrace it is,
> If a wife support her husband.

Ben-Sira also admonished the fathers not to let their sons remain single too long but to let them marry when young:

> If thou hast sons, correct them,
> And give them wives in their youth.

No wonder, therefore, that in the days of Ben-Sira, parents looked with concern at their marriageable daughters, and Ben-Sira exhorted the fathers:

> Get thy daughter married, and worry will vanish,
> But bestow her on a sensible man.[156]

Under these conditions there was no place for the old mohar institution. Fathers no longer expected any material gain from their daughters' marriages. On the contrary, fathers often gave rich dowries to daughters as an inducement to marriageable men.

Yet the mohar institution did not pass out of existence. It was reformed intermittently in the course of this period, adapting itself to new circumstances. The first stage in this process was to make the bride's father a mere trustee of the mohar. The money was then inherited ultimately either by the husband or by his children. This reform availed little, so the husband himself was made the trustee of the money, which was employed to buy household articles. This is the phase in the evolution of the mohar which we meet in the papyri of Elephantine. The money which As-Hor gave to Mibtachiah was spent mostly for clothing and household utensils. The last step in the reform of the mohar institution was made by Simeon ben Shatach, head of the Pharisees, who were the ruling party in the state during the reign of the Maccabean queen, Salome Alexandra (76–67 B.C.E.). Simeon ben Shatach declared that the mohar, which was ordinarily two hundred silver dinars (fifty shekels) for a girl, and one hundred for a widow, should merely be written in the k'subo, the marriage deed, as a lien of the wife on the estate of her husband, to be paid to her only if he divorced her, or at his death.[157]

This reform served two humane purposes. It made marriage easier, and divorce more difficult. A man did not need two hundred dinars in cash in order to marry a girl, but he needed this amount if he wanted to divorce her. The k'subo thus protected the woman from being arbitrarily divorced by her husband.

In the First Centuries of the Common Era

Wedlock and Bachelorhood . . . The conditions of life which militated against matrimony as far back as the Greek and Maccabean periods of Jewish history became more strained in the first centuries of the Common Era. The Talmud and Midrash, the Jewish literature of that period, contain many references to wedlock and bachelorhood. It was an epoch of bachelorhood in the Roman world at large, and also among Jews. Bachelors were common. One of the greatest Jewish sages, Simeon ben Azzai, who lived in the first half of the second century, died a celibate. Although bachelors were excluded from teaching in primary schools, there were generous bachelors who contributed to the maintenance of those schools. They were highly commended for supporting an institution in which they could not be directly interested.[158]

No wonder, therefore, that the Talmud and Midrash contain many exhortations to marry at an early age, and admonitions against staying single. For example:

"Any man who has not a wife is not a proper man (an Adam)."

"Any man who has no wife lives without joy, without blessing, and without happiness."

"Until the age of twenty, the Holy One, blessed be He, sits and waits: 'when will he take a wife?' But as soon as one attains the age of twenty and is not yet married, He exclaims: 'Blasted be his bones!' "

"Whilst your hand is yet upon your son's neck, marry him off, viz., between sixteen and twenty-two. Others state, 'Between eighteen and twenty-four.' "

There is an anecdote in the Babylonian Talmud about the three famous Amoraim, Rav Huna, Rav Chisda, and Rav Hamnuna, who lived in Babylonia in the second half of the third century (C.E.). Rav Huna was then the head of the great academy at Sura and Rav Chisda was his pupil and colleague. Once, in conversation with Rav Huna, Rav Chisda praised Rav Hamnuna as a great man. So Rav Huna said to Rav Chisda, "When Rav Hamnuna visits you, bring him to me." When Rav Hamnuna arrived, Rav Huna saw that he was not wearing the head-covering or turban customary for married men. "Why have you no headdress?" asked Rav Huna. "Because I am not married," was the reply. Thereupon Rav Huna turned his face away from him, saying, "See to it that you do not appear before me again until you are married." [159]

Bachelorship was disapproved severely as detrimental in every way. The bachelor was ridiculed. As long as he was young, he considered no woman was good enough to marry, but it did occur to him to marry at an age "when his nose is nipped, his ears are heavy, his eyes are dim, and no woman can be found that would marry him." [160]

There is no record of women celibates among Jews in that period, but we do hear of unmarried women who waited a long time to get married because the marriageable men were reluctant to wed.[161]

The main cause of this state of affairs were the political and economic conditions of the times. There was a difference between Palestine and Babylonia in this respect. Conditions in Babylonia, which was a part of the Persian kingdom, were much more favorable for the Jews than in Palestine, which belonged to the Roman Empire. Matrimony was a simpler matter for the Babylonian Jews than for their brethren in Palestine. In Babylonia in the third century, the religious teachers decreed that a man should marry first and study the Torah afterwards, whereas in Palestine, they said: "Can a man indulge in the study of the Torah with a millstone on his neck?" In that century of civil war and social chaos in the Roman

Empire, it was quite usual for men in Palestine to marry between the ages of thirty and forty.[162]

Marriage of Minors . . . A man's correct matrimonial age was from eighteen to about twenty-four. A girl was supposed to marry much earlier, at the age of twelve or thirteen. Fathers were reproved if they permitted their daughters to pass that age without giving them in marriage.

Theoretically, the son and the daughter had the decisive voice in choosing and concluding a match, but this theory was not always followed. There were inconsiderate fathers who betrothed their children, especially daughters, when they were still children. Among the Romans, girls often were married at the age of nine and ten, and this practice spread among Jews. From the third century on, loud voices of protest were raised against this inconsiderate attitude. Some religious teachers of Babylonia prohibited it, but the practice was not discontinued.

However, the betrothal of minor girls was the exception rather than the rule. A girl betrothed when still a minor had the right to make a declaration of refusal when she came of age. She could say that she disliked the man and did not wish to marry him; and then the betrothal was annulled.[163]

Making a Choice . . . Jewish girls of that period enjoyed much personal freedom. As in ancient Biblical days, they gathered at the wells and conversed as they drew their jugs of water. They also went to market, sold wares in the stores, and in general, occupied themselves in various ways. They were apt to meet and become acquainted with marriageable young men, and often chose their own mates.[164]

However, it was the parents rather than the children who had the deciding voice in making the choice, and who arranged the match.

There were many aspects to be considered in choosing a mate. First, there was the physical aspect, and, as in Biblical days, the main emphasis was laid upon the girl's eyes. As long as a girl had beautiful eyes, she passed as a beautiful bride. For the sake of the progeny, the physical characteristics of bride and groom were taken into consideration. It was inadvisable for a very tall man to marry a very tall woman, lest their offspring be tall "as the mast of a ship"; for a very short man to marry a very short woman, lest their offspring be dwarfs; for a very white man to marry a very white woman, lest their offspring be albinos; for a very dark man to marry a very dark woman, lest their offspring be pitch black. The character of the prospective bride's brothers was looked into, because of the current belief that most children take after their mothers' brothers.[165]

More important than the physical qualities and the progeny was the social rank of the prospective bride and groom and the nature of the groom's vocation. A distinction was made between a clean and a dirty occupation. As to the social rank, emphasis was laid upon culture. A man of learning should not marry the daughter of an illiterate under any circumstances. Nor should a man of learning give his daughter in marriage to an illiterate. A daughter of a kohen, a descendant of the priestly caste, was supposed to marry a kohen only. The marriage of a daughter of a kohen and an ordinary Jew was discouraged. The Talmud says: "If a man marries a wife who is fit for him, the prophet Elijah kisses him and the Holy One, blessed be He, loves him; but he who marries a wife who is not fit for him, Elijah binds him and the Holy One, Blessed be He, flagellates him." [166]

There were many degrees in the social scale even within the cultured and learned classes. Says the Talmud: "A man should sell all he possesses in order to marry the daughter of a scholar. If he cannot get the daughter of a scholar, let him marry the daughter of a prominent man of his day; if he cannot get the daughter of a prominent man of his day, let him marry the daughter of the head of a synagogue; if he cannot get the daughter of the head of a synagogue, let him marry the daughter of a director of charity; if he cannot get the daughter of a director of charity, let him marry the daughter of a teacher in a primary school, but he should never marry the daughter of an illiterate." [167]

Among Jews, nobility of culture and aristocracy of learning took precedence over nobility of blood or wealth, and the aristocratic families made every possible effort to separate themselves from the ignorant and illiterate masses.

K'tsotso . . . Not all men conformed with the social rules. Occasionally, a defiant young man married beneath his social rank, to the great embarrassment of his family. Sometimes the family was shocked into disinheriting the defiant member and severing all connection with him. This act of disinheriting a young man was marked by a ceremony called *k'tsotso*, which means severing, cutting off.

In the Talmud there is a description of this queer ceremony, performed in the following manner:

The members of the family came together, bringing a cask full of fruits. In the presence of the children, the open middle space in the cask was broken and the children picked up the fruit and called out, "Brethren of the House of Israel, hear! Our brother So-and-so has married a woman who is not worthy of him and we are afraid lest his descendants will be united with our descendants. Come and take a warning for future generations, that his descendants shall not be united with our descendants." [168]

Severance of all relations with the disinherited member was thus publicly proclaimed and impressed upon the memory of both the older and younger generation who participated in the k'tsotso ceremony.

Negotiating a Match . . . After the choice was mutually made, negotiations began between the two parents, usually through an intermediary. If the bride was of age, she carried on the negotiations personally. If she had not attained her majority, her father did this for her. The arrangement of marriage negotiations was permitted even on the Sabbath.[169]

There were various conditions and stipulations to be agreed upon, beginning with the dowry which the girl's father gave to his daughter and his prospective son-in-law. In this era of bachelorhood, fathers promised large dowries in order to attract suitors, often out of proportion to their means. As far back as the days preceding the second destruction of Jerusalem, it was not unusual for a father-in-law to promise a large cash dowry to his prospective son-in-law and refuse to carry out his promise after the betrothal. Cases came before the courts in Jerusalem in which the groom refused to wed the girl without the promised dowry and she remained betrothed but unmarried for life. Usually she could force the groom either to wed or divorce her.[170]

In those days, even more than in the days of Ben-Sira, a number of men married rich women merely for the sake of large dowries. This practice was sternly discouraged. "He who takes a wife for the sake of money will have unworthy children," says the Talmud.[171]

Not every man gave his daughter a dowry in cash, but each father was obliged to furnish a wedding outfit valued at fifty *zuz* (silver dinar), which was the minimum. Even an orphaned girl received that from the charity fund. Among the poor, the wedding outfit consisted of the barest necessities: clothes, house utensils, and furniture. Among the rich, slaves and real estate were included in the marriage gift. The daughter sometimes received a share of the parents' wealth as her own property. Her husband merely had the right to use and derive benefit from the property with her consent during her lifetime.

Paramount in the negotiations was the amount of money on which the wife received a lien in the marriage contract, the k'subo, in the case of her husband's death or in the event that he divorced her. If the groom had no property as security, someone else guaranteed it for him. The minimum amount was two hundred silver dinars for a girl and a hundred for a widow.

In priestly families and in some aristocratic lay families, four hundred dinars were the minimum to be entered in the k'subo.

This primary amount of the k'subo was not a matter for negotiations. Every groom was obliged to grant it to his prospective wife, without regard to wealth, social rank, or dowry. It was the "additional k'subo" which came up for negotiations. The primary k'subo was the ancient mohar transformed into a promise, a lien clause in the marriage contract. The additional k'subo was the ancient matton transformed into a lien and varied according to circumstances. There was no limit to the amount of money to which the groom could increase the "additional k'subo" in accordance with his wealth and social position. The larger the additional k'subo, the more important the groom appeared. If the bride turned out to be a bad wife, the husband deeply regretted his generosity at the betrothal. It was embarrassing for a man to be wedded to an unworthy wife who had an enormous k'subo. On the other hand, a large k'subo protected the wife from any arbitrary attitude on the part of her husband, and kept him from divorcing her.

Negotiations revolved around various other provisions, mutual duties and rights. Many of these provisions were necessary only when the bride came from a different locality. If both lived in the same place, the many details of these mutual rights and obligations followed the local custom.[172]

Betrothal . . . After the terms of the marriage were settled, the betrothal was celebrated at the house of the bride's father. It was a highly festive occasion. In the Talmud we have a brief and vivid description of a betrothal celebration. There was much hustle and bustle in the house. The rooms were brightly illumined. In the room where the guests were received were beautifully upholstered sofas, upon which the guests might recline, as was the custom of the times. The women were meanwhile doing their handiwork. Drawing the thread from the distaff, they joyfully announced the name of the happy bride: "So-and-so is being betrothed today." [173]

At the betrothal, the groom gave the bride an object valued at no less than a *p'ruto* and declared orally in the presence of two witnesses: "Be thou consecrated to me, be thou betrothed to me, be thou my wife." She was also legally betrothed if he gave her this declaration in writing signed by two witnesses, without handing her anything of value. In late Talmudic times, the bride could be legally betrothed without receiving anything at all from the groom, if he just did some favor for her.[174] Thus, betrothal among Jews was no longer a commercial transaction, as among the Greeks and Romans. Even formerly it was merely the symbol of a purchase.

In Talmudic times, betrothal had assumed high religious significance. A new term for betrothing, *Kadesh*, came into vogue. Whatever this word may originally have meant, there was implicit in it, in this connection, the sense of sanctification.[175] In the Mosaic Law the prohibition of incest and licentiousness was promulgated as a prerequisite for "sanctifying oneself and being holy" (Lev. 20). This was the starting-point for spiritualizing the matrimonial union and for declaring it as preliminary to the sanctification of man's life. Thus the betrothal celebration was accompanied by a benediction proclaiming the purity of married life as a divinely ordained institution and concluding with praise to God "who sanctifies His people Israel through chupo and Kidushin." [176]

It was customary for the groom to send gifts to the bride shortly after the betrothal. Then the groom was entertained with a second betrothal feast by the bride's father.[177]

The betrothal continued to be a binding contract which only a formal divorce could dissolve. This was the practice among the Jews of Palestine and Babylonia. But among the Alexandrian Jews, apparently under the Greco-Egyptian influence, a betrothed woman was not regarded as married. The declaration of betrothal in Alexandria was conditional: "Be thou my wife when thou wilt go with me into the chupo." Betrothal among the Egyptian Jews could be dissolved without divorce.[178]

In regard to the interval between the betrothal and the wedding, there was a variation in local custom even in Palestine. In Galilee, bride and groom were kept strictly apart. In southern Palestine, Judea proper, the groom was permitted to visit the bride at the home of her father during the time between the betrothal and the wedding.[179]

The Wedding . . . As in Biblical times so also in the period with which we are now concerned, the wedding consisted of escorting the betrothed to the home of the husband. We know more about the wedding and wedding customs in this period than in the preceding era, but the customs practiced in this later era were not entirely new. Some of them dated back to Biblical days.

The maiden was allowed a year's time to prepare her trousseau for the wedding. A widow was allowed only thirty days. Girls were usually married on Wednesday, and widows on Thursday. With the exception of the Sabbath, festivals and fast days, other days of the week were not ruled out.[180]

On the Sabbath preceding the wedding, festivities took place at the home of the bride's father. This was called "the first Sabbath of the wedding." [181]

Participation in the celebration of the wedding and contributing in any way to the joy of the bride and groom was regarded as a mitsvo (a religious act). It was a mitsvo to take part in the wedding procession and also, if the bride was poor, to provide her with festive raiment and adornment.[182]

The bride was seated in a beautifully decorated chair while her female friends or older relatives helped dress her. They washed her, heavily perfumed her and sumptuously adorned her with twenty-four ornaments. Her hair was braided and garlanded. The bride and the groom both wore crowns before the disastrous days of the Jewish wars against Rome, when this practice was abolished.[183] However, only the crown of the groom was definitely abolished. The garland of the bride was resumed in the Middle Ages and is still in vogue today.

Before the bride left her parents' home, a feast was arranged for the guests. When it was over, the father bestowed his blessing upon the bride, and the bridal procession set forth into the streets of the town.

The bride sat in a litter carried by the most eminent of the guests. The townspeople fell in at the end of the procession. Even elderly men and women followed the sound of the drum. They were prompted by curiosity as well as by the desire to attain the great religious merit of participating in the joy of a wedding. Even distinguished rabbis interrupted their discourses on the Torah, and, with their pupils, joined the wedding procession.

While the bride was being prepared for the great event, the groom was attended by his friends, especially his most intimate friend and best man. His friends prepared the chupo. This was a pavilion hung with precious tapestries in the house of the groom or his father. These hangings were usually of white linen, embroidered in gold and purple. Fruits and sweetmeats were suspended from the chupo. In some localities the chupo was constructed from the lumber of trees which had been planted at the birth of the bride and groom (p. 21).

The groom, in festive array, accompanied by his friends, went to meet the bride. His most intimate friend, carrying a myrtle branch, played the chief role. They were met by ten maidens, friends of the bride, who carried torches or lamps. The maidens marching ahead of the bridegroom introduced him to the bridal party.

Joined by the groom and his retinue, the throng moved on, singing and dancing, shouting and clapping, playing harps, flutes and zithers, and beating timbrels. Wine and aromatic oil emitting sweet odors flowed in profusion from large vessels. In honor of the bride and groom a cask of wine was carried before them. In some places a cock and a hen were carried as a symbol of fertility. Nuts, parched corn, and other sweetmeats were scattered in their path.[184]

Even high dignitaries, myrtle branch in hand, danced and

sang in honor of the bride, praising her. In the Talmud, a fragment of a wedding song is preserved, "No paint, no powder, no beautification and yet a graceful gazelle."

But not all who participated in the procession sang the praise of the bride. Sometimes ridicule and jeers were directed at the pair. For instance, if the groom happened to be handsome and the bride ugly, scoffers derided him, saying: "This nice young man is ruined by this basket" (the litter in which the bride was carried), and vice versa.[185]

The joyous throng continued the merrymaking until it reached the house of the groom or his father. The gaiety was then transferred from the street to the house, reaching its highest point at the wedding feast. The house was illumined by countless oil lamps. At the head of the room sat the groom. Food and wine were served lavishly. Songs were sung and merry tales and fables were told. Some even made ribald jokes about the bride and the chupo. This was sternly condemned by the religious leaders. In the first half of the second century (C.E.), religious leaders protested vehemently against singing the odes of the Song of Songs at wedding feasts,[186] and in time this custom was discarded. By that time the Song of Songs was included among the Sacred Writings and was not interpreted literally but allegorically, as a dialogue between God and Israel (see p. 132).

Notwithstanding the wine and the jests, the wedding feast now assumed a religious character. A special wedding benediction, still in use today, was recited over a cup of wine, expressing a lofty religious view of the institution of marriage and the joy of the wedding. If learned men were present, discourses on the Torah were given. Religious merit was attached to the participation in a wedding feast. In Jerusalem there was a special brotherhood for the purpose of attending betrothal and wedding feasts, just as there was a special brotherhood to attend circumcision feasts (see p. 26 and p. 240).

The banquet lasted until past midnight. As in ancient Biblical times, the merriment continued for seven days. On each day the wedding benediction was repeated for new visitors who had not previously attended the wedding festivities. On the Sabbath it was repeated even without visitors; the Sabbath and holidays were regarded as visitors. If the bride was a widow, the merriment lasted only three days; sometimes only one day.

As a counterpart of the feast on the Sabbath preceding the wedding, a post-wedding feast took place on the Sabbath following the wedding, "the second Sabbath of the wedding." [187]

xiv

In the Middle Ages

So far the history of Jewish marriage has been traced through ancient times, from Biblical days to the early centuries of the Common Era. Within that time the Jewish marriage institution passed through various changes in regard to human relations as well as outward form. Notwithstanding those modifications, the procedure and celebration of marriage remained essentially the same throughout the epoch. Later, in post-Talmudic times and in the Middle Ages, the ancient betrothal and chupo gave way to a new mode of marriage celebration.

Matches and Matchmakers . . . In the Middle Ages, the sexes were kept strictly apart, and romance was almost unknown. The time for love between husbands and wives was after marriage. Before marriage the couple hardly knew one another. Jewish religious authorities prided themselves on the modesty and obedience of Jewish daughters, who, even after twenty, relied entirely upon their fathers to arrange a match for them, and in no way interfered or expressed themselves upon the matter.

If occasionally a girl expressed herself, she was considered bold and arrogant. Parents therefore had no scruples in selecting a mate for their daughter while she was still under age. The marriage of minors, especially of minor girls, was widespread among the Jews in the Middle Ages, in spite of the Talmudic prohibition (see p. 148). The reasons were mainly economic and political. A religious authority of the age of the crusaders said explicitly: "The custom that now prevails of marrying off our daughters when they are still minors is a result of the persecutions which increase daily, for though today a man may be able to afford a dowry for his daughter, he may by tomorrow be unable to give her anything, and she might consequently remain unmarried." [188]

Dowries for daughters were a matter of course. A man seldom married even a cousin "by the hair of her head," the current expression for marrying a woman without a dowry. However, in arranging a match, the amount of the dowry was less essential than the genealogical record and the social position of the family. In the Middle Ages, as in Talmudic times, stress was laid not only upon the conduct and moral qualities of the bride, but also upon those of her brothers.

Since boys and girls had no opportunity to meet and become acquainted with one another, and matches were arranged entirely by the respective fathers, the matchmaker naturally played a significant role in effecting a marriage. We met the matchmaker in the Talmudic era. We cannot ascertain whether matchmaking was then a vocation or merely an act of kindness on the part of some friend or relative. In the Middle Ages, matchmaking became a well-paid profession, and Jewish law fully recognized the matchmaker and the remuneration which he received for his service. The amount paid to the *shadchon* (the Talmudic term used for the matchmaker) varied in different localities from one to three per cent of the dowry. There was also a difference in various localities in regard to the time when the shadchon was to be paid. In some localities he was paid after the wedding; in others, he received his compensation soon after the match was arranged. [189]

The shadchon was, as a rule, a very dignified person, held in high esteem. Even renowned rabbis occupied themselves with matchmaking. The most famous was Maharil, the great rabbi and head of the y'shivo in Mayence in the first half of the fifteenth century, to whom we have already referred in an earlier chapter (see p. 40). Although Maharil was the rabbi of Mayence, he made a living from matchmaking. He gave the money derived from his congregational services for the support of the students in the y'shivo. Maharil was not the only rabbi engaged in matchmaking; rabbis apparently were best fitted for this occupation. In the Middle Ages, parents sought a gifted y'shivo student for their daughter, and no one was better able to make the right selection than a great rabbi of a Talmudic academy.

Not all matchmakers were as conscientious as the famous Maharil. Many of them were unscrupulous persons who did not hesitate to use dubious tactics and gross exaggerations.

There are numerous stories, proverbs, anecdotes, and jokes in Jewish folklore about this degraded type of shadchon, who resorted to any available means to attain his ends. He has been the perennial target of Jewish jesters and humorists.

The Decline of the Betrothal . . . We have already noticed in the history of Jewish marriage a continuous breaking away from the outward forms of purchase. This entailed a gradual diminution in the importance of betrothal. In later Talmudic times the betrothed woman was no longer regarded as actually married. She belonged to the household of her father. The writing of the final terms of the k'subo was accordingly shifted from the betrothal to the wedding.[190]

The betrothal was thus on the decline at the beginning of the Middle Ages. However, as in the case of many social and religious institutions and practices which persisted long after they had lost their original significance, the betrothal celebration might have continued had it not been gradually absorbed by the wedding. Both ceremonies were ultimately united in one celebration to comprise the new, transformed wedding ceremony that emerged in the later Middle Ages.

There were many reasons for the breakdown of the independent betrothal ceremony. Based originally on the conception of marriage as a purchase, the betrothal became outdated and antiquated in the Middle Ages. Besides, for the poorer classes two separate celebrations and feasts were too costly. It was embarrassing, too, to keep the couple apart after they were nearly married. Then too, in times of persecutions, especially if the bride and the groom came from different localities, the betrothal of a daughter who might be unable to join her husband was too precarious.

In about the eleventh and twelfth centuries there was a period of transition when the betrothal and the wedding were performed on the same day, with an intermission of a few hours—the betrothal in the morning and the wedding toward evening. But this arrangement was burdensome, because the feasting lasted the whole day and was quite a financial burden on the bridegroom and his family. Finally, in the following centuries, the betrothal and wedding were performed simultaneously as a single event.[191]

The Marriage Ring . . . In the same period which saw the collapse of the betrothal, the ring, as a new symbol in the marriage ceremonial, appeared. As far back as the seventh or eighth centuries, among the Jews of the Orient, the ring began to supersede the coin as a symbol of marriage. Apparently the custom of using a ring spread westward. In about the twelfth century, among the Franco-German Jews, the betrothal ring contained no precious stone. In the following centuries, the coin was finally dislodged, its place definitely taken by the ring which became the symbol of conjugal love and fidelity.[192]

When the use of the coin was abandoned, the last vestige of the outward forms of purchase disappeared from Jewish marriage.

To the Synagogue . . . In Talmudic times, marriage had already assumed a religious character. Nevertheless, it was still exclusively a ceremony performed in the home, not in the synagogue. True, the betrothal and wedding feasts were both marked by special benedictions, recited in the presence of a religious quorum of ten; but these were recited at the home of the bridegroom or his parents. Only in post-Talmudic times, in the eighth or ninth centuries, did the wedding celebration become a community affair associated with the life of the synagogue. Then the entire congregation shared the joy of the bridegroom, paying its respects to him at the synagogue services.

On the Sabbath following the wedding, the newly married man was honored by the congregation. In the morning the groom was escorted to the synagogue by a solemn procession. Religious hymns were sung. The services on this Sabbath were amplified by special *piyutim* (liturgical poems added to the regular prayers for festivals and outstanding Sabbaths). When the week's portion of the Pentateuch was read, the precentor, chanting Hebrew hymns, called the groom to witness the reading of the Torah and to recite the benedictions over it. A special portion of the Pentateuch, the story of the wooing of Rebekah, was chanted in his honor. The cantor also chanted on this Sabbath a special Haftoro (Isaiah 61:5, which contains allusions to the festive bridal attire and the rejoicing of the bridegroom and the bride). This custom of reading a special portion of the Pentateuch and a special Haftoro in honor of the bridegroom was discontinued by European Jewry, although the custom still prevails among Oriental Jews.

The actual marriage ceremony, however, was still performed at home. The rabbi did not officiate at the ceremony, and the benedictions were recited or chanted by several people, each benediction by another man. Not until the beginning of the fifteenth century do we first hear of a marriage ceremony performed by a rabbi in the synagogue.[193]

By that time the marriage ceremony had been entirely transformed. The betrothal, the wedding, and the chupo were united into one ceremony.

The Transformation of the Chupo . . . Not only did the ancient form of betrothal disappear in the Middle Ages, but likewise the chupo, as a bridal chamber. In the later Middle Ages, the ancient custom of leading the bride into a chamber or tent, where she remained in strict privacy with the groom, became repugnant to the European Jews. Besides, among the Jews in Western lands it was the groom who went from his father's house to the house of the bride's father. The old wedding procession at the conclusion of which the bride entered the chupo thus became devoid of meaning, for entering the chupo had signified that the bride passed from her father's house to that of her husband, whereas now in actual life, the groom went from his father's house to the home of his father-in-law.

However, the chupo idea did not entirely pass out of existence. Many symbolical substitutes for the ancient bridal chamber arose. In one region, the veil with which the bride covered her face when she left her father's house was called chupo. In another, both the heads of the groom and the bride were covered by one kerchief which was called chupo. In Germany, the name chupo was applied to the custom of wrapping the bride and groom in a talis (prayer-shawl).

Even as late as the sixteenth century, religious authorities could not determine the signification of chupo. Among the Jews of the Orient, chupo still signified the strict privacy into which the couple was inducted immediately after the marriage ceremony. In Poland, which was the main center of Jewish life and learning in that period, as well as in the West European countries, various symbolic substitutes for the original chupo were used among Jews. The most popular symbolic substitute was the portable canopy. The canopy was a combination of a curtain, spread over the heads of the bride and groom, and a tent. This symbolic chupo was almost universally accepted by the European Jews. We hear of communities in Germany in the 15th century, where, early on Friday morning, the bridal pair were seated under a canopy in the courtyard of the synagogue. This ceremony will be described later. At a somewhat later date the b'rocho (benediction), as the marriage ceremony was then called, took place inside the synagogue, without a canopy.

In Poland, in the 16th century, the marriage ceremony was

performed under a canopy, and this latter form of the chupo became universal. The bride and groom were led not *into* the chupo, as in the olden times, but *under* the chupo. With great pomp, with lighted torches and music, the groom, followed by the bride, was led under the canopy which was placed inside the synagogue, or outside at the entrance. There the groom betrothed the bride with a ring, and the benedictions over the betrothal and the wedding were chanted solemnly by the rabbi of the community in the presence of the guests who had gathered to witness the ceremony.[194]

Thus at the threshold of modern times, the entire character of the Jewish wedding was changed. The wedding was now characterized by a procession which led the bride and groom into the synagogue instead of into the bridal chamber.

Synagogue and Courtyard . . . Originally the marriage ceremony was transferred to the synagogue. It was performed within the edifice, and there the canopy was erected. In order to secure better accommodations for a large company, some people preferred to have the ceremony in the courtyard, in front of the entrance to the synagogue. In the sixteenth century, Jews in Poland were still divided on that subject. Some were in favor of the synagogue, and others in favor of the courtyard. Ultimately the courtyard became more popular through a new symbolic interpretation of the chupo under the open sky. A marriage ceremony performed in the open air, under the shining stars, was a good omen that the progeny of the couple would be as numerous as the stars in heaven.[195]

In the course of time, performing the marriage ceremony at the entrance of the courtyard of the synagogue became the accepted practice, and when, in the nineteenth century, Reform Jews shifted the marriage ceremony back to the synagogue, they were opposed by Orthodox Jewry. In America, where synagogues seldom have spacious courtyards, Orthodox Jews tacitly acquiesced in this innovation and even more sweeping innovations. Often the marriage ceremony does not take place even in a synagogue, but at the private residence of the rabbi or at a hall where the dance and the feast are held.

The Knas Mahl . . . In the same manner in which the ancient chupo had been superseded by the canopy, the betrothal ceremony of the Middle Ages was superseded by a new kind of engagement which the Jews in Germany called *knas mahl*. *Knas* is a Hebrew-Talmudic word meaning penalty; *mahl*, a German word meaning meal or feast. The German Jews compounded a hybrid name for the engagement party, calling it knas mahl, penalty meal; i.e., a feast at which the penalty to be paid by the person who broke the engagement was stipulated. At this feast all the conditions of the match were set down in a written contract.

The knas mahl was provided by the groom and marked by much feasting and merrymaking. As an outstanding feature of the celebration a piece of crockery was dashed to the ground and broken, as a reminder of the destruction of Jerusalem. It was customary for the guests to take the fragments of the broken dish with them.

As in Biblical and Talmudic times between the betrothal and the wedding, so also in the Middle Ages between the knas mahl and the wedding, the groom was not supposed to visit his bride, nor even to see her. The origin of this custom had long been forgotten. The motive for it had been the promotion of chastity. Occasionally, ordinances were issued by rabbinical synods against laxity in this custom. We are unable to tell how strictly these customs and ordinances were adhered to in actual life.[196]

Wedding Preliminaries . . . The favorite day for weddings was Friday for a maiden, and Thursday for a widow. In some small communities, Wednesday was the wedding day for girls as in Talmudic times, because the out-of-town guests who attended the wedding needed several days in which to travel home before the Sabbath. In larger communities, accommodations were provided for out-of-town guests, and they could remain for the Sabbath. The larger communities had a communal guest house, and a communal dance hall for weddings. The wedding celebration began on Friday and lasted until Sunday morning. By means of this arrangement the expense of an extra celebration on the Sabbath following the wedding was saved.

Only the actual wedding began on Friday. The preliminaries began on the Sabbath preceding the wedding. As far back as in the first centuries of the Common Era, this Sabbath was marked by festivities (see p. 154). Among the German Jews this celebration was called *Spinholz*, a medieval German term, the meaning of which cannot be ascertained. The usual explanation is that "Spinholz" refers to the distaff of the spinner, an important article in the trousseau of every German bride in the Middle Ages. We would then have to assume that among the German Jews the Sabbath before the wedding was the day when the bride received the spinner's distaff as a gift. But this is merely a theory. In earlier times, the two preceding Sabbaths were celebrated, the first called "Little Spinholz" and the second "Great Spinholz." Later the "Little Spinholz" was discarded and only the Sabbath immediately preceding the wedding was marked by a celebration.[197]

On the Thursday before the wedding the bride received presents from the groom. These were not brought by the groom, but by the rabbi or some other dignified member of the community, who gave them to the bride in the name of the groom. The presentation of the gifts was accompanied by the following words: "Listen to me, pretty bride. Through me your groom is sending you these presents, but you should regard them as your property only after the chupo." As betrothal could legally be effected by proxy, this stipulation was necessary in order that the presentation of the gift should not constitute a legal betrothal the day before the wedding.

At that moment, the bashful bride, too shy to accept the presents with her own hands, usually asked one of her female relatives to receive them for her. The gifts consisted, as a rule, of a girdle inlaid with gold, a veil, and similar articles. Usually, the bride gave the groom a ring and shoes, to which the bride's mother added a girdle inlaid with silver. Since clothing in the Middle Ages was without buttons, the girdle was an indispensable article and among persons of distinction it was made of the costliest material, sometimes even wrought with gold and adorned with gems.

At every wedding, music was provided by Jewish musicians called *klezmer* or *klezmorim*. Klezmer is a distortion of the two Hebrew words *klei zemer* meaning musical instruments. In the course of time, klezmer became the name for those who played the musical instruments. It was, and still is, used both in the singular and in the plural. The special plural form, klezmorim, was more frequently used. As Jewish law forbade the playing of musical instruments on the Sabbath, it was customary among the German Jews to engage Christian musicians to play on the day after the marriage ceremony. Engaging a non-Jew to work on Saturday was not considered a violation of the Sabbath rest, for, although it was forbidden by the rabbis as a minor transgression, it was permitted in cases of emergency. Among the German Jews, instrumental music was indispensable to the celebration of a wedding and to the observance of the religious precept—the mitsvo—of gladdening the bridegroom and the bride. Therefore, German rabbis relaxed the rigidness of the Sabbath rest and permitted non-Jewish musicians to be engaged for the Sabbath following the wedding ceremony. In the Orient, however, conditions were entirely different. The Oriental Jews did not consider instrumental music indispensable to the joy of a wedding. The rabbis objected to and actually suppressed the practice of engaging non-Jewish musicians on the Sabbath. The Jews of the Orient satisfied themselves with vocal music on the Sabbath following the wedding.[198]

In the later Middle Ages, the professional jester and merrymaker performed with the klezmorim. As far back as the thirteenth and fourteenth centuries, the professional jester was mentioned by his Hebrew name, *letson* (scoffer, jester). Later, he was called *marshalik* (from a German word for a buffoon or droll fellow at a feast), or *badchon* (a Hebrew-Yiddish name for a public merrymaker and entertainer). The badchon was a folk-poet and a preacher, a jester and an exhorter, a singer and an improvisator, as well as a rhymster and a learned man. A badchon had to have learning because his jests and witticisms were based upon and interwoven with verses from the Bible and passages from the Talmud. Weddings were not the only occasion on which the badchon entertained the public, for he was employed also on other occasions. There were some great rabbis who sternly frowned upon the unrestrained drolleries of the badchon, believing them incompatible with religious life. But the antagonism of these rabbis was of no avail, and, until recent times, the popularity of the badchon persisted in Eastern Europe.

In the midst of the tumultuous joy and of the hustle and bustle of the wedding, many tricks were played upon the groom and his friends by the practical jokers of the town. The ordinary procedure was for the bridegroom to bribe the wild lads not to play these pranks. In order to keep the sum demanded by the mischief makers within limits, the rabbis decreed that it should not exceed six florin.[199]

Cutting the Bride's Hair . . . Throughout the Middle Ages and until very recent times, Jewish women cut off their hair immediately before they were married, and thenceforward always wore a covering on their heads.

In Biblical times, this custom did not prevail among Jews. But at the beginning of the Common Era, Jewish married women covered their hair when they went out into the streets. It was considered unchaste for a married woman to go out bareheaded, as did girls. Some extremely pious and chaste women never showed their hair even within the four walls of their homes. Later, under the influence of the Greco-Roman world, this practice spread among the Jews and became the universal rule among Jewish women. Among the Greeks and the Romans, elderly women wore caps on their heads, and some cut off their hair. Boys and girls too cut off their hair just before they were married, and offered their tresses as a sacrifice to the gods. This Greco-Roman custom suited the modest, chaste character of Jewish women, and was universally adopted by them as a rigid rule.[200]

In the sixteenth century, the wig, for both men and women, was introduced among the Christian peoples of Europe. Soon the Jewish women, too, adopted the fashion of wearing a wig. But the rabbis could not agree upon the propriety of this custom. Some of them protested against women wearing wigs which resembled their own hair. Other more liberal rabbis claimed that the rule did not apply, as long as the hair was false. Notwithstanding their protests, the wig became popular among Jewish women. Only the ultra-conservative women rejected the innovation, clinging tenaciously to the hair-cap or the kerchief on top of the head.

One or two generations ago in Eastern Europe, cutting off the bride's hair was a feature of the wedding. But this custom was discarded. At present, even among Orthodox Jews, married women do not observe any more the custom of cutting off their hair and wearing wigs.

The K'subo . . . In the foregoing chapters we have followed the origin of the k'subo, through its development in Talmudic times. We shall now consider the k'subo in post-Talmudic times.

The wording of the k'subo was not fixed, but varied in the periods of Jewish history, not only in the various lands where Jews lived, but also among the different sections and groups into which Jews were divided.

For instance, the k'subo had been consistently written in Aramaic, but there were even some exceptions to that. The Samaritans and Karaites wrote it in Hebrew. The S'fardim never recognized the validity of the ban of Rabbenu Gershom against polygamy as strictly as did the Ashk'nazim. Even in our own day, they insert a special clause in the k'subo, stating that the future husband cannot marry a second wife without the first wife's permission. The k'subo of the S'fardim also contains a clause in which the future husband cannot sell or give as a pledge any of his wife's possessions, nor can he make a journey beyond certain specified limits, nor any voyage by water unless, before starting out, he gives his wife a conditional *get* (bill of divorcement) and sufficient means for her sustenance.

There were other special clauses consistent with the time and the place. In a recently discovered k'subo of the eleventh century, the bridegroom, a Jew, pledged his bride, the daughter of a Karaite, that he would not compel her to have a light in the house on Friday night, a practice which the laws of the Karaites forbade. The bride, on the other hand, pledged observance of the festivals with him according to the calendar of the Rabbanite Jews, without profaning her own Karaite holidays.[201]

Tithes of the Dowry . . . One additional custom of bygone days should be mentioned, that of giving a tenth part of the dowry to charity, which was an obligation that was enforced. At the end of the eighteenth century, this laudable custom still prevailed in some communities, but it has since been discontinued.[202]

A Wedding in Mayence . . . In a previous chapter we witnessed the ceremonials of a b'ris and a pidyon ha-ben in Mayence in the fifteenth century. It was the famous rabbi of Mayence, Maharil, who officiated as sandek at the b'ris and who also conducted the ceremonial of the pidyon ha-ben (see pp. 41, 49). We are going now to witness the ceremonial of a wedding in Mayence at which this same great rabbi officiated.

The wedding we shall witness differs in many respects from

the well-known traditional Jewish wedding of later times. To begin with, the marriage ceremony takes place in the early morning, and is not performed in the courtyard of the synagogue, but on the central platform in the interior of the building. Nor is the marriage ceremony performed under a canopy. But instead of checking on all the differences, let us carefully watch the entire procedure of the marriage ceremonial at Mayence.

After the preliminaries on the preceding day, the actual wedding celebration begins on Friday morning. At dawn, when the beadle of the community, in his daily round from house to house, knocks on the doors with his wooden mallet to awaken the people for morning services, he invites them to the wedding celebration. The entire community gathers to witness the wedding and share in the joy of the occasion.

Maharil and a few notables of the community go to the home of the bridegroom to bring him to the courtyard of the synagogue. The bridegroom leads the way, followed by Maharil and the notables. The musicians, playing their instruments, and a large group of the townsfolk, carrying lighted torches, follow. After the bridegroom is escorted into the courtyard, the crowd and the musicians go to the home of the bride to escort her and her retinue to the wedding. As soon as the bride arrives at the entrance of the courtyard of the synagogue, Maharil and the group of notables bring the bridegroom forward to meet and greet her. He and his bride stand with hands clasped, while the assembled guests toss grains of wheat over their heads, three times pronouncing the Biblical blessing, "Be fruitful and multiply!" Coins for the poor to pick up are mixed with the grains of wheat. The couple then walk together as far as the door of the synagogue where they remain seated for a time. Then the bride is taken back to her home, where she places a sargonas, a white shroud, over her attire, and covers her face with a veil. The white shroud is a reminder of the burial shroud, and serves the purpose of restraining the bride from being over-joyous. Instead of the usual cloak, she places over the white shroud the wide mantle with tight sleeves which married women wear on festive occasions. The mantle has a fur lining and is lavishly embroidered in silk. Meanwhile the bridegroom is led into a room in the synagogue building where he dons Sabbath clothes over which he throws a cowled cape, the cowl covering his head. This hood is worn by both Jews and non-Jews on various solemn occasions.

The bridegroom is now seated by the Holy Ark, in the northeast side of the synagogue, and the congregation is chanting the morning prayers, omitting the penitential prayer, for this is a joyous occasion. While this is taking place in the synagogue, the friends of the bride are busy with her at her home, braiding her hair and presenting her with rings as gifts.

The morning services are over, and soon the marriage ceremony begins. The synagogue is crowded. All relatives and friends of the bride and groom wear their Sabbath attire. Maharil, who officiates at the wedding, wears his Sabbath clothes; but his talis is the one which he wears on week-days. Only at the wedding of his own daughter did he don his Sabbath talis.

Now to the strains of music the bride is conducted from her home to the door of the synagogue. She pauses while Maharil leads the bridegroom to the platform in the center of the synagogue. There, lifting the cowl, Maharil strews ashes on the head of the groom, in the place where the phylacteries are laid. This is in memory of the destruction of Jerusalem. Then Maharil, followed by the notables of the community, proceeds to the door to receive the bride. The rabbi, taking her by her robe, leads her to a place at the right of the groom because it says in the Psalms, "At thy right hand doth stand the queen" (Ps. 45:10). The bridal pair stand with their faces turned toward the south. Their mothers stand on the platform near the bride. The corner of the bridegroom's cowl is stretched over the head of the bride as a chupo. At the wedding of his own daughter, Maharil took the end of her veil and threw it over the couple as a chupo. Maharil claimed that using the veil as a chupo was the older custom.

Two wine glasses are held in readiness, one for the benediction of the betrothal and the other for the benediction of the wedding. The two glasses differ in shape, depending upon whether the bride is a maiden or a widow. At the wedding of a widow or a widower, the marriage ceremony takes place on Thursday, not inside of the synagogue, but in the courtyard at its entrance.

After Maharil chants the benediction of the betrothal, he calls forward two witnesses, showing them the marriage ring and asking: "You see this ring; do you think it has some value?" They answer in the affirmative. He then bids the witnesses to listen closely to see whether the bridegroom recites the correct formula for betrothing the bride. The groom places the ring on the forefinger of the right hand of the bride. Maharil calls two additional witnesses to testify to the k'subo and to the marriage stipulations drawn up at the knas mahl. He does not read the k'subo and the stipulations publicly, only assuring himself that the witnesses give it proper attention.

Maharil, his face turned to the east, chants the wedding benedictions. Then he holds the glass of wine, first to the lips of the groom and then to those of the bride. After they have each sipped the wine, he gives the glass to the bridegroom who turns northward and then dashes the glass against the wall, shattering it. Immediately, the bridegroom is rushed home by his companions who hilariously escort him to the house of the wedding, trying to arrive before the bride.

After arriving there, the married couple eat an egg and a hen. In former times it was customary for them to eat in a separate room with only one person, a female relative, in attendance; and only after a while did the joyous relatives and guests enter the room. Our historical record informs us that this custom has been forgotten and that all immediately flock into the room where the couple partake of their repast.

Maharil always insisted upon music at every wedding. On Friday night following the wedding ceremony the bridal pair did not go to the synagogue. Instead, the younger men gathered at the home of the couple for the evening services.

On the following Sabbath morning, the services at the synagogue had special features in honor of the bridegroom, as was already previously described (p. 162).[203]

A Wedding in Worms . . . The historical record of the wedding in Mayence just given is limited in its scope. Intent on describing religious ceremonies and ritual, the author gives minute and tiresome details of the wedding ceremony only, paying little attention to the joy and hilarity, the hustle and bustle before and after the wedding ceremony. In this respect we are fortunate to have a good complement in the historical record, describing a wedding in the ghetto of Worms in the seventeenth century. In the description which follows we have a vivid picture of life in a German ghetto three hundred years ago.

Worms is very near to Mayence. Yet, in many respects the Jews of Worms differed in their customs from the Jews of Mayence. They had age-old customs of their own and consistently observed them.

In Worms, even as late as the seventeenth century, the marriage ceremony, performed by the rabbi of the community, did not take place in the synagogue, but in the communal dancing house. A wedding was not merely a family affair. The whole town was astir with it. The day for weddings was Wednesday. It was only in unusual cases that a wedding was performed on Friday.

The wedding festivities covered a period of ten days, beginning a week before, and ending three days after the wedding day. During these joyous days many festive meals were served by the bride and the groom, and the communal dancing hall resounded with music, dancing, and singing. A favorite song was Yigdal, the hymn of the morning services which elaborates poetically in thirteen verses the thirteen articles of the Jewish faith laid down by Maimonides.

There were many wedding festivities but few clocks in those days. Besides, what clocks there were, were very inaccurate and unreliable. So someone had to announce to the people that the time had arrived for this or that ceremony or festivity. This task fell to the beadle of the synagogue.

A week before the wedding, the bride invited all her friends for a meal. "Soup-meal," it was called. From that day on until the wedding the bride did not leave the house.

The Sabbath preceding the wedding, called Spinholz by the German Jews (see p. 166), was a great day in Worms. On the Friday night preceding that Sabbath, the bridegroom in his best clothes attended the evening services in the synagogue, where special honor was paid to him. The chazan sang certain liturgical poems with a special tune called "Spinholz melody." After the evening meal, the beadle strode through the streets of the ghetto, calling aloud, "Zu der Spinholz!" (to the Spinholz celebration), and relatives and friends soon gathered, first in the house of the groom and afterward in the house of the bride. The next morning, the bridegroom was again the hero of the day at the services in the synagogue and the friends of the bride and groom again gathered in their respective houses for refreshments. After the midday meal, the beadle again went through the streets calling, "Zu der Spinholz!" The bride and the groom, in separate processions, were then led to the dancing house where the afternoon hours were spent in dancing, singing and merrymaking. But soon the hour of Mincho arrived and all left the dancing hall, the bridegroom going to the synagogue to attend the afternoon services. After Mincho, the voice of the beadle was again heard in the streets calling, "Zu der Spinholz!" But now only boys and girls went back to the dance house.

On the following Monday a special meal was served for relatives only. On Tuesday, the bride and groom each separately invited their friends to a dairy dinner. The eve of the wedding was dedicated to the delivery by the rabbi of the mutual gifts of the bride and the groom to one another, a ceremony already described (see p. 166). The gifts were called by the Talmudic term *sivlonos*, and the festive meal served on this evening—"sivlonos meal."

On Wednesday, early in the morning, after unlocking the doors of the synagogue and the dancing house, the beadle— unlike the beadle of Mayence who called the people to the wedding when he knocked on the doors with his wooden mallet to awaken them for morning services—walked through the streets, calling loudly, "Zu der Maien!" (to the wedding celebration). A large throng, led by musicians and torch bearers, escorted the bridegroom to the dancing house. The bride followed, to be met and greeted there by the bridegroom and his entourage. The main feature of this ceremony on the morning of the wedding was the throwing of grains of wheat over the bride and groom and the calling out of the blessing, "Be fruitful and multiply!" In Mayence it was performed in the courtyard of the synagogue; in Worms—in the dance house. From the dance house the bridegroom was escorted to the synagogue for the morning services. In an earlier chapter it was related that the synagogue of Worms was provided with a special door to carry in the child for the b'ris. It also had a special small side entrance for a bridegroom. But the latter was often saved the trouble of walking in. He was pushed in by the mischievous lads of the town. In the synagogue a special honorary place was reserved for him. On the book-rest in front of him twelve braided candles were kindled.

After the services the crowd went back to the dance house. For dinner the young men were invited to the bridegroom's house and the girls to the house of the bride. After dinner both fathers went to the rabbi for the payment of the dowry. It was a precaution in case of any conflict between the two parties. The dowry was then sealed and deposited with the rabbi.

Then the beadle again strode through the streets, calling aloud: "Di kalo flechten gehen!" (going to braid the bride's

1. Silver M'zuzo—*The Jewish Museum, New York*

2, 3, and 4. Wedding Rings

5. Silver T'filin Cases—*The Jewish Museum, New York*

CARRYING THE LAW by William Rothenstein
Johannesburg, South Africa, Art Gallery

hair), and the notable women of the community, led by the rabbi's wife, thereupon went to the home of the bride. While the women braided her hair she held a large bowl in her lap into which relatives and friends threw gifts: silver rings, spoons, veils and also coins. These presents were called "Einwurf" (throwing in).

Now, again the loud voice of the beadle was heard in the streets calling, "Zu der b'rocho!" (to the benediction of the wedding). A large crowd gathered at the dance hall where the ceremony was to be performed. The chupo still consisted of a corner of the bridegroom's cowl which the rabbi pulled over the head of the bride, as in Mayence in the time of Maharil.

The high point of the wedding feast was the drosho, the discourse on Torah, delivered by the bridegroom. Jewish learning was apparently wide-spread in Worms in the seventeenth century, as every groom was expected to deliver a drosho at his wedding. Before the drosho, a collection was made, the proceeds of which were given to the bridegroom to distribute among the poor. After the drosho, gifts were given to the bridegroom, usually rings. Then grace was recited and again there was dancing and singing. The bride and groom, exhausted with fasting and excitement, wanted to leave the wedding company. But they had to redeem themselves with "sugar" (sweet candy). It was only after they had distributed the candy that they were escorted home, to the music of Yigdal.

But the wedding festivities were not yet over. The next day, Thursday evening, a festive meal was served for the relatives. On Friday evening a festive meal was served for the entire community. The next morning great honor was paid to the bridegroom at the services in the synagogue as has already previously been described (see p. 162). On this Sabbath following the wedding, it was customary in Worms to send wine or brandy as a present to the bride and groom. On the departure of the Sabbath the newly married man himself had to

recite the benediction of *havdolo* (the prayer over wine, marking the distinction of the sacred day of the Sabbath from the
profane days of the week). He then served a meal of fish.
From the meal the gathering proceeded again to the dance
house to dance and sing. With this the wedding festivities
were officially ended.[204]

In Modern Times

Getting Married in an East European Community . . . We shall now leave the German-Jewish communities of the later Middle Ages. Proceeding swiftly through the latter centuries of Jewish history to the last decades of the nineteenth century, we visit a Jewish community in Eastern Europe.

The Age of Marriage . . . Old folks often tell quaint stories about bygone years when boys and girls still in their childhood were married. Married couples, so the story went, played in the sand and indulged in childish games. In those days simultaneous celebration of the bar mitsvo and the wedding was regarded as meritorious.

All that is a thing of the past. During the period which we now describe, a girl was at least fifteen or sixteen years old, and a boy seventeen or eighteen when they married. A girl who was still unmarried at the age of twenty-five was considered an old maid. Very few men or women remained single. For the poor and unattractive girl, no longer young, some elderly, pious women could always be found, who considered it their sacred duty to collect a fund for her dowry. Sooner or later they married her off to some ne'er-do-well or to an elderly widower who could not afford a younger or more beautiful wife. As long as she was married to someone, all was well.

The Shadchon . . . Falling in love was considered an extraordinary and abnormal phenomenon, a sort of mental disease occurring once in a great while among the very wealthy or the very poor—the only groups who dared to flout the conventions of social decency. As a rule, matches were arranged by parents with the tacit consent of the children. The shadchon, therefore, was still an important figure in effecting a marriage. Sometimes a relative or friend of the family of the boy or the girl acted as the go-between. For the most part, the intermediary was a professional shadchon, paid for his endeavors.

There were very few matchmakers exclusively employed in arranging marriages. Usually the shadchon had some additional vocation. A rabbi rarely occupied himself with matchmaking, but a m'lamed sometimes practiced it as a sort of side-line. Often the shadchon held some office in the synagogue. He may have been the sexton, the precentor, the reader from the Scroll of the Torah, etc. Now and then a woman was the go-between in arranging a match, although there were no women among the professional matchmakers.

Matchmaking required a special aptitude. A professional shadchon had to have an air of importance and dignity in order to arouse confidence. He usually wore good clothes and carried a cane. He led up to the subject very cautiously and made every proposal in a tortuous and indirect manner. He was skilled in hiding and distorting facts, especially when the bride and groom were from two different localities. His most arduous task was to forestall slander by malicious foes of the family of the bride or the groom. A match could easily be ruined, and the shadchon was on guard from the very outset. "Even a cat can spoil a match," is a Yiddish saying.

Sometimes two matchmakers arranged one match—one for the family of the lad, and the other for the family of the girl. Each tried to outwit the other; both would exaggerate the qualities of the young people to their future in-laws. Occasionally, there was a whole group of shadchonim who tried to arrange one match, particularly where a large dowry was involved. Everyone who in any way helped effect the match pretended to be a co-matchmaker in order to claim a share of the reward accruing to the shadchon.

The amount of the dowry which the girl's parents expected to give their prospective son-in-law was one of the main points in negotiating a match. Next in importance was the *kest*, the pension which the girl's parents often obligated themselves to give to the couple after their marriage. When the groom was a good student of the Talmud, this was given for periods as long as one to ten, and sometimes even twenty-five years. There were even cases, though very rare ones, where a particularly brilliant student was given "eibige kest," a life pension. However, the dowry and the pension were not of paramount importance. As in Talmudic and medieval times, it was the pedigree, the social rank of the respective bride and groom that counted most. The age-old Jewish love and respect for learning still asserted itself. Families and descendants of famous rabbis were of the highest social rank. The very greatest discredit to a family was to have among its members, no matter how remote, an apostate from the Jewish faith. When a member of an impoverished family of high social rank was forced to take a mate from a family of low social standing, it was considered a great personal tragedy.

Parents of a grown-up son, distinguished in the y'shivo, the Talmudic academy, were besieged by matchmakers. Parents of such a son refused even to bargain. They would not consider the girl unless her parents promised a dowry of a thousand *kerblech* (Yiddish slang for rubles) and ten years' pension. The physical attributes of the *bochur* (youth, lad) evoked small consideration as long as he was a distinguished student of the Talmud. Nor was the physical appearance of the girl of great importance. The young lad had never looked closely at young women and no matter what the girl's appearance, she was a graceful and charming bride for him. Her moral qualities were what really counted. Ordinarily her education consisted of being able to read the siddur (Hebrew prayer book), to write a letter in Yiddish, and to calculate according to the fundamentals of arithmetic. It was also regarded as advantageous if she could speak the language of the country, for if her groom was a student of the y'shivo, she would have to conduct some business in order to provide for the family, while he spent most of his time in the beis ha-midrosh (the house of study).

If the bride and groom were from different localities, they were put to a test. The girl's father would send a Talmudic scholar to test the Talmudic knowledge of the bochur. The examiner had ready a number of difficult and intricate passages in the Talmud which tested the versatility and the casuistic acumen of the bochur. On the other hand, the girl was tested for patience and skill by the women of the groom's family. She was given a tangled skein of thread which she was expected to unravel, or told to prepare a large sheet of dough and to cut it patiently into fine, thin noodles.

The negotiations were often protracted for a long time. There was a great deal of haggling, a long series of making up and changing of minds. More than once the negotiations were on the verge of being broken off altogether, and the shadchon had to exert all his tact in order to save the situation.

T'no-im . . . At last the negotiations were brought to a conclusion and the date set for celebrating the *knas mahl*, also called t'no-im (conditions) because of its main feature, the setting down in writing of all the agreed stipulations.

T'no-im was usually celebrated on a Sabbath night, or during the week-days on a semi-holiday, as Lag Bo-omer or one of the two Chamisho Osors. Only the close relatives were invited. Since it was not marked by any religious ceremonial, the presence of the rabbi was unnecessary. The precentor, or sexton of the synagogue wrote the t'no-im in medieval, corrupt Hebrew. The written agreement was corroborated and made more binding by the ceremony of symbolic affirmation. This ceremony was performed by one who, for a moment, held a kerchief jointly with the two parties of the contract.[205] The precentor read the t'no-im aloud in the presence of all the guests, and when he had finished, the shadchon jumped up, shouting, "Mazol Tov!" and dashed a piece of crockery to the ground. At that moment all the guests threw on the floor plates, platters and bowls which they had brought from their homes. Ordinarily, every woman brought some broken earthenware dish with her. Now and then a more pretentious aunt or cousin, in order to demonstrate her importance in the family, brought to the t'no-im a large new platter or bowl. The loud crash of the shattered dishes filled the air, and the mass of shattered fragments covered the entire floor. This custom was regarded as a reminder of the destruction of Jerusalem.

Within a short while the shattered crockery was removed from the room, and delicious foods and drinks were served. After the feast, the bride and groom received their first gifts from each other. The bride received a ring, and the groom a watch and chain.

One of the stipulations of the t'no-im was the amount of money to be paid as a penalty by the party who broke the engagement. Sometimes the stipulated amount was half of the dowry. However, it was regarded as a misdemeanor to break the t'no-im.

If the prospective bride and groom were from different localities, one traveled to see the other on a visit for the holidays. They also wrote letters to one another. These letters were distinctive in character, consisting of high-sounding, stereotyped phrases. In most cases, the betrothed couple did not write their own letters, but delegated the task to a man in the town who had a beautiful handwriting and the ability to use pompous language. He used the same phraseology and the identical expressions in most of the letters which he wrote for betrothed couples, and he did it either as a favor, or for remuneration. If the pair lived in the same town, they paid one another official and infrequent visits.

Preliminaries to the Wedding . . . Sometimes after the t'no-im, the date was set for the wedding and the dowry was deposited with the rabbi or one of the leading members of the community. A last attempt was made at bargaining for a lesser sum than the dowry originally agreed upon. If the groom lived in another town, both the father and the mother of the bride traveled there to deposit the dowry.

Friday was the wedding day for a maiden; Tuesday or Thursday for a widow or divorcee. Weddings occasionally took place on Sunday, too, but never on Monday or Wednesday, which were regarded as unlucky days.

The favorite Fridays for weddings were the Friday following Tisho B'Ov and preceding Sabbath Nachamu, the one following Shovuos, and the one between Yom Kippur and Sukos.

Sometimes, when the bride and groom were from different towns, the wedding was performed in a roadside inn somewhere between the two towns. Such a wedding was naturally less pretentious, and took place on Tuesday or Thursday in order that the guests who attended might be able to return home for the Sabbath. In most cases the bridegroom and his entourage traveled in large wagons to the town of the bride, to remain there from Friday until Sunday, housed by the bride's family.

As soon as the date was set for the wedding, both families, particularly the family of the bride, prepared for the great occasion. The bride's parents arranged the wedding and bore all costs. The bride herself was the busiest person, occupied with the preparation of her trousseau, particularly with her chupo dress. If her parents were rich, the dressmaker came to her house to work on her dresses; otherwise she went to the dressmaker's.

The celebration on the Sabbath before the wedding was called *Aufruf* (calling up), because its main feature was the calling up of the bridegroom at the synagogue to *maftir* (the reading of a portion of the Prophets at the conclusion of the reading from the Torah). The chazan or sexton called up the bridegroom to the bimo with a louder and more sonorous voice than he used in calling up the others. As soon as the bridegroom ascended the bimo, a shower of raisins, almonds and nuts descended upon his head from the women's section in the synagogue. The children, with noisy joy, rushed for the fruits. After the services, a crowd of relatives and friends accompanied the bridegroom to his home where they were served with cake, brandy, and various delicacies.

The preparations reached their highest point in the last few days before the wedding. There was a constant hustle and bustle, and continuous cooking and baking at the home of the bride. Every family in the community invited to the wedding sent a *lekach* (plain cake) or a *tort* (a rich cake) to the bride or the groom. But these cakes were not sufficient, and were supplemented by the many lekachs and torts that were being baked at home. Other confections to be served required professional skill and so a cook was engaged to prepare them. In addition, the family hired a sarver (waiter) who served the foods and drinks and acted as general handyman. Both received a stipulated sum from the bride's parents and additional tips from close relatives.

Well-to-do families arranged a feast for the paupers of the community a day or two before the wedding. On this occasion, the poor folks were served with a meal abounding in fish, meat, beer, and in some instances, even mead and wine. The bride and groom were seated at the head of the table with the paupers who were waited on by the parents and some of the distinguished relatives of the bride and groom. After the meal, the bride and groom danced with the poor folk, and distributed coins among them.

On Thursday, the wedding atmosphere pervaded in every nook and cranny of the house. Even the air was saturated with the pleasant odors of freshly prepared foods and sweetmeats. The door of the house kept opening every few moments to receive a cake sent by some relative or friend. A child or a poor woman carried the cake to the celebrants. The child received a piece of cake and the poor woman a coin. The same poor woman ran many errands bringing cake after cake; and each time she was given a coin by the bride or her mother, who took the cake from her. The same message was sent every time a cake was delivered, "Tell your father and mother," or "Tell So-and-so not to be late for the wedding."

The relatives and friends of the bridegroom sent their wedding cakes to his home, although the wedding was held in the home of the bride.

On Thursday evening there was a quiet celebration at the home of the bride, for on that evening the bride was led to the ritual pool. Only girls were invited, friends of the bride and the girls from the bridegroom's family. They came to bid farewell to the bride on her passing from the unmarried to the married state. The celebration was merely a preliminary to the wedding, and the bride wore some of her festive clothes. Sweetmeats were served and the girls danced. They knew that they must depart early in order that the bride might go on her way to the pool.

One or two generations previously, the bride had been led to the ritual pool accompanied by klezmorim. In the period which we now describe, the procedure was more private. The bride's only escort to the bath-house were the two mothers and the bath-house attendant. A man was engaged to stay in wait near the bath-house so that he should be the first to meet her eyes on her way home. If she cast her first glance on an unclean animal, a dog or a cat, she had to return to reimmerse herself in the pool.

The Klezmorim and the Badchon . . . Klezmorim were the indispensable concomitant of a wedding, particularly the wedding of a maiden. "A wedding without klezmorim" is an expression in Yiddish, characterizing any social arrangement devoid of color and beauty. The minimum number of musicians in a band of klezmorim was three: one played a fiddle, one bass, and a third, usually a young chap, accompanied the two, beating on a small drum with two little sticks. Barring exceptional cases, the klezmer was an amateur musician, with very little theoretical knowledge of music. He had only a very limited repertoire of tunes which he always played by ear, as he was unable to read musical notes.

There was neither room nor need for music in the ordinary, dull life of the people. Barring weddings, there were only two other occasions on which klezmorim were employed: on the very rare occasions when a Sefer Torah was donated to the synagogue or when the Talmud Study Circle celebrated the "Grand Completion" of the entire Babylonian Talmud which occurred once in about seven years. The long intervals of idleness between festivities made it necessary for the klezmorim to engage in some other trade. A band of klezmorim could be found only here and there in some of the larger towns, from which they occasionally traveled to the smaller communities when they were engaged to play at a wedding. They received a stipulated sum sometimes augmented by tips from the guests.

At this period the badchon was not as indispensable as the klezmorim. However, the role he played was still an important and integral part of the wedding celebration, particularly in Poland and the Ukraine. He, too, had to be imported from a large town. In wealthy families two badchonim were engaged as entertainers at a wedding. The badchon had a double task: to evoke laughter from the guests and tears from the bride and groom.

The "Unterfuerers" . . . Two married couples, one for the bride and one for the groom, were honored by being selected in advance as the "unterfuerers," a new name for an old institution. In the Biblical story of Samson, mention is made of the groom's best friend. In Talmudic times we also hear of the best friend or two best friends, one for the bride and one for the bridegroom. At the period with which we are now occupied, these particular people were privileged to lead the bridal pair to the chupo. They were always four in number, two couples who had been married only once. If the bridegroom had brothers and sisters who were married for the first time, they had precedence over all others. If there were no brothers or sisters eligible for this privilege, other relatives were appointed. The unterfuerers were expected to give more costly wedding gifts than any of the other guests. They also had to pay for the honor with enormous tips to the cook and the sarver, and especially to the klezmorim and the badchon.

The Wedding . . . Before noon on Friday, the whole town is astir. "There is a wedding today, a wedding today!" Young and old, aware of the great occasion, look forward to it with keen interest and inner joy.

About nine or ten o'clock, the klezmorim start on their round to the houses of the close relatives and friends of the bride and groom. If a badchon has been engaged, he goes with the klezmorim. A list with the names of the wedding guests to be visited is handed to them. A few lads join them in the street, for curiosity's sake, showing them the way to each house. After they have played, a silver coin is given to them, and they depart for the house of another relative. Now and then one of the relatives is accidentally omitted from the list. A few hours later the rumor has spread that Uncle So-and-so and Auntie So-and-so are terribly offended because the klezmorim have not been sent to their home, and that they are not coming to the wedding. Immediately the bride's or bridegroom's parents, depending upon which side the offended relatives belong, depart on an appeasement mission and finally convince the uncle and the aunt that the omission is all the fault of the klezmorim. Who, they plead, can rely upon people who drink whisky before reciting the morning prayers, and who stare at strange women at weddings?

Now it is noon, and the bridegroom is from another town. A number of relatives and close friends of the bride ride to meet him and his entourage. This ride to meet the bridegroom is an important feature of the wedding and is carried out with much commotion and spectacular splendor. The best available coaches with bells attached to the splendid harness of each horse are hired or borrowed for the parade. The participants are already dressed for the wedding. Usually, the coaches depart with great speed to meet the wagons of the bridegroom and his entourage on the outskirts of the town. Hilariously the two parties meet, greeting each other with exclamations of "Mazol Tov!" After partaking of cake and brandy, the bride's party, with the bridegroom now in its midst, hurry back to the town with the wagons of the bridegroom's entourage lagging a little behind. The coaches roll quickly through the town, the horses gallop, the jingling bells reverberate and the occupants of the coaches, all in their best attire, beam with joy. Immediately, the news spreads from house to house and from street to street, "The bridegroom is coming! The bridegroom is coming!" Almost the entire populace, men and women, old people and children, rush to the street, to the windows, to the doors, and to the open porches to watch the procession of the bridegroom and the wedding guests. The coaches stop at the house where the bridegroom is lodged for the period of the wedding celebration.

Most of the houses were small and unfit for a wedding celebration. There were only a few with sufficient space to accommodate a large gathering. The owners of these houses, usually as an act of kindness, accommodated the rest of the people, for it was regarded as an act of great religious merit to contribute to the joy of the bridegroom and the bride. Two such spacious homes were needed, because the celebration before the chupo, and the festivity and dance on Saturday night were engaged in separately by the men and women. Often the two homes in which these parties were held were located at opposite ends of the town.

Let us watch the changing scene, first catching a glimpse of the bridegroom and the male guests in the house where they are lodged.

The bridegroom in his best attire and with serious face is seated at the head of a table, surrounded by the guests, with the rabbi of the community, who officiates at all marriage ceremonies, in a place of honor. On the table, covered with a fine tablecloth, are placed bottles of brandy and wine, platters of cakes and abundant cigarettes, which the bridegroom offers liberally to everyone. There is little solemnity, as this party is just a *kabolas ponim* (a reception) for the bridegroom. Even people who are not invited to the wedding drop in for a little while at the kabolas ponim to greet the bridegroom with "Mazol Tov!" and to partake of the cake and the brandy.

Let us now leave the bridegroom and his party and betake ourselves to the bride around whom an elaborate ceremonial centers in these solemn hours before the chupo.

About noontime the girl friends of the bride come to her home to help her dress for the wedding. After a while the girls are joined by the married women, and all accompany the bride to the house where she will be lodged for the period of the celebration.

The first ceremony performed here is called *bazetsens* (seating the bride). One or two generations before the time of which we write it was customary to seat the bride in the center of the room on a kneading bowl stuffed with pillows. This custom was later discarded. The bride of whom we speak is seated on a chair, covered with a white sheet and decorated with flowers, particularly with myrtle. On her head over the veil which hangs almost to the floor the bride wears a garland of myrtle. The richer and more aristocratic the bride, the longer the veil which she wears. On each side of the chair stands a row of girls, each holding a candle in one hand and a handful of raisins or hops in the other. A generation previously, the hair of the bride was shorn at the ceremony of bazetsens, but as previously mentioned, this custom was discarded. Married women did not crop their hair but they wore wigs covering and matching the color of their own hair.

The seating of the bride is accompanied by the music of the klezmorim who play melancholy tunes which stir the hearts of the women. The klezmorim are followed by the badchon who, in grotesque rhymes and a peculiar singsong, exhorts the bride, reminding her of the solemnity of this day which, for her, is similar to Yom Kippur. He then turns abruptly to the humorous and ludicrous, concluding with burlesque. When he ends, the klezmorim immediately begin to play a gay tune, while the women with tears still on their cheeks, dance about in jovial mood. All are merry now except the bride who, sitting on the bridal chair in the center of the room, weeps copiously on this day of her destiny.

The next ceremony after bazetsens is *badekens* (covering the bride's face). A group of women of the bride's party, preceded by the klezmorim and the badchon now pay a visit to the bridegroom, inviting him to badekens. The women are treated to delicacies, the klezmorim play a tune, the badchon exhorts the bridegroom, and then all return to the bride, preceded by the klezmorim and the badchon.

In the street, children call loudly, "Here comes the bridegroom, here comes the bridegroom!" and the rows of maidens beside the bride's chair immediately light their candles.

The bridegroom, escorted by his father and the rabbi, walks between the two rows of girls holding the lighted candles until he approaches the bride's chair. The two mothers stand in front of the chair holding a plate of raisins or hops covered with a silk kerchief. The rabbi and the bridegroom seize the kerchief by two corners, lift it hastily, and cover the bride's face. At this moment a mass of raisins and hops is showered upon both bride and groom.

Then the bridegroom and all the males return to the house where they are lodged. Only the klezmorim and the badchon remain for the third ceremony, called "mazol-tov-dance" or "kosher dance." The badchon calls aloud the name of each woman present, who then embraces the bride and completes a circle with her. The wedding guests are amused by this dance, but it is a great strain on the bride. Weakened by fasting the entire day, she grows dizzy with the continuous whirling to which she is subjected.

If the bride is an orphan, the chazan now recites the prayer for the dead, "Merciful God, etc.," chanting it in the accepted mournful tone. The klezmorim after each sentence reply antiphonally in the same tone, accompanied by floods of tears and the loud sobbing of the women, especially the bride.

The klezmorim then depart for the house in which the bridegroom is lodged. If the bridegroom is an orphan, the above ceremony is repeated except for the sobs and tears.

The pre-chupo ceremonies are now completed, and in the two separate houses, the bride and bridegroom prepare themselves for the high and solemn moment of their lives. Both fast and recite mincho (afternoon prayers) with the addition of the long confession of the Yom Kippur prayers. The bridegroom, for the first time in his life, wears the talis which he has received as a gift from the bride. He also wears a *kittel*, a white robe, under the talis. In some regions before the chupo, it was customary to untie all knots in the garments of the groom and the bride so that no one could "bewitch" them by means of the knots.

Meanwhile the sexton of the synagogue places the portable canopy close to the entrance of the courtyard of the synagogue. The canopy, a piece of communal property, always stands folded in the anteroom of the synagogue. As soon as the sexton takes it out into the courtyard, a number of lads are on hand to hold the four poles. As there are more lads available than the chupo has poles, two or three of them hold each one of the poles.

Leading the Couple to the Chupo . . . Every person who can spare a little time in the late Friday afternoon now rushes to the courtyard of the synagogue as if by appointment. The entire courtyard, particularly around the entrance to the synagogue, is soon crowded with people.

Soft, sad music is heard in the distance. Soon the procession of the bridegroom and his entourage becomes visible, emerging from one of the side streets which leads to the synagogue. Preceded by the klezmorim, the bridegroom is led to the chupo by his unterfuerers and his parents, followed by the male guests at the wedding. The solemn procession moves slowly. As the bridegroom approaches the chupo, the chazan or sexton calls loudly, "Boruch habo!" (blessed be he who comes). The bridegroom is then led under the canopy, and the klezmorim depart in haste to bring the bride's party.

Meanwhile the bridegroom, dressed in his best attire, stands motionless under the chupo, shy and awkward, exposed to the piercing gaze of the large crowd. The mischief makers of the town seize this opportunity to play all sorts of tricks on the bridegroom and the wedding guests. In winter, they throw hard snowballs, and in summer they toss burrs which cling to the clothes and even to the hair of the wedding guests.

However, this interval until the arrival of the bride's procession does not last long. Soon melancholy strains of music again fill the air, and the more imposing procession of the bride and her entourage enter the courtyard of the synagogue, preceded by the klezmorim, whose music accentuates the stern solemnity of the moment. There is a hushed silence about this procession, too. As the bride approaches the chupo, the sexton calls loudly, *"Hachnosas kalo!"* (induction of the bride) and the chazan chants a short greeting to the bridal pair, beginning with "Mi adir al ha-kol" (Who is mighty over all?). The parents and the unterfuerers, followed by a few of the close relatives, carrying candles, now lead the bride seven times around the groom. A restrained silence prevails. The rabbi then chants the benediction of the betrothal over a glass of wine, passing the wine first to the groom and then to the bride. The rabbi lifts the veil from the bride's face for a moment to allow the groom a glimpse of the bride before betrothing her, a vestige of earlier days when the groom never saw the bride until after the chupo. The Talmud declares that a man must not marry a woman unless he has seen her. So this custom was introduced to afford the groom an opportunity to see his bride. The bridegroom immediately betroths the bride by placing a ring upon the index finger of her right hand, reciting slowly, word for word, the ancient formula of betrothal. This is followed by the ceremony of breaking a glass. The rabbi hands the bridegroom the glass over which the benediction of betrothal is recited, or sometimes a very thin glass brought for this purpose, which the bridegroom dashes to the ground. If it does not break, he tramples upon it with the heel of his shoe. If the glass still remains unbroken, some of the wedding guests come to the assistance of the bridegroom. Some exclaim "Mazol Tov!" when the crash of the glass is heard, but in a quiet manner, because it is in the midst of the marriage ceremony. The rabbi reads the k'subo in its old Aramaic version and, in addition, performs the ceremony of corroborating the marriage contract by holding a kerchief jointly for a moment with the bridegroom (see p. 182). Then he chants the wedding benedictions over the second glass of wine, passing the wine first to the bridegroom and then to the bride.

At this moment, the whole atmosphere abruptly changes as if a blanket of gloom and fear had been lifted. The silence is broken by loud cries of "Mazol Tov" on all sides. The bride uncovers her face, the klezmorim strike up their liveliest and gayest tune, and lead the procession, which now moves quickly back to the bride's home. All are merry and hilarious. The two mothers, behind the klezmorim, sway and dance and clap their hands. The dancing mothers are followed by the bridal pair walking side by side. The two separate parties mingle in one happy crowd. Approaching the home of the bride, the mother or some other close relative comes out to meet the couple with a large, white, braided loaf lifted high in her arms. Turning and swaying in a dance, she hoists the loaf higher and higher, joyously shouting repeatedly, "Mazol Tov!" The bride's entourage sees to it that the bride crosses the threshold of the house before the bridegroom, believing this to be an omen of her mastery over him.

After the Chupo . . . The bridal pair who sit alone at a table now break their fast with a light repast.

As in Mayence in the time of Maharil, on this Friday evening the bridegroom does not go to the synagogue. The male guests gather around the bridegroom at the bride's home, recite the Friday evening services with a religious quorum of ten, the "minyon." After the services, the sarver serves the "chupo supper" on two separate tables, one for men and one for women, the bridegroom eating with the men and the bride with the women. A conspicuous feature of the meal is the soup eaten by the bridal pair called "The Golden Soup."

The hilarity and excitement of the wedding are entirely suspended during the Sabbath. There is no music nor dancing until nightfall. The only ceremony which marks the Sabbath following the wedding is connected with the morning services at the synagogue. In the Middle Ages the bridegroom was led in a solemn procession to the synagogue on Sabbath morning; now, the bride enjoys this honor. The bridegroom quietly goes to the synagogue early in the morning escorted only by both fathers and both male unterfuerers. The bride is led to the synagogue a little later, at the time of the reading from the Torah. The reading lasts a long time because almost every one of the male wedding guests is called up to the Torah. The portion of the Pentateuch read on the Sabbath is not divided into seven sections, as on all ordinary Sabbaths, but into very small passages, each one consisting of not less than three verses. There is ample time during the reading to allow for the ceremony of leading the newly married woman to the synagogue.

As soon as the reading from the Torah begins in the men's section, the bride's mother in the women's section calls loudly, "Who is going to lead the newly married woman into the synagogue?" Almost all the women present answer the call. One of them, the rebitsin (the rabbi's wife), is obliged to go.

At the home of the bride, the women usually partake of refreshments set out on a table. In a quiet procession the bride is then led to the synagogue where she is seated by the side of the rebitsin. She sits silent during the services, reciting no prayers. The motive of this custom is not to shame an illiterate bride. When the bridegroom is called up to the Torah, all the women approach the bride and greet her with "Mazol Tov!" After the services most of the men go from the synagogue to the home of the bride for b'rocho (the Kiddush recited before the morning meal). A great number of men who did not attend the wedding celebration proper go to the b'rocho. Again a table is set with refreshments—this time for the men.

At the end of each of the Sabbath meals, beans or peas, cooked and salted, are served. After the meals, Grace is recited with special amplifications in honor of the wedding, and after Grace, the wedding benedictions are again recited over a cup of wine.

At the departure of the Sabbath, after the reciting of Havdolo, the wedding celebration is resumed, and again men and women celebrate in two separate houses and in different manner. The men are entertained by the badchon and the chazan who sing chants, droll tunes, Yiddish folk-songs and liturgical melodies. Among the women there is continuous dancing to the accompaniment of the klezmorim. The mischief-makers are busy, playing tricks on the wedding guests. They are generally bought off with large slices of cake and other delicacies.

Sunday, the day following the wedding, is called the *Rumpel* (from a German word meaning tumult) and is marked by specific entertainments. A festive farewell meal is served in the afternoon after which the wedding gifts are publicly announced. The badchon or the sarver call loudly the name of the giver and the nature of the gift. At the close of the Rumpel, there is a specific farewell dance. The wedding gifts are called d'rosho geshank (the gift for the discourse) although it is no longer customary for the bridegroom to deliver a discourse at the wedding feast (see p. 177).

The Rumpel is the day on which the klezmorim, the badchon, the sarver, and the cook receive their pay and their tips.

The "seven days of the feast" are not celebrated. The newly married man, however, does not go to work during the week following the wedding, and in the morning services at the synagogue, in which he participates, the whole congregation omits the "penitential prayer" on his account.

The wedding of a widow or divorcee took place on Thursday. The chupo was not put up in the courtyard of the synagogue, but inside the house, and klezmorim were not present. It was not designated a wedding and people did not say, "So-and-so is celebrating her wedding today," but "So-and-so is setting up chupo today."

xvi

Marriage among the S'fardim in Palestine

The history of Jewish marriage in the Middle Ages as out-lined in the preceding chapters applies only to the Ashk'nazim (German and East European Jews). The S'fardim (Spanish-Portuguese Jews) shared the first stages of this long develop-ment and stopped in the middle of the way. They linked the wedding with the synagogue only in regard to the morning services on the following Sabbath. Their marriage ceremony proper still remains a home celebration as it was among the Ashk'nazim in the early Middle Ages. The chupo did not fully develop among the S'fardim, remaining a combination of both the canopy and the talis. For many centuries, the S'fardim lived in an Oriental environment which affected their mode of life. We can easily understand why the procedure of marriage among the S'fardim in Palestine differs in so many points from the traditional procedure of the Ashk'nazim.

Arranging the Match . . . The S'fardim in Palestine do not employ the name or the ceremonial of t'no-im described above. In arranging the match, the fathers merely jot down the main points of the agreement. This is called *kin'yanim* (agreements) and is not marked by any festivity.

A few weeks after the kin'yanim the bridegroom and the bride send gifts to one another and the day when the presents are delivered is marked by a joyous celebration. On the Sab-bath following this day, the bridegroom is called up to the Torah in the synagogue and the relatives and friends visit the bridegroom and the bride. This celebration is called *siman* (a sign, that the girl is engaged).

Preliminaries . . . There are many preliminary wedding festivities. Two weeks before the wedding, the bridegroom sends a shoemaker to the bride to make shoes for her, as a sign that the wedding date is set.

Eight days before the wedding, there is a celebration at the bride's home called *Ashugar*, a Spanish word for the trousseau. The bride's entire outfit is arranged and displayed as if on an exhibition. Many men and women attend this celebration. Expert appraisers estimate the value of each article and the scribe jots the figure down on paper. The figures are then added and the sum total doubled. To this, the sum of the dowry is added. To this total, something is added in honor of the bride's parents and something in honor of the family. This whole sum becomes the amount set down in the k'subo (except that they pronounce it k'tuba). Care is taken to add to the sum as much as was needed to make the last four digits fives, because it is believed that an evil eye has no power over the number five. (Arab villagers in Palestine also celebrate the purchasing, delivering and viewing of the bride's outfit. The women of the village gather in the bride's house to survey the entire trousseau, celebrating the occasion with song, dance and refreshments.)

On the Sabbath preceding the wedding, the bridegroom, accompanied by his friends, visits the rabbis of the town. He kisses their hands and receives their blessings. The bride, escorted by her mother and mother-in-law, pays a visit to the wives of the rabbis and she also kisses their hands and receives their blessings. She does not do this until two weeks after the wedding and, in Jerusalem, her visit is preceded by a visit to the Wailing Wall.

On Wednesday evening preceding the wedding, there is a gathering of girls in the bride's house. The bride, wrapped in a long veil, sits on a chair as motionless as a marble statue, while her friends, seated on benches around the wall of the room, merely play all sorts of silly games.

The following day, Thursday, is the day of bathing. The

bride in a beautiful dress is spectacularly led to the bath-house in the midst of a long line of married women and girls. The women are followed by men carrying lighted torches in their hands. In the rear of this procession there is instrumental music, singing and dancing. All women who participate in the procession bathe at the expense of the bride.

About an hour later, the bride returns home, and again a line of women is formed to the accompaniment of singing and dancing. All the doors of the houses which the procession passes are opened and the mistresses of the houses stand with trays of sweetmeats and glasses of lemon water in their hands. In passing, the bride and her entourage taste the refreshments offered them. This queer custom was taken over by the S'fardim in Palestine in its entirety from their Arab neighbors.

On the eve of the wedding day, Thursday night, a queer celebration takes place at the bridegroom's home. In the presence of relatives and friends, a Jewish barber cuts the hair of the bridegroom and receives a tip from each person present. The haircut is followed by singing and joyful entertainment which lasts late into the night.

The Chupo . . . The marriage ceremony takes place on Friday, early in the afternoon, and, as already noted, has no link with the synagogue. Two canopies are set up for the wedding, one in the house of the bridegroom and the other in the house of the bride. Both canopies are improvised from the curtains of the Holy Ark of a synagogue. The marriage ceremony is performed under the canopy at the bride's home. The canopy is set up against the wall. The part of the wall enclosed is covered with the silken curtain of a Holy Ark.

If the bridegroom is a learned man, he delivers a discourse on Torah before the marriage ceremonial is performed.

The chupo, as already remarked, is a combination of both the talis (prayer garment) and the canopy. First the bridal pair wrap themselves in a new talis provided with tsitsis (ritual show-fringes) and the bridegroom recites the benediction over the talis and the tsitsis and the benediction Shehecheyonu (see p. 29). The canopy is spread over their heads and in spreading it the wedding guests recite the verse, "So God give thee of the dew of heaven and of the fat places of the earth, and plenty of corn and wine" (Gen. 27:28). The chupo ceremony is then performed in the same manner as among the Ashk'nazim. Among the S'fardim more importance is attached to the breaking of the glass. The glass is wrapped in a kerchief in order that no fragment will be lost. When it is broken, the wedding guests recite two verses of the Psalms, first, "The snare is broken and we are escaped," and afterwards, "If I forget thee, O Jerusalem, let my right hand forget its cunning" (124:7; 137:5). The splinters of the broken glass wrapped in a kerchief are cautiously buried or put in an inaccessible place, for it is believed that the bridegroom could be bewitched with these splinters.

After the Chupo . . . When the chupo ceremonial is over, the bridal pair kiss the hands of their parents and relatives and of all the wedding guests, and receive their congratulations. Unlike the Ashk'nazim who congratulate with the words "Mazol Tov," the S'fardim congratulate with the words "Siman Tov" (a good omen). The relatives of the bridegroom place gold coins in the hands of the bride, and the relatives of the bride put gold coins in the hands of the bridegroom.

The bridal pair and their entourage march to the bridegroom's home. During the "seven days of the feast" the chupo remains in the bride's house with a candle burning under it. No one dares to sit there because it is regarded as a sacred place.

When the bride approaches the house of the bridegroom, her mother-in-law scatters sweetmeats from a plate, and holds a loaf of bread and breaks it above the head of her daughter-in-law, as an omen of good fortune.

At the meal following the chupo ceremonial, the guests sing *piyutim* (liturgical poems) in Hebrew and in Arabic composed especially for this occasion. After the meal, the pair are seated side by side on chairs in the center of the room, with lighted torches in their hands. Around them, the guests dance, sing and make merry, and continually try to put out the light of the torches. When the light of the torch which the bridegroom holds in his hand is out, he is compelled to kindle it with the torch of the bride. Then the guests put out the light of the torch of the bride, compelling her to kindle it with the torch of the man whom her parents have chosen as her husband. This game is repeated numerous times.

During the seven days following the wedding, the newly married couple sit under the chupo in the house of the bridegroom, who is never left alone. A number of young men, his best friends, guard him constantly and play various games with him. The most popular game consists of filching the bridegroom's kerchief, a ring or any other thing

As the bridegroom does not leave the house during the week following the wedding, his relatives and acquaintances gather at his home at the time of prayers in order that he could recite them with a minyon. Only on Sabbath morning does he visit the synagogue. On this occasion he enjoys greater honor than among the Ashk'nazim. On Sabbath morning the bridegroom is seated under a beautiful canopy of silk, made and kept especially for bridegrooms. When he is called to the reading of the Torah, he goes to the bimo with much pomp. The custom of reading to him an extra section of the Pentateuch, the story of the wooing of Rebekah, still prevails. At the same time, the sexton moves about among the assembled people, sprinkling rose-water on their hands from a perforated silver vessel.

On the day after the wedding, both mothers and all the women relatives visit the bride and bring her presents.

Musical instruments are not played at weddings. The Oriental dances are performed to the accompaniment of vocal music by female voices while the women beat little drums.

Cropping the hair of the bride was discarded by the S'fardim also.[206]

Among the Jews of Yemen . . . While the marriage customs of the S'fardim in Palestine remind us of Jewish life centuries ago, marriage among the Jews of Yemen remind us of even more ancient days.

Among the Jews of Yemen, the ancient custom in which the groom betrothed the bride at the engagement and gave her a divorce in case the engagement was broken, was discarded only recently. Among the Persian Jews and among some Jews of the Caucasus this ancient custom still prevails.

Among the Yemenite Jews, the fathers of the groom and the bride arrange the match. The children are not even consulted. Often they are too young to comprehend. The mothers are not informed of the affair until the match is completely effected.

The Jews of Yemen follow the ancient Biblical custom in which the groom, or rather his father, pays a certain amount of money to the father of the girl. He also gives the girl many presents, the value of which is recorded in the k'subo. Her father, however, does not usually keep the money he receives from the groom, but gives it to his daughter for her dowry.

As in Talmudic and medieval days, the pedigree of the family is more important than money. There are families among the Yemenite Jews who claim that their ancestors had come to Yemen prior to the destruction of the First Temple. Such families do not intermarry with families of low rank.

The interval between the engagement and the wedding lasts not less than a year, and sometimes even two years, particularly in a case when the bride is too young. During this time the groom and bride cannot see one another (see p. 130).

Shortly before the wedding, the bridegroom goes with his parents to buy the presents for the bride. These consist of garments, ornaments, cosmetics, soap, rose-water, a comb and many other things needed for the wedding. They also include waxen candles which are lighted at the wedding.

The bridegroom bears the cost of the wedding, which is a

heavy burden for him, or rather for his father. In addition to three or four large feasts which include many guests, he has to give many smaller parties for the close relatives during the "seven days of the feast."

In case the bride comes from another town, the bridegroom has to provide riding animals for all the guests of the bride's family. Among the poor classes a lad waits until he or his father have saved the money to cover the expense of marriage. Parents among the Jews of Yemen, therefore, never worry about marrying off their daughters, but they do worry about marrying off their sons.

For a period of two weeks before the wedding, the bride may not show herself on the street in daylight. If she has to pay a visit, she does so after dark.

The day for weddings is Wednesday. But the entire week before the wedding is a time of great joy. Each day has a special observance and is a joyous occasion.

The last three days before the wedding are the days when the bridal pair are colored with paint, a custom generally practiced by the Oriental Jews. Among the Jews of Egypt this custom was practiced as far back as the time of Maimonides. The groom is painted only once with henna, but the bride is painted several times with henna and with other materials. The paint is daubed on her face, her feet, her arms, and the inside of her hands and is an occasion of great hilarity. The bride is seated high on cushions. Many cotton wicks burn in a large bowl of oil placed before her while the women in the room sing and dance. Painting the groom's arms and feet is an occasion of still more boisterous joy.

The wedding day is crowded with various ceremonies and processions. The greatest solemnity and hilarity takes place before the chupo when the groom's hair is being shaved. Only his long ear-locks are left. The hair of the bride is cut short on the front of her head.

The chupo ceremony among the Jews of Yemen is altogether different from the chupo of the Ashk'nazim or the

S'fardim. They do not employ the canopy at all and still call the room where the bridal pair is left in privacy, chupo. The wedding ceremony takes place in the house of the bride. During the ceremony the bride sits in a separate room. Where such a room is not available, she sits in a corner of the same room, separated by a curtain, with only two women friends or relatives with her. First the k'subo is read aloud and the bridegroom with two witnesses, who are not members of his family, sign it. The bridegroom himself recites the benediction of betrothal over a cup of wine. The two fathers, followed by lads carrying candles in their hands, lead the bridegroom into the room or the corner where the bride sits. The bridegroom recites the betrothal formula, placing a new glittering coin or a ring in the painted palm of the bride's hand. He also hands her the cup of wine which she sips under her thick and heavy veil. The wedding benedictions are then recited and the wedding ceremony is over. The Jews of Yemen do not break a glass.

After the chupo ceremony, the bridal couple are led into a separate room and remain there in the company of the best men and two of the bride's friends. They break their fast with a repast and the groom presents the bride with a ring. Then the door is opened and the wedding guests crowd in.

With the coin, with which the groom betrothed the bride, her mother buys her raisins and almonds which the bride alone is allowed to eat. She must not let a crumb of these delicacies drop to the ground.

The wedding feast, accompanied by discourses in Torah, is served immediately after the chupo ceremony or, in some regions, on the following day. On each evening of the "seven days of the feast" a meal accompanied by singing and dancing is prepared for close relatives and friends. In this week following the wedding, the bridegroom stays indoors.

The Jews in Yemen today retain ancient Jewish marriage customs. Some of their customs are not Jewish in origin, but were taken over from their Arab neighbors; others are derived from a common source, the ancient Orient.[207]

xvii

Beliefs Connected with Marriage

Predestination of Marriages . . . The doctrine of the Pharisees, that every action of man was foreseen by God, became in time the common belief of the masses of the Jewish people. According to the Talmud "a man will not injure his finger without a decree from heaven." No wonder, therefore, that such an important step as the choice of a wife was believed predestined. According to the Talmud, the match was made in heaven even before the young man and woman were born. "Forty days before the creation of the child, it is proclaimed in heaven: 'This man's daughter shall marry that man.' " [208]

That this belief was wide-spread may be inferred from several anecdotes in the Talmud and the Midrashim.

There is a story concerning a Roman lady who somewhat impishly asked the Tanna Rabbi Jose ben Chalafta whether God had anything to do after He created the world. Rabbi Jose answered that He was busy in arranging marriages. "I could do it as well myself," replied the lady. "I have numerous slaves and could match them off in no time." "You may think it is easy, but for the Holy One blessed be He, this is as difficult as dividing the Red Sea," retorted Rabbi Jose. The lady then gathered a thousand men-servants and as many maid-servants, and paired them and declared them married. On the following day, they appeared before her a sorry lot. One's head was bruised, the other had a black eye, the third had a fractured arm, the fourth a broken leg. When she asked what had happened, they all loudly said that they wished they were not married. The lady then sent for Rabbi Jose and admitted that the arrangement of matches was an extremely difficult task. [209]

The belief in the predestination of marriage was expressed in a story about Raba, the famous Amora who lived in Babylonia in the fourth century, c.e. Raba once heard a man praying that he might win a certain woman in marriage and he rebuked the man with the words: "If she is destined for you, she will be yours; and if she is not destined for you, your prayers flaunt the will of Providence." [210]

The most striking illustration of the belief in the predestination of marriage is found in the Midrashic tale of King Solomon and his beautiful daughter.

King Solomon had a daughter who was the fairest in the whole land of Israel. Her father once scanned the stars to discover whom she was destined to marry and he saw that her future husband would be the poorest man in Israel. He built a high tower by the sea, and surrounded it on all sides with walls. Then he placed his daughter in the tower with aged guardians to watch her. He supplied them with provisions and then sealed the tower so that none could possibly slip past the guards. He said, "I shall watch the work of God."

In the course of time, the poor man who was his daughter's destined husband walked near the tower one night. His garments were ragged and torn and he was on the verge of fainting from hunger, thirst and fatigue. Looking about for some shelter he beheld the skeleton of an ox lying on a field close by. The poor youth crept into the skeleton to shelter himself from the cold. As he slept, a great bird swooped down and picked up the carcass in which lay the unconscious youth. The bird flew with it to the roof of the tower to consume the carcass. When the poor youth awoke, he found himself on the roof and there the princess found him when she came up on the roof to sun herself. When she had recovered from her surprise, she asked: "Who are you and who brought you here?" He answered, "I am a Jew of Acco, and a bird brought me here." The princess ordered her servants to clothe him and anoint him with oil, and then she saw that he was the handsomest youth in all Israel. He was intelligent too, and learned, and the princess loved him with her heart and soul. One day she said to him, "Will you marry me?" and he answered, "I wish it might be so!" They decided to marry, and as there was no ink with which to write the k'subo, he used a few drops of his own blood as ink, and when he recited the marriage b'rocho he said, "Let God and Michael and Gabriel be my witnesses today."

When the guardians learned of the marriage, they summoned Solomon. The king came at once in a ship, and calling his daughter to him, asked her to tell him what had happened. "The Holy One, blessed be He, sent me a youth, who is handsome and learned, and he married me." She then called the lad, who appeared before the king and showed him the k'subo which he had written. The king inquired about his father and mother and the town from which he had come, and from the young man's replies he realized that this was the very man whom the stars had shown as the destined husband of his daughter. Solomon then rejoiced greatly and exclaimed, "Blessed be the Lord who chooses a wife for every man." [211]

There is still another illustration of God's design taken from a Hebrew book of the twelfth century. It concerns a girl who persistently refused to adorn herself. People said to her, "If you are not well dressed, no one will notice you or want to marry you." But she answered firmly, "It is the Holy One, blessed be He, who arranges marriages; so I need not be concerned." She was properly rewarded for her faith, for she married a learned and pious man. [212]

The belief in the predestination of marriages has persisted in Jewish life and Jewish lore even to our own day. According to the popular belief no one must intervene in a marriage and preventing a predestined match is a sin which entails punishment from Heaven. [213]

Unlucky Days and Seasons . . . Various peoples did and still do believe that some of the days of the week, the periods of the lunar month, and the seasons of the year are unlucky

THE WEDDING under the Chupo by Moritz Oppenheim

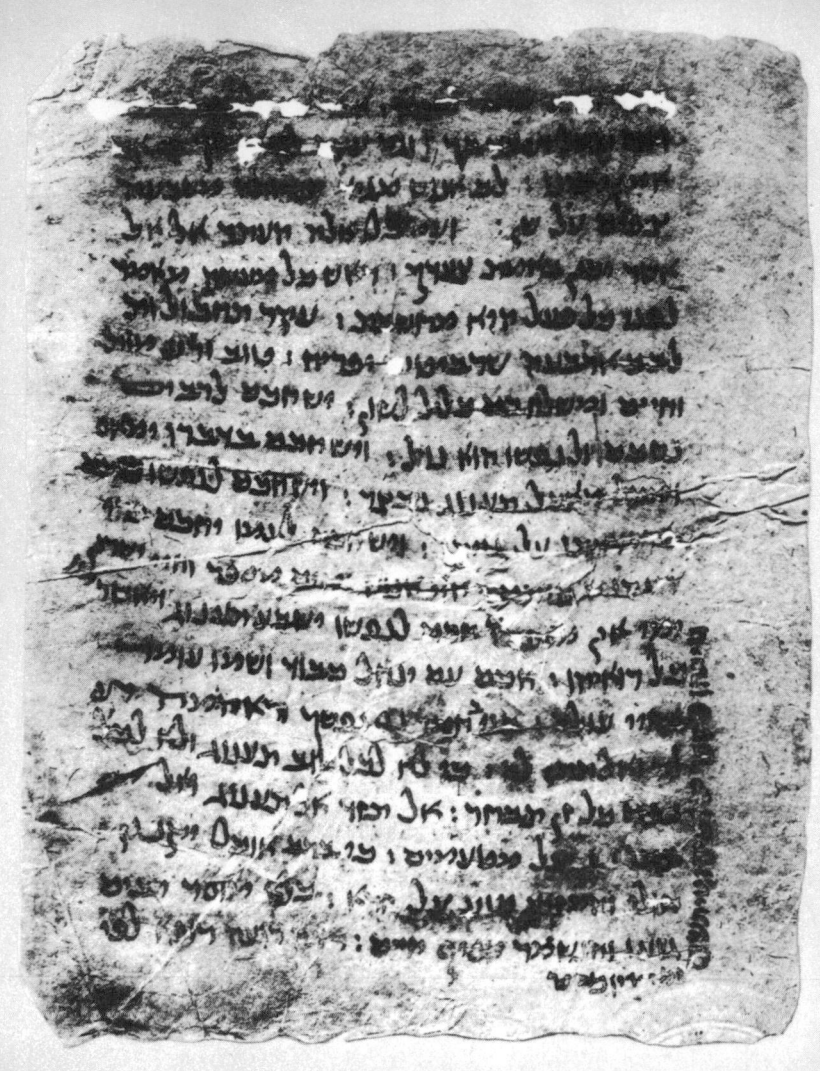

or ill-omened, and that it is hazardous to start any new undertaking during such times. The various peoples did not agree as to which of the days, periods, and seasons were unlucky. For instance among the Germans, Friday was considered an unlucky day, while among Jews, weddings were performed on Fridays as far back as Talmudic times, and, since the Middle Ages, Friday became the favorite day for weddings. Apparently, there was an economic reason for this preference, as the poor were thus spared extra expense by combining the celebration of the wedding day with the celebration of the Sabbath following the wedding. In olden times, Wednesday was regarded as a lucky day, the favorite wedding day for maidens. In the Middle Ages, apparently through some foreign influence, Monday and Wednesday were both declared to be unlucky days, and even today East European Jews do not perform weddings on those two days.[214]

Some peoples believed that the phases of the moon had an influence over life on the earth. Among the Jews and many other Oriental peoples, weddings were performed at the New Moon or at the Full Moon, but never in the period when the moon was absent.[215]

There were two seasons of the year in which weddings were not performed—one between the fast of the seventeenth of Tamuz and the fast of Tisho B'Ov, and the other between Pesach and Shovuos. The former was a season of mourning and needs no explanation. The latter was declared to be a season of mourning based upon the Talmudic legend which says that Rabbi Akiba, the great Tanna of the second century (c.e.), lost thousands of his pupils who were all stricken by a plague during this season from Pesach to Shovuos. However, critical scholars have agreed that the connection with the mortality of Rabbi Akiba's pupils was merely a later and remote interpretation given to an old custom, the origin of which had been forgotten. Originally, the period between Pesach and Shovuos was not a time of mourning because of any sad events in Jewish life, but was merely regarded as an unlucky season. According to some scholars, it coincided approximately with the month of May in which marriages were forbidden among the Romans. This Roman custom adopted by some European nations was also adopted by the Jews who later tried to Judaize it by linking it with the Talmudic legend regarding the wholesale death of Rabbi Akiba's pupils. This later interpretation was not universally accepted. In the Middle Ages, other less tenable interpretations were also offered by some rabbis.

In the Middle Ages there was a variety of customs in regard to the duration of the period. In some Jewish communities, marriages were forbidden during the period from the New Moon of Iyor until Shovuos. In other communities it was forbidden to perform a marriage on any day between Pesach and Lag Bo-omer (the 18th day of Iyor). Again in other communities, the curb on marriages lasted from Pesach until Shovuos, with the exception of the day of Lag Bo-omer. Among some East European Jews today, the restriction is in full force from Pesach until Shovuos, except Lag Bo-omer, Rosh Chodesh Iyor, Rosh Chodesh Sivon, and the three days preceding Shovuos.

The prohibition also extended to the cutting of hair, and in some communities women refrained from doing any work after sunset on those days.[216]

Origin of Marriage Customs . . . The customs connected with marriage are very old. While the religious ceremonies associated with marriage are a product of a higher spiritual culture, the popular customs stem from primitive times. For quite a time they were a topic of discussion among scholars of primitive culture and comparative folklore. Various theories have been offered to explain their origin. But each theory explains only some of the customs without necessarily excluding the other theories. Sometimes a single custom may spring from different motives and admit of more than one explanation.

In the following we shall briefly touch upon these theories

as far as they are applicable to Jewish marriage customs.

Some of the Jewish marriage customs involve no primitive beliefs. They are mere symbols of unison and concord between the bridal pair. Such symbols are the drinking of wine from the same cup by the bridal pair at the marriage ceremony and the exchanging of gifts between them. Marriage signifies also the union of two families. This is symbolized by the wedding feast eaten together after the marriage ceremony.

We have to treat at a little greater length another set of marriage customs derived from the belief that on the wedding day the bridal pair was menaced by evil powers. Primitive man feared evil spirits at every critical moment and every important step of his life, particularly at the three important moments of his earthly career: birth, marriage, and death.[217]

Guarding the Bridegroom . . . The Oriental peoples believed that male demons desired to marry the daughters of men, and vice versa, and that the demons were envious of the bridal pair, especially of the bridegroom, their ostensible rival, whom they sought to destroy. The bride whose five or seven successive bridegrooms were killed by a demon on the wedding night was the theme of many popular tales. We find this theme in Tobit, one of the books of the Apocrypha. One protagonist of the story of Tobit is Sara, the pious daughter of Raguel, who lived in Ecbatana, a city of Media. This pious Jewess had been married to seven successive men whom the evil spirit Asmodeus had killed on the wedding night. She was ultimately married to Tobias, the son of the pious Tobit, who succeeded in escaping death at the hand of Asmodeus by employing a charm against him prepared at the direction of the angel Raphael. The charm consisted of smoke made by the heart and liver of a fish, burnt on coal and placed on the ashes of perfume. Asmodeus, smelling this smoke, fled into the furthest parts of Egypt.[218]

Hiding the Bridal Pair . . . It was already remarked in a previous chapter that primitive man devised a varied strategy in this warfare against evil spirits. He tried to shut them out by hiding the threatened person. He tried to deceive them and to frighten them, and he even tried to appease them with offerings, with gifts. These various strategems employed by primitive man in his warfare against the evil spirits explain the origin of many marriage customs as well as they explain the origin of many customs connected with the birth of a child (see p. 65).

The first precaution taken was to prohibit the bridegroom and the bride from going out alone during the week preceding and, in some regions, also during the week following the wedding, especially at night when the demons spread their terror. Precaution was also taken to keep the bridal pair from sight on the wedding day. Veiling the face of the bride was a prevalent custom, employed among Jews and other Orientals since ancient days. At the wedding in Mayence previously described, the bridegroom also hid his head under the cowl of his cape during the marriage ceremony, although it was mostly the face of the bride which had to be concealed from the jealous eyes of the demons. There may have been another motive for the use of the veil, as every snarl and knot was regarded as a magic safeguard against evil spirits, based on the popular belief in the magic power of knots.[219]

Keeping the bridal pair out of sight may have been prompted by another motive. It has already been previously noted that, in the belief of primitive man, the bride and the groom had an evil eye for one another. Among some peoples, the bridal pair were not allowed to see one another in daylight for several days after the wedding. According to this belief, there was in general something sinister about the glances of the bridal pair which ought therefore to be avoided (see pp. 130, 131 and 203).

Combating the Evil Spirits . . . Another strategem employed in combating the evil spirits was to deceive them in such a manner that they should not recognize that a wedding was being performed. Various ruses were devised to make the demons believe that this was an occasion of mourning. This procedure explains why the traditional Jewish wedding of former days was marked by so many signs of mourning. The bride did her best to weep as much as possible. Both the bride and groom wore white shrouds at the marriage ceremony as a reminder of the burial shroud. The custom of having the bridegroom wear a kittel (white shroud) under his talis during the marriage ceremony was in force until recently among East European Jews. He also covered his head with ashes. This was an ancient sign of mourning which became a wedding custom in Talmudic days and persisted as such in Eastern Europe until our own time.[220] A few centuries ago, in some Jewish communities, the bridegroom wore a black kerchief on his head during the marriage ceremony as a sign of mourning.

No traces of joy or gaiety were present in the traditional Jewish wedding procession until the marriage ceremony was over. These signs of sadness and mourning were later divested of their original magic character and new interpretations given to them. The signs of mourning remained only as a reminder of the destruction of Jerusalem. The white shroud, a reminder of death rather than of national disaster, was declared a means of restraining the bridal pair from excessive joy.

In a special category is the fasting of the bridal pair until the wedding ceremony is over, as if it were a day of mourning. Jewish religious authorities in the Middle Ages were not in agreement as to whether the bride should fast, some believing the fast incumbent on the bridegroom only. Later this procedure was universally accepted for both bridegroom and bride. The fasting of the bridal pair could not be interpreted as a symbol of national mourning; so other explanations were offered. Most popular was the explanation that the day of the wedding is a day of destiny, a day of atonement for the bridal pair on which they must fast as on Yom Kippur. It was this explanation which caused the custom to persist, but it may have originally been based upon two other motives. Besides the necessity of making the wedding day appear as a day of mourning, there was also a popular belief that abstinences of various kinds practiced by the bridal pair on the wedding day are a means of averting evil from them. Among some peoples it was the custom for the bridal pair not to speak on the wedding day or at least not to speak aloud.[221]

One additional ruse employed to deceive the evil spirits at weddings must be mentioned. People believed that disguises confounded the evil spirits so that they did not know who was who. This explains the custom of painting the faces of the bridal pair, still prevalent among Oriental Jews. The bride and groom were painted in order that the evil spirits should not recognize them. At weddings, the bridegroom and the bride even interchanged clothes. Although the interchange of garments between sexes was forbidden by the Mosaic Law, it was still in vogue among the Jews of Egypt at the time of Maimonides (twelfth century). Apparently, under the influence of the non-Jewish environment, among the Egyptian Jews the bride was dressed like a man and the bridegroom like a woman. Maimonides abolished this practice. However, in the seventeenth and eighteenth centuries mention is again made of an ordinance, among the Jews of Italy, against masquerading at weddings and at circumcision celebrations. Apparently this practice was due to the influence of non-Jewish surroundings. However, in the interchange of clothes between the bride and groom one more motive may have been involved. It may have symbolized the complete union of the bridal pair.[222]

But even these means of concealment, supplemented by tricks of deception, were not deemed adequate protection from the evil spirits. Primitive men used numerous talismans and charms to frighten the demons and put them to flight in case they dared appear. We have cited the story from the Book of Tobit in which the demon Asmodeus was driven away by the smell of the smoke made by burning the heart and liver of a fish. The smell of smoke was generally believed efficacious in dispelling evil spirits. Smoke was a protection against injury from an evil eye, and among some peoples it was customary before the wedding to fumigate the bridegroom and bride. A similar custom was the bathing of the bride before the wedding, for, according to primitive man, spirits recoiled before water, because they could not cross it. The Caucasian Jews led both the bride and the groom to the bath before the chupo.[223] However, among the Chasidim in Eastern Europe immersion before the chupo is part of the physical and mental preparation for marriage as a sacred rite.

There are additional charms already mentioned, which we note again in connection with weddings. Light was a popular charm. The demons, who held sway only in darkness, shunned the light. This explains the lighted torches and candles at weddings used from ancient times to the present day. The closed circle was a popular charm, explaining the encirclings around the bride under the chupo. This magic circle may also have motivated the marriage ring, not excluding other motives. Iron, salt, legumes and weapons were regarded as charms against evil spirits. This explains many marriage customs among Jews. Among the Jews in some parts of Germany in the Middle Ages, a piece of iron was placed in the bridegroom's pocket before he was led to the marriage ceremony. In olden times, salt was put in the garlands of the bride and the bridegroom. In Biblical times, weapons were brandished in the wedding procession. Among the Jews of Egypt, in the time of Maimonides, the bride, dressed like a man, danced with a sword brandished in her hand. At the weddings of the East European Jews, it was customary as late as a generation ago to serve cooked and salted beans and peas just as it was done at the birth of a child.

Plants with a strong odor, i.e., garlic and myrtle, were among the magic means employed against evil spirits and witchcraft. The amuletic character of the myrtle was enhanced by its unwithering leaves. This accounts for the plant's popularity at weddings as a bridal garland, and also as an adornment of the wedding guests.[224]

Frightening away demons with loud noise may have been the original motivation for breaking of the glass at the marriage ceremony, a custom mentioned as far back as the twelfth century. In the sixteenth century, the custom arose among the Jews of Germany to break dishes at the knas mahl also. This custom was apparently due to the non-Jewish environment, for in southern Germany the Germans broke dishes at the engagement, whereas in other parts of Germany, the tumultuous breaking of dishes took place on the evening preceding the wedding, which was called *Polter Abend* (evening of noise and clattering). In recent times, the order of this observance within the chupo ceremony was changed. In most communities instead of breaking the glass after the wedding benedictions at the very end of the marriage ceremonial, the bridegroom broke it in the midst of the ceremony, after he had recited the betrothal formula. This custom of breaking a glass at the marriage ceremony, and earthen dishes at the knas mahl, was later interpreted as a reminder of the destruction of Jerusalem, an explanation which seems forced and untenable when we remember that breaking dishes was accompanied by a loud and joyful "Mazol Tov" from all present. The magic origin of this custom explains why the S'fardim in Jerusalem hide every splinter of the broken glass, and why the breaking of the glass is accompanied by the recitation of the verse of the Psalms, "The snare is broken and we are escaped" (see p. 201).

However, the primitive idea of driving away demons by noise does not fully explain the custom of breaking the glass at the marriage ceremony. Originally, the bridegroom dashed the glass against a wall with the wine still in it, spilling the wine. This displayed a second motive for this custom—propitiating the evil spirits by offering them gifts. Wine and oil were prominent among the gifts which effected the withdrawal of the demons.[225]

Appeasing evil spirits with gifts may have motivated the custom prevalent in Talmudic times when wine and oil flowed in profusion, and nuts, parched corn and other sweetmeats were thrown before the wedding procession of the bridal pair. The wine and oil were also used as an expression of honor accorded to men of fame on their entry into a town. The nuts, parched corn and other sweetmeats thrown before the bridegroom and the bride may have had an entirely different meaning, for in primitive belief they were considered omens of fertility and an abundant life.[226]

Omens of Fertility . . . Mention has been made of the primitive belief in sympathetic magic, the belief that every activity called forth its counterpart. If water was poured, rain would come; if one ate sweet dishes at the beginning of the year, sweetness was presaged for the entire year; if bread was the first thing brought into a new dwelling, bread would never be lacking there. Magic rites of this kind, which presaged fertility and an abundant life, have always played a prominent role at weddings among the Jews as well as among other peoples.

The grains of fertile plants were among the omens of fertility. In Talmudic times, a short time before a wedding, seeds of barley were planted in an earthen pot on behalf of the bridal pair. When the seeds began to sprout, the pot was brought to the bridal pair with the words, "As these barley seeds sprout, so you shall be fruitful and multiply." [227] At the weddings in Mayence and in Worms described above, grains of wheat were thrown over the heads of the bridal pair. Among East European Jews, this rite of sympathetic magic was practiced at weddings a generation ago where raisins, hops, rice, nuts, and almonds were used.

The hen played a prominent part in the magic rites of fertility. As far back as the beginning of the Common Era, Palestinian Jews carried a hen and a cock before the bridal pair in the wedding procession, and as late as the fifteenth century, the Jews of Posen caused a hen and a cock to fly over the chupo after the marriage ceremony. At the wedding in Mayence, described above, the bridal pair broke their fast after the marriage ceremony with an egg and hen.[228]

The fish was also regarded as a symbol of fertility. In the Middle Ages, the bridal pair ate fish on the day after the wedding. In some Jewish communities of the Orient, the women bring two fish in a silver vessel to the wedding ceremony and place the vessel on the earth close to the canopy.[229]

Not all the practices of sympathetic magic at weddings pertain to omens of fertility. Some of them are omens of general good luck as the large loaf of white bread with which the bridal pair were met on their return from the chupo ceremony and the kneading bowl on which the bride was seated (see pp. 190 ff.). Among the S'fardim, the gold coins given to the bride and bridegroom by their relatives after the chupo ceremony were omens of good fortune. The custom of mixing coins with the grains of wheat thrown over the heads of the bridal pair, practiced among the German Jews in the Middle Ages, may have been similarly motivated, representing a twofold omen in which the grains of wheat presaged fertility, and the coins, material fortune. The coins, however, were used for charity, and were picked up by the poor.

"Mazol Tov" and "Siman Tov" . . . In previous descriptions of weddings the readers have noticed the two formulas of congratulation used among Jews since the Middle Azes: Mazol Tov among the Ashk'nazim, and Siman Tov among the S'fardim. Both formulas can be traced to ancient beliefs cherished by all peoples in bygone days.

Originally, mazol meant a constellation of the Zodiac and also a planet, which is the Biblical and Talmudic meaning of the word. Because of the universal belief that the fate of men and the success of their enterprises depended upon the position and aspect of the stars, the word mazol in the Talmud and Midrash acquired a secondary meaning—star of destiny, and destiny in general. In the Middle Ages among the Franco-German Jews, "Mazol Tov" became an expression synonymous with "good luck," until gradually all traces of its astrological background were forgotten.

In olden times, the fortune of man was read not only in the stars, but in countless objects and occurrences, especially extraordinary ones, which were interpreted as good or bad omens. "Siman Tov," good omen, is a current expression in the Talmud and Midrash. Although the original background, the belief in good or bad omens, has been lost, the expression is still retained among the S'fardim as a formula of congratulation.[230]

PART FOUR

Death, Funeral, Burial, and Mourning

xviii

In Biblical Times

In Biblical times, the Jewish outlook on life and death differed from that of a later day. In those days the Jew looked for his salvation and centered his thought not on heaven, but on the earth with its abundance of fruit, corn, wine and oil. He identified himself with his kindred in the earthly life which he lived upon the good land the God of his ancestors had given him. He dwelt among his own people and was gathered to them after his death.

When a man felt that he was about to "go the way of all the earth" and be "gathered unto his people," he called his children to him and blessed them, charging them to execute his will, particularly in regard to his burial. The just and God-fearing man commanded his children to keep the way of the Lord, to do righteousness and justice after his death. The leader of the people sometimes delivered an address of great import when he felt his end was approaching. In the Bible, Moses and Joshua addressed the people before their death.[231]

When death came, all the relatives and friends gave vent to their grief, aloud. They moaned and smote their breasts. They sobbed and lamented wherever they were—on the flat roofs of the houses, or in the streets.[232]

Gestures of Mourning . . . With the coming of death, many duties and observances were incumbent upon the mourners. The first thing to be done was to close the eyes of the deceased, and to kiss him. Then the mourners rent their outer garments and attired themselves in coarse sackcloth. They laid aside their head ornaments, tore their hair and plucked their beards or made a bald spot in them. They covered their heads, or at least the upper lip, strewed dust and ashes on their heads, removed their shoes, and sat on the ground in the dust. They even made incisions in their flesh.[233]

The Funeral . . . Among the ancient peoples of the Orient, including the Jews, a corpse was regarded as the ultimate defilement.

The burial, therefore, took place on the same day as the death. In the Bible, the bier on which the corpse was carried in the funeral procession is called *mito*, the Hebrew word for bed, apparently the deathbed. The mito was followed by the mourners who lamented the deceased with loud weeping. Learned women, who were professional wailers, were hired to add their voices to the lamentations of the women of the household. This custom is still prevalent in the Orient. There were men who were known as accomplished mourners, but women mourners predominated, apparently superior to men in their ability to display grief and to bring tears to all eyes. David, in his elegy over Saul and his son Jonathan, addressed himself not to the sons but to the daughters of Israel, bidding them weep (II Sam. 1:24). Jeremiah, sensing impending destruction, bade his people call forth the mourning women that they might "take up a wailing for us, that our eyes may run down with tears and our eyelids gush out with waters" (9:16–17). These professional wailers walked before the bier, with shrilly dramatic lamentations. They sang a dirge (kino) composed according to an established rhythm and beginning with the word *echo* (how). One woman led the chanting of the dirge, and the rest responded in a chorus. The chant was accompanied by the playing of pipes. Ejaculations were uttered as: "Alas, Alas! Ah, my brother! Ah, my sister! Ah, Lord! Ah, His glory!" [234]

Burial . . . The dead were always interred. Cremation was regarded as an abuse of the dead, and was applied only to certain criminals condemned to death, to enhance their punishment. It was a disgrace and a calamity to remain unburied. Even a criminal was buried on the same day on which he was executed.[235]

The clothed corpse was laid in the grave uncoffined. The dead were buried in the clothes they wore in life, which accounted for the prevalent belief that the deceased could be recognized by their costume in *Sheol*, the nether world.[236] Embalming was not a Jewish practice. The embalming of Jacob and Joseph referred to in the Bible was an Egyptian custom as was the use of a coffin in the Biblical phrase, "Joseph was put in a coffin in Egypt" (Gen. 50:2, 26).

At the burial of rich people, particularly princes, a great fire was prepared. Fragrant spices, and apparently the bed and many other possessions which the deceased used in life, were burned in the blazing flame.[237]

In the ancient graves excavated in Palestine, many empty clay vessels were found, such as jars, plates, bowls and lamps. The archaeologists infer from this that the Jews, as well as their Canaanitic predecessors, placed food in the graves.

In the Bible we hear of giving food for the dead. When a man "has made an end of tithing all the tithe of his increase," he declared in the sanctuary, "I have not eaten thereof in my mourning, neither have I put away thereof, being unclean, nor given thereof for the dead" (Deut. 26:12–14). In Tobit, an Apocryphal book of the time of the Second Temple, we continue to hear of food offered to the spirits of the dead. Before his death, it is told, the pious Tobit called his son, Tobias, and among many other things, commanded him, "Pour out thy bread on the burial of the just, but give nothing to the wicked" (Tobit 4:17). Food for the dead was not always genuine food. Fine white sand used as a substitute for flour was found in excavated graves.[238]

Period of Mourning . . . The mourners fasted for the dead, eating a meal which was called "the bread of mourners" only in the evening of the day of burial. According to prescribed custom, the mourners could not prepare their own food, which was therefore brought in by the neighbors, who joined in a common feast. With the food, the neighbors gave the mourners a cup to drink, called "the cup of consolation." Sometimes the fast lasted for seven days and was only interrupted in the evenings.[239]

The mourning lasted at least a week. During these days acquaintances visited the mourners to comfort them. A father or a mother, or great and famous men, were mourned for thirty days with less intensiveness.[240]

These marks of mourning and modes of burial, many of which now appear very strange, were not peculiarly Jewish, but were common to most of the peoples of the ancient Orient. The Jews who took them over in their entirety from their Canaanitish neighbors did not extend and embellish them. Although their origin had long faded from memory, they still retained a touch of ancestral worship which the Jewish religion so sternly opposed. Some of these customs of mourning, i.e., tearing the hair, and making incisions in the flesh, were rigidly forbidden by the Mosaic Law, but only in the course of time were these practices actually discarded by the people.[241]

Graves . . . When one departed from life, he "lay with his fathers" or "was gathered unto his people." These phrases of the Bible may be taken literally, because the dead were usually buried in a family grave, a burial chamber where all the members of the family rested side by side. This grave was "a possession of burying place" on ground which was the property of the family. There were single graves, but no cemeteries existed as we know them, as a common field of interment for the entire community.[242]

No one wished to be buried in a strange place. Barzillai, the Gileadite, refused to go with King David to Jerusalem, because he was fourscore years old and wished to die in his own city and be buried in the grave of his father and mother

(II Sam. 19:36). Those who lived in a strange land charged their children before dying to carry them to their native land, and place their bodies in the burying place of their ancestors. This is illustrated in the Bible, in the stories of Jacob and Joseph. No matter how long a man lived in a strange land, his real home remained the place where his forefathers rested in the family grave. Nearly one and a half centuries after the destruction of Jerusalem, Nehemiah said to the Persian King Artaxerxes, "Why should not my countenance be sad, when the city, the place of my fathers' sepulchres, lieth waste?" (Nehemiah 2:3). To be buried far away from the family sepulchre was a severe punishment.

Family ties endured even in the grave. The sepulchre was originally in the immediate neighborhood of the family dwelling place, in the garden or court of the house. In the course of time the tendency developed to remove the graves from the dwellings of the living, especially in the cities, where it was impossible to have the sepulchre near the house. The kings of Judah whose sepulchres were in the grounds of their castle were an exception in this respect. Even the grave outside the gates of the city remained a family grave, bearing an inscription with a warning that no stranger should be interred within.[243]

The numerous natural caves in Palestine were used as the first family graves. The sepulchral caves were extended as the need arose. Artificial grottos were dug where natural caves were unavailable. Later, the Jews adopted from the Phoenicians the custom of hewing graves from the stony slopes of the mountains. The Palestinian mountains consist of limestone which is easy to cut and is durable. There, single graves were hewn out of the mountains' stony ground as well as wide, deep burial chambers which served as family sepulchres. These hewn graves were naturally expensive, and used only by the richer classes. The poor continued to use the caves for burial. In the burial chamber, the dead were interred in niches, cavities dug horizontally in the perpendicular wall. There were other modes of burial for poor people without "a possession of a burying place" who humbly laid their dead in a common field of graves. In the Bible, mention is made of a field of graves situated near Jerusalem called "the graves of the common people" (II Kings 23:6; Jer. 26:23).

In Biblical times, the graves of the Jews, unlike the Egyptian tombs, were of the utmost simplicity, without ornamentation and embellishment in or outside the burial chamber. Before the Greek period, the Jews did not mark each grave with a stone. That was a Phoenician fashion. In the Bible, King Saul and Absalom, the son of King David, set up monuments for themselves while they were still alive, and not as monuments for their graves. The Bible mentions a "sign" of a grave, but this was not a monument to commemorate the dead, but a sign to mark the site of an unnoticeable grave or the grave of a distinguished person.[244]

XIX

In the First Centuries of the Common Era

The rites and customs of burial and mourning, as well as many other aspects of Jewish life, changed in many respects in the course of the centuries between ancient Biblical days and the period with which we are now concerned. The change was due in part to the influence of Greco-Roman civilization, but more essentially to the inner development of religious concepts and beliefs among Jews, particularly those concerning death.

In Biblical times, the rites and customs connected with death stood entirely apart from the Jewish religion. Jewish leaders were rather hostile to the customs practiced when death occurred. Some of the mourning customs were sternly prohibited by the teachers and spokesmen of the Jewish faith who considered them primitive and heathen in nature, not befitting a people holy unto the Lord. Other customs, which were not considered particularly heathenish or repugnant, were tolerated as outbursts of grief. Such customs, still remembered as originating in the primitive belief in the spirits of the dead, could not become an integral part of the established rites and ceremonies of the Jewish religion and retained their existence only as popular customs.

In the era of which we now speak, this situation was entirely changed. The origin of these customs had been almost forgotten. The Jewish monotheistic religion, firmly established and deeply rooted, was in no danger any more of being submerged by heathen beliefs and cults. Thus, official sanction was given now to many popular customs and practices. The whole outlook on death had been changed by the belief in the future life in heaven and in the resurrection of the dead with the coming of the Messiah. The majority of the Jews, the followers of the Pharisees, believed that death is not the total extinction of man's life as it was conceived in ancient Biblical days (see further on pp. 237 ff.).

The rites, customs, and practices connected with death, burial, and mourning, assumed a new aspect. They no longer stood apart from the Jewish religion, but became an integral part of Jewish religious life, with the rabbis of the Talmud regulating all minute details.

As Death Drew Near . . . At this period written testaments were already in vogue, although any oral will made by a man mortally ill was as valid and binding as a written will.

At the end of a man's life, besides testaments in regard to property, he often charged his offspring to carry on his ideals and his way of life. We do not find any ethical wills in writing, but we do hear of many verbally delivered testaments of this character. In ancient Biblical times, in some rare instances, leaders had addressed the people before their death. Now religious and moral exhortations had become popular, especially among the religious teachers of the people, the rabbis of the Talmud. Some of them who remained conscious until the moment of death uttered statements from the Torah, recited psalms and prayers, and made a confession of their sins.[245]

When Death Came . . . When death came, the eyes and mouth of the deceased were closed, usually by the oldest son. The kinsfolk gave the departed a farewell kiss. All who were present at the deathbed tore their garments. Under foreign influence, many innovations were introduced in regard to the treatment of the corpse. It was laid on the floor on sand, or on a layer of refrigerated salt in order to prevent rapid decay in the hot climate. Cooling vessels of metal were placed on the dead body for the same purpose. An oil lamp or a torch burned at the head of the corpse. In general, great care was taken not to dishonor the dead.

The news of a death was announced by the sound of a trumpet. All the inhabitants of the locality were in duty bound to refrain from their usual labors, unless there was a burial brotherhood which took care of the burial.[246]

Preparations for the Funeral . . . There was only a short interval between death and interment, the burial taking place on the same day as the death, as in Biblical times. Delay of the burial until the next day was permitted only if the delay contributed to the honor of the departed one in order to notify people of the surrounding towns and villages of the funeral; or if the professional wailing women had to be brought from another locality; or if the coffin and shrouds could not be prepared on the same day. In Jerusalem, under no circumstances, was a corpse allowed to remain within the gates overnight. The corpses were deposited in open graves and carefully inspected for several days in order to ascertain that death had really occurred.

Among the Greeks and Romans, and also among the Jews, the corpse was washed and anointed with scented oil. The kinsfolk and friends of the family performed this rite unless there was a burial brotherhood in the community. In the case of persons of high rank, and among the well-to-do in general, the body was anointed with various expensive spices such as myrrh, aloes and many others. Burning coals laden with spices were placed before the dead, and vessels with spices were carried before the bier. Garlands of fragrant myrtle twigs were also laid on the coffin.[247]

Shrouds and Coffins . . . The dead were not buried uncoffined in the clothes they wore in life, as in Biblical days, but they were interred in coffins and wore garments especially prepared for the grave.

It became a popular belief that the dead would rise from their graves in the same clothes in which they were buried, and this fact may have played a part in regard to the garments of the grave. People provided fine garments for the dead for that great day of the Messianic Era.

There was extravagant expense and display in dressing the corpse, which was usually wrapped in three garments made of byssus. Funerals and burial were such an expense for the poor classes that at times the burial expense was a greater calamity to the relatives than the actual death. Many poor people deserted their dead and disappeared. Following the second destruction of Jerusalem, Rabbon Gamaliel, the Patriarch of Jabneh, sought to lighten the funeral burden of the poor by disregarding the fashionable custom. In his testament he expressed the desire to be buried in cheap common linen and his example was followed by the people. Still people were reluctant to reduce the number of burial garments. Judah the Patriarch, grandson of Rabbon Gamaliel, on his deathbed, expressed his desire not to be buried in several garments. Eventually the corpse was wrapped in a single garment of cheap linen, and simplicity at funerals became the general rule. In Babylonia, in the fourth century, people used rough cloth worth a mere zuz (a quarter of a shekel) for burial shrouds. The poor and destitute even buried their dead in a mat of reeds, but this was regarded as a disgrace. According to the popular belief, the soul of a man who received such a burial was bound to the tomb, and could not join the company of invisible spirits who hovered over the world.

There was no exclusive color for burial shrouds. The prevalent color was white. Black was also used and even variegated colors. Before death, some of the Palestinian *Amora-im* (the sages of the Talmud from the third century on) expressed their desire to be buried in a white garment, while others preferred variegated colors. The Palestinian Amora, Rabbi Jeremiah (fourth century), expressed his desire to be wrapped in a white garment, with shoes on his feet and a staff in his hand, and to be buried in a roadside grave in order that he might be completely prepared for the resurrection.

The coffin was of wood, preferably cedar, but sometimes

of limestone or clay. A cover was spread on the bottom of the coffin and the corpse, dressed in his shroud, was laid on it, face upward. In former days there had been a class distinction in regard to covering the face of the corpse. The faces of the rich people were uncovered, but the faces of the poor people were covered, in order to hide the marks of poverty and hunger. After the disasters following the wars against Rome, this class distinction was abolished and the faces of both rich and poor were covered. Only the face of a bridegroom who died betrothed was uncovered.

Apparently under the influence of neighboring peoples, various objects which the dead used in life, as keys or a writing tablet, were placed in or hung on the coffin, especially in the case of one who died childless. When a man died betrothed, his inkstand and writing pen were laid in the coffin to show that in death he was ready to write the k'subo which he was not privileged to write in life. A Scroll of the Torah was placed on the coffins of distinguished scholars, demonstrating the zeal with which the dead studied and observed all that was written therein. Later, the Scroll of the Torah was merely carried in front of the bier. Abba Saul ben Batnith, one of the Tannaim (the sages of the Talmud in the first two centuries of the Common Era) who lived immediately after the destruction of Jerusalem, asked that the blue thread of his tsitsis be deposited in his coffin. Josephus relates that King Herod lay in a coffin with a diadem on his head, a crown above it and a sceptre in his right hand. Jews deposited valuable ornaments and treasures in the sepulchres of kings.

The coffin was carried to the grave on a bier. The rich provided an extravagantly lavish bier consisting of a richly adorned and highly decorated couch. King Herod was carried to his sepulchre on a golden bier covered with purple cloth, embroidered with many precious stones. The poor used a common frame made of reeds. This class distinction was also abolished in the period following the destruction of Jerusalem and all coffins were carried on cheap reed biers.[248]

The Funeral . . . The funeral procession went from the house of the departed to the grave, attended by almost the entire community, who considered it a religious duty to join and accompany a funeral procession. Even the study of the Torah could be interrupted to pay the last honor to the dead. If one could not join the funeral procession, he at least rose from his place when it passed.

The bier was carried on the shoulders of pall-bearers who walked barefooted. Carrying the bier was considered a religious act. A large number of pall-bearers surrounded the bier, and when one group was tired they were relieved by another. The mourners followed, barefooted, directly behind the bier. Men and women taking part in the funeral procession were separated. In some localities the men followed the bier behind the mourners and the women walked before it; in other localities, the men preceded the bier while the women followed the mourners, as was customary among the Greeks.

Hired mourning women were present at every funeral. Originally, they walked in front of the bier, as among the Egyptians. In this period, in Judea, the wailing women walked behind the bier; in Galilee, they walked before it. Musical instruments were used; two pipes and one woman who chanted were the minimum of indispensable vocal and instrumental music. At some funerals, dirges and lamentations were chanted by many hired singers. Musicians accompanied the singers with pipes, horns, and tambourines. Even in broad daylight, the funeral cortège was accompanied by torch bearers.

In this order the funeral procession, beginning at the house of mourning, went toward the burial place which was located at least fifty ells from the boundaries of the town. As the funeral cortège moved through the streets of the town, new people joined the procession, for to let a funeral procession pass without joining it was regarded as sinful.

On the way, many stops were made in order that the bearers of the bier could be relieved by others who wished to share in this religious act. At these stops, the bier was placed in the street or on the road. In the case of a deceased female no stops were made, so as to avoid an accident which might make the corpse visible.

At each stop, the hired mourners chanted their dirges and lamentations, beating their breasts, expressing grief in rhythmical movements of the hands and feet, and eulogizing the dead. If there was only one hired mourner, the women attending the funeral voluntarily responded in chorus. Some fragments of the funeral dirges of that period have been preserved in the Talmud. In Palestine the wailing women called on all who attended the funeral to join in the song of lament with these words: "Weep with him, all you of bitter hearts!" In Babylonia, the mourners chanted: "Hide yourselves and cover yourselves, you mountains, for he was the son of high and exalted ones," laying stress on the merits of the ancestors of the deceased.[249]

Funeral Orations . . . In addition to the songs of grief and lamentation, funeral discourses were delivered in which the life and good deeds of the dead were eulogized in the current style and manner connecting and interweaving those deeds with verses of the Bible. The significance attached to the funeral orations varied. Some regarded them as a consolation to the survivors, but for the most part, the eulogy was a mark of honor to the departed. The popular belief was that, as long as the stone was not placed on the burial cave, the dead in a sort of dream heard the praise uttered in their memory. Before his death, the famous Babylonian Amora, Abba Arikha or Rav as he was called for short, urged Rabbi Samuel bar Shelath to deliver an impassioned oration over his corpse. "For," said he, "I shall surely be there and hear your words."

Funeral orations were delivered at the stopping stations of the funeral cortège, or in a special building belonging to the family of the deceased, used in times of mourning and located near the burial place. Funeral orations were also delivered in the synagogue. Rabbi Judah the Patriarch died in Sepphoris, but his sepulchre was in Beth-Sh'orim. On the way from Sepporis to Beth-Sh'orim, the funeral cortège made stops at eighteen synagogues in order to hear the various funeral discourses delivered at each of them.

The funeral speaker was a rabbi or a relative of the deceased, or a professional funeral speaker hired for this purpose. Often the eulogies of these professional funeral preachers aroused the ire of many people. Anecdotes were told about hired funeral speakers who were given the last savings of the family to deliver the funeral eulogy. In the case of unimportant people, only a set formula of commemoration was pronounced. Embellishing the facts in eulogizing the dead was not uniformly the custom. In Judea, exaggerations were generally allowed; in Jerusalem, people kept strictly to facts.

Some fragments of funeral eulogies delivered at the death of distinguished rabbis have been preserved in the Talmud. When Samuel the Little (one of the Tannaim who lived after the destruction of the Second Temple) died childless, his key and writing tablet were hung on his coffin and Rabbon Gamaliel and Rabbi Eliezer pronounced the following eulogy: "Over this one we ought to shed tears, over this one we have to grieve. When kings die they transmit their crown to their children, the wealthy leave their wealth to their children, but Samuel the Little has taken with him all the precious things of the world and has gone." In the Talmud are also found some fragments of funeral orations delivered by professional funeral orators in Babylonia, couched in pure poetic Hebrew. Here are two of them:

"When the flame seized the cedars, what shall the hyssop on the wall do? When Leviathan was caught by the angler's hook, what shall the fishes of the pond expect? When the fishing line was dropped in the rushing stream, what shall the stagnant waters do?"

"Weep for those who are mourning and not for the one whom we lost; for he came to his rest and we remained moaning." [250]

The Last Funeral Rites . . . When the corpse was interred, final leave was taken from the departed with the words "*Lech b'sholom*" (go in peace). The funeral rites were not completed until certain rites were observed after the burial. At some distance from the grave, the participants in the funeral formed an aisle and as the mourners passed between, they uttered words of consolation. In some localities in Galilee, the mourners stood in the line and the people comforted them, the mourners standing at the left of the comforters. On the return from the grave, stops were made at a minimum of seven places. At these stops, praises of the departed were pronounced, which consoled the survivors, and speeches were made by the mourners to the assembled people. A signal was given for stopping and resuming the march. The formula for stopping was: "Sit down, worthies, sit down"; for resuming the march: "Rise up, worthies, rise up!" The signal was given by one of the worthies of the community or by the head of the burial brotherhood where such a brotherhood was in existence.

The rites of mourning lasted for seven days after the burial.[251]

The Meal of the Mourners . . . As in Biblical times, the mourners ate food brought to them by relatives and friends. On the first day, a mourner was not allowed to eat his own food. In the days preceding the second destruction of Jerusalem, the meal eaten after the funeral was a splendid public feast, the expense of which ruined the poor who strove to emulate the rich. Josephus relates that Archelaus, the son and successor of Herod as ruler of Judea, gave a very expensive funeral feast to the multitude of Jerusalem during the entire seven days he mourned his father, and apparently he was not the only man of high rank to display such lavishness. The rich used valuable dishes on which to serve the funeral meal to the mourners, and the class distinction in this respect was as marked as the difference in the shrouds and bier. Among the rich, the food was brought to the mourners on dishes of silver and gold, and wine was served in cups of rare and expensive white glass. Among the poor, food was brought in wicker baskets and the wine was served in cups of inexpensive colored glass. This class distinction also was eventually abolished, and both rich and poor brought food in inexpensive wicker baskets and served the wine in cups of cheap glass. The religious authorities declared that ten cups of wine be served the mourners in the house of mourning; three before the meal, three during the meal and four after the meal. Special benedictions and prayers were recited over the cups of wine poured after the meal in the presence of a quorum of ten, not including the mourners. A dish of lentils was prominent among the foods served to the mourners. The benedictions were recited at the meal eaten after the funeral, and also during the other seven days of mourning, if new visitors came to the house. The benedictions enhanced the religious aspect of the ceremony and integrated the rites and customs of mourning into the religious life of the Jews.

The Period of Mourning . . . The rabbis of the Talmud did not condone excessive grief and mourning for the dead, basing their exhortation on the words of Jeremiah, "Weep ye not for the dead, neither bemoan him" (Jer. 22:10). According to the Talmud weeping should be limited to three days, lamentation to seven days, and refraining from calendering the clothes and cutting the hair to thirty days. Exceeding these limits constituted a challenge to God, implying that human beings were more merciful than the Holy One, blessed be He.

The practices of strict mourning during the "seven days" and the less severe practices during the "thirty days" were minutely regulated, and many points were disputed among the religious authorities of the Talmud.

At this period as in Biblical times, many ancient customs of mourning were still practiced, as rending the garments, removing the shoes, covering the head and sitting on the ground. Some of the ancient customs had been changed and modified.

The custom of wearing coarse sackcloth was discontinued. Instead, sackcloth was hung at the door. The custom of placing dust on the head became merely a symbol, and instead of putting the dust on their heads, the mourners picked up some earth and threw it into the air. The primitive custom of making a bald spot in the hair was reversed, forbidding the mourner to cut his hair during the thirty days of mourning, and, in the case of the death of a father or a mother, until rebuked by his friends for his uncomeliness.

Among the new customs of mourning was the inversion of beds, couches and lamps in the house of mourning during the seven days, with the exception of the Sabbath. The mourners slept and ate on these inverted beds.[252]

The old custom of fasting for the dead was discarded. Mourners refrained only from meat and wine before the burial, but were prohibited from bathing and anointing themselves. The customs of mourning which had now become religious precepts regulated in their details by the rabbis of the Talmud did not allow the mourner to leave the house of mourning or to pursue his handicraft even inside of the house. Only in case of dire want was a mourner allowed to pursue his occupation in privacy after the first three days have passed. A mourner was not allowed to read the Bible with the exception of the books of Lamentations, Job, and the sad portions of Jeremiah, nor could he learn any branch of Talmudic lore, because it is assumed that the study of Torah brings joy. On the first three days a mourner might not put on phylacteries. During the first thirty days, the mourner might inquire for the peace of others, but others must not inquire for his peace.

One peculiar custom of mourning in that period required the baring of the shoulder, compulsory only in the case of the death of a father or a mother. In the case of the death of other kinsfolk, the mourner's decision regarding the observance of this manifestation of mourning was voluntary.

Even thirty days was not the maximum time of mourning. Only after twelve months was the state of mourning completely ended. When one met a friend in mourning within the twelve months, he was supposed to speak words of consolation to him, but not to inquire for his peace. In the case of the death of a parent, within the twelve months the mourner could not participate in any joyous feast unless the feast was of such a nature that participation was considered a religious act (a mitsvo).

These manifestations of mourning were not confined to death. They were also practiced on other occasions of distress and grief, as in the case of excommunication or on fast days.[253]

Comforting the Mourners . . . In the seven days of severe mourning, relatives, friends, acquaintances, and all the people of the community who were eager to do a pious deed, visited the house of mourning to console the mourners. If a man died leaving no survivors to mourn for him, ten men came to sit at the house where he died. In the first centuries of the Common Era a mourner did not leave the house of mourning even on the Sabbath to go to the synagogue. Instead, the people came to him. In this period, comforting mourners had assumed paramount religious importance. The homilists of the Midrashim believed the comforting of mourners entailed a singular religious merit which bestowed the Holy Spirit and rescued from Gehenna. In Jerusalem and in other cities and towns in Palestine, there was a special brotherhood who went to comfort mourners, similar to other existing brotherhoods whose duties entailed religious merit (see p. 26 and p. 156).

No one went to the house of mourning empty-handed. Everyone carried some food, a cruse of wine, loaves of bread, vegetables and legumes. Cooked fish and meat were brought in a pot. If there was a brotherhood which went to houses of mourning, its members took care of providing the mourners with food.

In the Talmud, in the second century C.E., we find a one-word formula for consoling mourners, consisting of the single

K'SUBO (Marriage Contract)
Hebrew Union College Museum, Cincinnati

Tombs in the Kidron Valley near Jerusalem

Hebrew word *tisnechomu* (be comforted). Anyone could say this word, but few were able to pronounce the long benedictions and prayers which were recited over cups of wine after the meal of the mourners, following the funeral, and on the other seven days of mourning, if new faces appeared in the house. If a homilist was present, he delivered a homily appropriate to the occasion. Here is the version of the benedictions and prayers recited in a house of mourning by a Palestinian Amora of the third century C.E.

"Blessed be Thou, God our Lord, King of the world, the God who is great in the abundance of His greatness, mighty and strong in the multitude of awe-inspiring deeds, Who reviveth the dead with His word, Who doeth great things that are unsearchable and wondrous works without number. Blessed Art Thou, O Lord, who revivest the dead."

"Our brethren, who are worn out, who are crushed by this bereavement, set your heart to consider this. This it is that standeth forever, it is a path from the six days of creation. Many have drunk, many will drink; as the drinking of the first ones, so will be that of the last ones. Our brethren, the Lord of consolation comfort you. Blessed be He who comforteth the mourners."

"Our charitable brethren, bestowers of lovingkindnesses, who hold fast to the covenant of Abraham, our father, our brethren, may the Lord of recompense pay you your reward. Blessed art Thou, who payest the recompense."

"Master of the worlds, redeem and save, deliver and help Thy people Israel from pestilence, and from the sword, and from plundering, and from the blast, and from the mildew, and from all kinds of calamities that may break forth and come into the world. Before we call, mayest Thou answer. Blessed art Thou who stayest the plague."

The benedictions praised God, comforted the mourners, blessed the comforters of the mourners, and ended with a prayer asking God to save the Jewish people from the calamities which threaten the world.

We are not sure whether these quoted benedictions were the accepted version or the composition of an individual Amora. Whatever the accepted version in the first centuries of the Common Era, in post-Talmudic times different versions of the benedictions of mourners were in vogue, the predominating motif of which was mourning for Zion, longing for the coming of the Messiah, and the rebuilding of Jerusalem. In the course of time this rite of reciting special benedictions in the house of mourning was completely discarded.[254]

Burial . . . In Rome, cremation was used more than interment. In Babylonia where the fire-worshippers ruled, interment and cremation were both interdicted on the ground that neither the earth nor the fire should be contaminated by a corpse, which was exposed on an elevated place to be devoured by birds of prey. Unlike the Romans and the Persians, the Jews exclusively disposed of the dead by burial. Since their attitude was distinguished from their non-Jewish neighbors, their interment of the dead assumed among them a religious aspect. They declared that the earth atoned for the sins of the dead.

This quality of expiation they attributed particularly to the soil of the Holy Land, basing the belief on the words of the Bible, "And doth make expiation for the land of His people" (Deut. 32:43). A Babylonian Amora expressed it in the sentence, "Being buried in the Land of Israel is like being buried under the Altar." In addition to this quality, it was believed that in the Messianic Era it would be advantageous for the dead to be buried in Palestinian soil. Only in the Land of Israel would the dead rise from their graves, whereas in the lands of the dispersion, the dead would have to roll through caverns under the ground until they reached the Land of Israel. The dearest wish of every pious Jew was burial in the Holy Land. The coffins of many Princes of the Exile in Babylonia were brought for interment to the Land of Israel. The Jews of Babylonia had a special reason for wishing to be buried in

Palestine. They were not secure in their graves in Babylonia, for often the fire-worshippers, in their fanatical zeal for the tenets of their faith, dug up and despoiled Jewish graves.

In those times, people walking in the streets of Palestinian towns often saw a coffin brought there from abroad. Sometimes a small casket containing only the remaining bones of the corpse and not the coffin with the corpse was transported to the Holy Land. It was customary to place a handful of earth on the coffin as soon as it reached the soil of the Land of Israel, as an act of expiation for the sin of having lived and died "in an unclean land." [255]

A suicide was buried in silence, without any solemn rites or public manifestations of grief and mourning. Only the rites entailing honor to the survivors were observed. There was no manifestation of mourning for one who was executed by the Jewish court, but all rites and honors were accorded to those who were executed by the Roman government for political offenses. An apostate was never mourned even by his nearest kindred.[256]

The Second Burial . . . In the Greco-Roman period of Jewish history, Jews of Palestine reburied their dead after the corpse had been reduced to mere bones. The first burial in the family sepulchre was only temporary. After a lapse of a year or more, the niche in the cave or burial chamber hewn in a rocky mountain was opened and the bones were gathered and reburied in the same burial chamber or transferred to another burial place. The Talmud calls this second burial *likut atsomos* (gathering of bones).

The work of gathering the bones was done by a grave-digger whose vocation was the building of graves, by a brotherhood organized especially for this purpose, or by the relatives. Children were forbidden to gather the bones of their parents. The gathered bones were wrapped like a mummy with bands of linen, or placed in baskets or sacks after sprinkling them with wine or oil. The bones of men were gathered by men, the bones of women by women. The bones of two persons were not to be intermingled.

At the second burial, the bones, placed in a special receptacle, were reburied in a cave or a field, a family possession. The rites and customs of mourning were partially repeated, but only until sunset.

The receptacles in which the bones were permanently buried were chests made of cedar, clay or soft stone. These little coffins were first unearthed, mostly in the vicinity of Jerusalem, in the seventies of the nineteenth century. More recently, hundreds of them were found around Jerusalem.

All were boxes of white limestone, with covers decorated with rosettes, colonnades, palm branches, and geometric drawings, and often bearing the name of the dead person in Hebrew or Greek. When these queer chests were first discovered, archaeologists were not able to explain their original nature and purpose. Finally, scholars were convinced that these boxes did not contain hidden valuables, but were ossuaries, receptacles for the bones of the dead.

The second burial was not a universal custom among Jews, but was confined to Palestine in the Greco-Roman period. Even within the bounds of Palestine it was not practiced by all the Jews. The custom was practiced among the Greeks and the Romans. Some scholars see the influence of the Greco-Roman civilization in this practice of the Palestinian Jews; others ascribe it to the fact that the population of Palestine had increased enormously in the last two centuries of the Second Temple and there was not enough room in the family graves for all the dead. The two factors do not exclude one another; both had some influence in the development of this practice among the Palestinian Jews.[257]

The Burial Brotherhood . . . The burial brotherhood of this period was the predecessor of the *Chevro Kadisho* (Holy Brotherhood) of our days. Originally, relatives and friends of the deceased took care of the corpse and the funeral. This proved embarrassing for the survivors, and in the Roman period, influenced apparently by the Roman burial societies, brotherhoods for burying the dead were founded in the larger Jewish communities. The burial brotherhood announced the news of the death, washed, anointed, and dressed the corpse; appointed pall-bearers, engaged musicians, chanting women and funeral orators, and in general, took care of the proper order of the funeral. There was a *m'mune*, a supervisor of funerals, who was the head of the brotherhood.

The burial brotherhood took up a collection of money when death occurred in a poor family which could not defray the burial expenses. Sometimes the money collected exceeded the sum needed for the burial and the Tannaim expressed various opinions regarding the use to be made of this surplus. One felt the remainder belonged to the heirs of the deceased; another, that it should be used for a monument on the grave; a third, that the money remain unused for an indefinite time ("until Elijah will come"). In order to forestall the exigency in case of death in a destitute family, a special communal fund was established for helping the poor to bury their dead.[258]

Graves and Monuments in Palestine . . . In Palestine, Jews of this period had no cemetery, i.e., no common graveyard for the community, as in Biblical times. The dead were still interred in family sepulchres. Some few common graveyards existed as an exception to the rule—the graveyard for those executed by the court, the field for the burial of strangers, and the field of graves for those who died in battle who were to be buried in the field where they fell.

The dead were interred in sepulchres which were the property of the respective family, barring burial of all strangers. According to the Talmudic law, if one sold his family sepulchre, his kinsfolk might bury him in it, for it was a discredit to the family to bury a member outside.

The graves had to be located at least fifty ells from the town and not on its western side, in order to forestall the polluting of the air by the western winds blowing from the Mediterranean, which predominate in Palestine, especially in the summer.[259]

The sepulchre, regarded as the house of the dead, resembled its counterpart, the house of the living. The burial ground was, and still is, called "house." The Bible terms it "house," "eternal house," "the house appointed for all living." In the Talmud and Midrash it is also called "eternal house" but mostly "house of graves." "Eternal House" (Beis Olam), the "House of Life" (Beis Chayim) are the terms by which Jews still designate a cemetery.[260]

The sepulchre was influenced in many ways by the progress of civilization. In ancient pre-Greek times, Jewish graves were very simple, devoid of any ornamentation. In the Greco-Roman period, more stress was laid on the adornment of graves. The sepulchres of that period discovered near Jerusalem show the influence of Greek and Egyptian art, although even at this period, Jews were far less extravagant than other nations. Jews built burial chambers of white marble or laid with marble plates, and the area on and around the burial ground was planted with trees and roses.

In the Greco-Roman period it became fashionable to put up monuments on graves. We hear of a magnificent structure erected by Simon the Maccabee at Modin on the grave of his parents and his brethren. According to the First Book of Maccabees and Josephus, this structure, built of white, polished stone, rose to a great height in order to make it visible from afar. The structure was surrounded by arcades and provided with great monolithic pillars which could be seen from the Mediterranean Sea. In addition, Simon erected seven large and beautiful pyramids to commemorate his parents and brethren. This monument was still in existence in the fourth century (c.e.). Josephus also mentions the monument on the grave of John Hyrcanus, Simon's son, that on the grave of Alexander Janneus, Simon's grandson, and the three pyramids on the grave of Queen Helena of Adiabene and her sons. He also tells us that King Herod built a monument of white stone on the ancient grave of King David. There were various kinds of sepulchral monuments consisting of massive blocks of stone or monoliths. Some were built in the shape of houses resting on pillars and were provided with a compartment for the living, for the survivors, when they visited the grave, or as a regular dwelling for a watchman of the grave. Only two of these grave monuments have been preserved.

These monuments were entirely different from the tombstones of our day and should not be confused with them. Some of them may have had the name of the dead on them, but their inscriptions did not describe the qualities of the deceased, give his or her age and the date of death. Nor did they bear the name *matsevo* by which the tombstones have been called since the Middle Ages. A monument on a grave in Talmudic times was called *nefesh*, the Hebrew word for soul (plural *n'foshos*).

These expensive monuments were confined to the wealthy families. In the period following the second destruction of Jerusalem, spending great sums for the adornment of graves was not a popular practice. The rabbis of that period expressed their opposition to the erection of monuments in the Talmudic saying, "No monuments should be erected for the righteous, because their words are their memorial." Displeasure against the adornment of graves and erection of magnificent monuments may also be found in the statement of the Talmud that Amon and Moab, hostile neighbors of the Jews, told Nebuchadnezzar that Jewish graves were more splendid than his palace. The rabbis of the Talmud projected the conditions of their own days into the distant past.

The authorities marked spots in fields which might possibly contain the bones of dead. Signs were placed at both ends of these areas warning people not to tread on them and thereby incur impurity. These signs were whitewashed every year on the fifteenth of Ador, when the rainy season was over, in order that the pilgrims going to Jerusalem should avoid these spots.[261]

Graves were frequently visited, a practice still customary in the Orient, especially on fast days. The rabbis of the Talmud differed as to the purpose of this custom. One believed it signified "We are before Thee as dead." According to another opinion, visiting graves was permitted in order "that the departed ones should pray for mercy on our behalf." In post-Talmudic times many people gathered at the graves of scholars on the anniversary of their death. When a grave was visited, phylacteries could not be worn, a Scroll of the Torah could not be carried and the ritual threads (tsitsis) not worn close to the earth. For to do these things was a mockery of the dead and a transgression of the saying of Proverbs: "Whosoever mocketh the poor blasphemeth his Maker" (17:5).

A special benediction was recited when graves were visited.

Graves were visited only in broad daylight. To stay overnight in a burial ground, the haunt of the ghosts of the dead, was believed to be extremely dangerous. If a man was courageous enough to brave the danger and stay among graves overnight, people believed he might overhear conversation between the spirits of the dead and so procure advance information on fateful decisions made in heaven.[262]

Graves and Monuments in the Diaspora . . . From Palestine we turn to Babylonia which had become the seat of Jewish life and Jewish learning, by the side of the Land of Israel. Because of the nature of the terrain, which is free from caves and mountains, the Jews of Babylonia, unlike their Palestinian brethren, did not bury their dead in subterranean chambers, but in graves dug in the surface of the ground, with mounds of earth on top of them. These graves, level with a field, were not suited for family sepulchres. The burial grounds of the Babylonian Jews became the common graveyard of the community, the cemetery, in the present sense of the word.[263]

From the East we turn west to Rome, where the settlement of the Jews dated back to the Maccabean age. The Jews of Rome retained their native custom of burying the dead in subterranean chambers. Many of these Jewish burial grottos in Rome were discovered and investigated in recent times. They were called by the Greek name—catacombs. The ancient Christian catacombs of Rome were discovered first. Later, older Jewish catacombs were discovered, proving that the ancient Christians had copied from the Jews the custom of interring the dead in subterranean graves.

The Jews who had emigrated to Rome retained this native Palestinian custom, although in other respects they did adapt themselves to their heathen environment. Many Jewish catacombs have decorations, picturing scenes from Greco-Roman mythology. Some of the catacombs were without any pictures, some were decorated with Jewish motifs, as: a seven-branched candlestick, a Torah shrine, a shofor, an esrog, a lulov. There were also pictures, half Jewish, half heathen, as: a seven-branched candlestick in the hands of winged genii. Among the non-Jewish pictures found in the Jewish catacombs was a picture of Fortuna, goddess of fortune and fate.

In the catacombs, the dead were mostly buried uncoffined, but were equipped with jewelry and many useful objects. Bracelets inlaid with precious stones, amulets, lamps, gilded glasses, copper coins, and many other objects have been found. Giving a coin to the dead was a Greek custom, for the Greeks placed a coin under the tongue of the dead to pay Charon, the ferryman of Greek mythology, who ferried the deceased over the waters of death into the nether world.

In spite of the influence of the Roman environment, the Jews of Rome remained loyal to their people and their faith. This loyalty was proved by the sacred symbols of the synagogue which they depicted on their graves.[264]

XX

In the Middle Ages

While Jewish marriage was entirely transformed during the Middle Ages, the customs relating to death did not yield so much to the changes of time. These rites and usages, precepts and inhibitions in connection with death, fixed and regulated by the rabbis of the Talmud, have for the most part persisted until recent days. They are still being practiced among Orthodox Jews in America. In the long stretch of time separating the Talmudic era from the late Middle Ages, only a few of these practices were modified, or even discarded. The procedure of burial and mourning remained essentially the same. Whatever changes took place were due more to the change of environment than to the factor of time. During the Middle Ages the main scene of Jewish life shifted from the East to the West. Some of the practices which had been appropriate to the Oriental scene were out of place among the Franco-German Jews. The general tendency was to discard the sumptuous, extravagant and ostentatious practices of the Orient.

In the following pages we shall outline the most conspicuous changes made during the Middle Ages.

On the Deathbed . . . The *tsavo-o* (command), the last will left by the deceased, which in olden times was a verbal charge, became a literary product, occasionally an elaborate treatise on ritual and morals. The vidui (confession of sins before death) gained great importance in late and post-Talmudic times. When a Jew was about to die, he was advised by the friends who visited him to make a full confession of his sins. Lest he become alarmed at the apparent imminence of death, they casually told him that many people who recited the confession recovered from their illness, while others passed away without repenting.[265]

Preparations for the Funeral . . . In the Middle Ages, the ancient custom of giving the deceased a farewell kiss and anointing the corpse was discarded. Occasionally, at the beginning of the fifteenth century, red *tachrichim* (shrouds) were used, but in the sixteenth century, white linen became the exclusive material for the shrouds.

A great change took place regarding the coffin. In Talmudic times it had been regarded as a dishonor to be buried without a coffin; but in the Middle Ages there was no general rule as to whether one was buried with or without a coffin. The custom varied in the various lands and communities. In Spain, the coffin was not in vogue. Among the French Jews the coffin was made from the table which had witnessed the hospitality and generosity of the deceased. In the sixteenth century, under the influence of the Cabalists, the notion became prevalent both inside and outside of the Holy Land that it was more meritorious for the dead to be in direct contact with the earth. The words of the Bible, "for dust thou art and unto dust shalt thou return," were then literally fulfilled. Among the Christians in the Middle Ages, the dead were generally interred uncoffined.

Interment without a coffin became the rule strictly adhered to by Orthodox Jews in Eastern Europe to the present day. In America and in Western Europe, Orthodox Jews were forced by the municipal administration to reintroduce the coffin.[266]

The Funeral . . . Displaying objects on the coffin symbolizing the life of the deceased and the burning of incense had fallen into disuse. The flutes and the professional mourners had been discarded in the lands of the West, although in the East mention is made of the chanting women as late as on the threshold of modern times. A peculiar custom prevailed in the

Jewish community of Saragossa, Spain. The mourners attended the services in the synagogue even on the first seven days of mourning and returned home accompanied by the whole congregation. On the way, a wailing woman chanted a dirge, accompanying herself on a tambourine. The other women responded to the chant vocally and with the clapping of hands. (This custom is recorded in the fourteenth century.) [267]

The Mourners' Meal . . . The meal of the mourners had become an ordinary meal brought to the house by strangers, and was no longer a public feast with ten cups of wine and the solemn recital of special benedictions. Eggs replaced lentils as the main dish.

Signs of Mourning . . . The old customs of inverting sofas and covering the head, provoking ridicule from their non-Jewish neighbors, were discarded by the European Jews. In France and Italy, covering the head was discarded in the twelfth and thirteenth centuries. In the Rhineland, at the time of Maharil, in order to keep his head covered, the mourner wore his cowled cape during the first seven days of mourning. After the first seven days of strict mourning, the mourner went about with the cowl over his head for twelve months if he mourned a parent, and for thirty days for other kindred. In the Rhineland this old Oriental custom was thus retained by substituting the hood for the turban. In the Orient, as late as the sixteenth century, a mourner kept his head covered with a talis or a turban reaching to his mouth during the seven days of mourning. Only when visitors came to the house of mourning to bring him comfort did he uncover his head.

In the Middle Ages, no mention is made of baring the shoulder, a custom obligatory even in Talmudic times only at the death of a parent. In the East, the gruesome practice of cutting the flesh as a sign of mourning was not entirely extinct, even as late as the seventeenth century.

In some communities the mourners were provided with food during the entire week of mourning from the chest of the community or of the Chevro Kadisho (burial fraternity). The rich shared alike with the poor in order not to shame the poor who were forced to become public charges during this week. Afterward the rich returned more than had been given them originally.[268]

In the Synagogue . . . In Talmudic times, the rites of mourning, as well as the circumcision ceremonial and the wedding celebration, were all exclusively home affairs. The mourner did not leave the house to go to the synagogue even on the Sabbath of the first week of mourning, nor was any prayer or doxology recited or chanted in memory of the dead during that time. In post-Talmudic times, mourning was linked with the synagogue and the old custom underwent a change. The congregation no longer went to the mourner, for he attended the synagogue on the Sabbath, where he stood in an anteroom behind the door, or in an isolated nook. After the chazan had finished *Musof* (the additional prayer on Sabbaths and festive days), he went to the place in the synagogue where the mourners stood and pronounced a benediction, and recited Kaddish. This usage was not uniform. In communities in Babylonia and Spain the mourner went daily to the synagogue during the first week of mourning, while in other regions he visited the synagogue only on the Sabbath. In the Rhineland on the Sabbath of the first week of mourning, the whole congregation accompanied the mourner from the synagogue to his house. Maharil praised this custom as a consolation for the mourner.[269]

The rites of mourning became more closely connected with the prevailing custom whereby an orphan recited Kaddish in memory of his dead parent. In general, prayers for the dead became a part of the services in the synagogues. These rites and customs, which developed prominently in recent times, will be dealt with at length in a subsequent chapter.

Graves and Tombstones . . . Every Jewish community, no matter how small, had its place of worship, the synagogue, but only the larger communities owned their fields of graves, and there, the Jews of the small communities brought their dead for interment. Transporting a corpse from one town to another was not always an easy matter. A special permit had to be obtained from the police, and in some places, a high toll was collected from the cortège for the privilege of entering the environs; also for passing through the town.

It was apparently under Roman influence that in the early Middle Ages the custom arose to erect a tombstone with an inscription, commemorating the name and status of the deceased. This commemorative stone has been termed "matsevo," the Biblical name for the sacred stone. For a long time, the use of the matsevo was not a universal custom, and in the twelfth century, numerous graves were found without it. In the fourteenth century, however, the matsevo had become a necessary supplement of the burial, although even a generation ago, in Eastern Europe, a grave without a matsevo was not unusual. Only recently has the matsevo been accepted universally as an integral part of the grave.

Two different ways of erecting a matsevo evolved in the Middle Ages. The German Jews placed the stone in an upright position, while the Jews in southern France and Spain laid it flat upon the grave. This difference in the position of the matsevo still prevails among the Ashk'nazim and the S'fardim.

The Hebrew epitaphs of the early Middle Ages were brief and simple. Later, they became more detailed and high-sounding. On some of the tombstones in Germany, in the late Middle Ages, emblems representing the vocation of the dead were added to the inscriptions—a pair of shears for a tailor, a violin or harp for a musician, etc.

The resting place for the dead was as crowded as the space for the living in the ghettos. Small wonder, therefore, that two, and even more graves were placed on top of one another, and often as many tombstones were found on the same grave.

The cemetery, called "eternal house" or "house of life," was usually surrounded by a protective wall which did not always afford adequate protection. The graves, as well as the houses of the ghetto, were not secure against desecration. Frequently Jews were driven from a town, their field of graves taken away and the tombstones used for building purposes. When after a time, they were readmitted, they had to reacquire their graveyard for an enormous price. When a fanatical and incited mob assaulted the Jewish quarters, the wives and children were hidden in the graveyard while the men tried to resist the attackers.[270]

Visiting Graveyards . . . The Jews of the Middle Ages like the Christians and Mohammedans often visited graveyards to pray at the graves of distinguished persons, notwithstanding the stern protest of the great rabbis who considered this a transgression of the Mosaic Law which forbade communication with the dead (Deut. 18:11). How frequently graves were visited can be best attested by the fact that Judah the Pious, the famous mystic of Regensburg (died 1217), prohibited the visiting of a grave twice in one day. There were occasions, as on Tisho B'Ov, when the entire congregation repaired to the cemetery, encircling it in a procession. This latter custom was still prevalent in Eastern Europe in our own day (see p. 270).

Whenever exigencies of sickness or danger arose, people resorted to the graves of the righteous and pious, invoking aid from the dead for the living. In Babylonia, as far back as the third century C.E., dust from the graves of famous rabbis was applied as a remedy for fever. In the Middle Ages these superstitious practices assumed vast proportions. Vows were offered, torches or tapers lighted, incense burnt, dances performed at the graves of pious people, and votive offerings were hung on the trees in cemeteries.

The belief in ghosts accompanied these superstitious practices. Scores of wild and horrible tales of encounters and conversations with dead souls were told and believed by the people. One story told of a ghost who was met on a road on a moonlit night. Another related how a man had fallen asleep in the synagogue at night and was locked in by the beadle. At midnight he awoke and saw the dead souls wrapped in prayershawls, with two men who were still alive standing among them. These two men died shortly. "The Book of the Pious" (Sefer Chasidim) is replete with stories of this kind. So deeply rooted was the belief in ghosts that Judah the Pious enjoined the people not to accept any gifts from a ghost who appeared in a dream. These gruesome beliefs and tales persisted to some extent in Eastern Europe and the Orient even in recent days.[271]

Chevro Kadisho . . . We have already met the burial brotherhood at the beginning of the Common Era, but we are not sure of the form of its organization in those times, whether there was only one fraternity for this purpose in town or the community was divided into several sections, with a burial brotherhood in each section. Of the fourteenth and fifteenth centuries we have historical records, telling of a single burial society which served the entire community. It was called *chavuro*, the Talmudic name for a society or brotherhood, and it had its regulations and ordinances, according to which the family of the deceased paid for the burial in proportion to its economic standing. Only poor families were served free of charge. Lots were cast among the members of the brotherhood to ascertain whose turn it was to dig the grave. If the lot fell to a poor member, the brotherhood paid him for his day's work. If a member of the brotherhood died, he was succeeded by his oldest son, if the latter had attained his majority (thirteen years). The brotherhood took care of everything pertaining to the burial as well as the mourners after the funeral, providing them with meals and with a minyon to recite prayers in the house of mourning during the first seven days.

In the sixteenth and seventeenth centuries the burial society was called Chevro Kadisho, Holy Society or Brotherhood.

This title, originally given also to other religious societies, became in the course of time the exclusive title of the burial society.

The Chevro Kadisho became the strongest society in the Jewish communities. Because the brotherhood owned the cemetery, exacting high prices for the graves from the survivors, it also became the richest society. With functions widely ramified, it looked after the orphans and took care of the sick poor. In the course of time the task of caring for the sick was vested in a *Bikur Cholim* (visiting the sick society), a brotherhood which branched off and became independent of the Chevro Kadisho.[272]

XXI

In Modern Times

In Eastern Europe . . . In the previous chapter, we have noted between the Talmudic era and the late Middle Ages a small number of changes in the customs relating to death. Still less was the change between the Middle Ages and recent days. The following description of the customs observed in Eastern Europe a generation ago applies as well to the late Middle Ages.

Resuscitating the Sick . . . Even in the face of approaching death, hope was not lost. After all natural therapeutic means were exhausted, recourse was had to supernatural powers. Various remedies and means drawn from higher spheres of religion as well as from the realm of magic and superstition were applied.

To begin with, prayers for the sick were recited by the congregation which gathered in the synagogue to recite psalms and special prayers composed for the occasion. Psalm 119 was believed to be particularly efficacious, if recited in a certain order. This psalm is an acrostic of twenty-two stanzas containing the twenty-two letters of the Hebrew alphabet in their order. The stanzas were arranged and recited so that their beginning letters constituted the full name of the sick person with his or her mother's name.

Charity in the form of bread or money was distributed to the poor, interpreting literally the sentence of Proverbs, "righteousness delivereth from death" (Prov. 11:4). In post-Biblical times, ts'doko, the Hebrew word for righteousness, was interpreted to mean alms-giving. All the garments worn by the sick person were distributed to the poor.

Some of the kindred, especially the women folk, ran to the synagogue with supplications, storming the Holy Ark containing the Scrolls of the Torah. With their heads placed inside the Holy Ark, the supplicants, weeping hysterically, invoked the mercy of God for the sick. From the Holy Ark in the synagogue, the women went to the graves in the cemetery where, with loud cries and moans of anguish, they urged the family dead to intercede in heaven for the one hovering between life and death. After pouring out their hearts at the graves, the women "measured the field," a custom described in a previous section (p. 54).

Adding a new name was a very popular means of averting the threat of death, a practice previously described (p. 75).

Chevro Kadisho . . . If the condition of the sick became critical, the *Chevro Kadisho* were called.

The Chevro Kadisho was the largest and most important of all the brotherhoods in the community, with a membership composed of two groups, consisting of a small number of full members and a considerable number of "assistants" (shamoshim), who performed the menial tasks. The full members were elderly, dignified men, whereas every married man was qualified to be a shamosh. The head of the shamoshim was a *shamosh rishon* (chief assistant), who gave the orders and supervised their work. After many years of service, an assistant might be promoted to the rank of shamosh rishon and a shamosh rishon, in his advanced age, might be promoted to the rank of a full member. Only a man highly distinguished for his learning and piety could be promoted to the rank of a full member while he was still young. The entire brotherhood was under the direction of three *gabo-im* who were counted among the most eminent men of the community.

There were also female members and assistants in the Chevro Kadisho who attended to the burial of women. The men dug the grave, and the women made the tachrichim.

One day of the year was a Chevro Kadisho day. In some

communities it was the fifteenth day of the month of Kislev; in others, the seventh day of Ador, the traditional anniversary of the death of Moses; and in some it was on Lag Bo-omer. This day was observed with fasting and penitential prayers by all who belonged to the brotherhoods, shamoshim as well as members. They visited the field of graves to ask forgiveness from the dead for any dishonor that might have been done them at their death. At dusk, between the Mincho and Ma-ariv services, the rabbi or some learned layman delivered a discourse of moral exhortations at the synagogue. In the evening, after the Ma-ariv services, a feast was held at which new "shamoshim" were admitted to the brotherhood or some of the shamoshim were promoted to the rank of shamosh rishon or of a member.

The Chevro Kadisho was the collective owner of the field of graves and all the implements of burial.

The Ma-avar Yabok . . . Usually a member of the Chevro Kadisho visited the sick man as soon as his condition was critical, carrying the Ma-avar Yabok (a book written by the Cabalist Aaron Berechiah of Modena, in Italy, at the beginning of the seventeenth century). The name, *The Ford of Yabok*, was derived from the story in Genesis which tells how Jacob took his wives and children and passed over the Ford of Yabok. The author indicated that death was a passage from a lower to a higher, a heavenly stage of existence. The book contains, in addition to numerous passages from the Bible and confessions to be recited on the deathbed, a description of all rites and usages, also meditations and prayers connected with burial. It was reprinted in numerous editions during the last three centuries, and is still the manual among Orthodox Jews in all matters pertaining to death and burial.

In Anticipation of Death . . . Jews never believed in the remission of sins through an intermediary. Their sins were expiated on Yom Kippur and at their death, if they sincerely repented. They needed no intermediary. A member of the Chevro Kadisho recited the confession from the Ma-avar Yabok, while the dying person repeated the words after him. The last words which came from the lips of the dying were the declaration of the Jewish faith in Hebrew, "Hear, O Israel, the Lord our God, the Lord is One." If the dying person was in a coma, the member of the brotherhood recited the confession for him. (In the case of a dying woman, a woman member of the Chevro Kadisho recited the confession.)

Chairs were placed around the deathbed in order to prevent a limb from protruding over the edge of the bed, basing the custom on the story of Genesis in which Jacob "gathered up his feet into bed and expired." If a limb emerged, it could not be moved, because Talmudic law forbade the touching of a dying person lest it accelerate death. No matter how protracted and tormenting the death, nor what the circumstances, nothing could be done to hasten it.

Custom forbade that a dying person be left alone. It was considered advantageous for the dying to have a ritual quorum of ten present at the moment of death. If death was protracted, one of the Chevro Kadisho remained constantly in the room.

To be present at the moment of *y'tsias n'shomo* (departure of the soul) was regarded a religious act. When death was imminent, numerous people gathered in the house, reciting the psalms and other passages from the Bible prescribed for the occasion in the Ma-avar Yabok.

Candles were lit near the dying. The religious authorities offered various explanations for this custom. Light caused the demons to flee. A more recent explanation expressed the thought that the light of the candles was illumination in honor of the *Sh'chino*, the Divine Presence, that comes to meet the departing soul. According to a third explanation, light was a symbol of the flickering human soul.

When Death Came . . . To establish death, a feather was placed against the nostrils to see if the breath of life still remained. After death was confirmed, the oldest son closed the eyes of the dead. The windows were opened immediately and all the water in the house poured out. The same process of pouring out the water was carried out in the three adjoining houses on each side of the house of death. Religious authorities offered two explanations for this; the first, that the pouring of water was an announcement of the death, and the second, that the Angel of Death cleansed his dripping knife in water, and that therefore all water must be poured out in order to prevent the spread of death.

All present at the moment of death made a rent in their coats, the mourners on the outer side, and strangers in the lining. They expressed their resignation to the will of God by exclaiming, "Blessed be the true Judge!"

The dead body, covered with a black cloth, was then laid on the floor in the garments in which he or she had died, feet towards the door. A living person, as a matter of custom, never lay with his feet toward the door.

Behind the head of the corpse one large candle burned. Under no circumstances was the corpse ever left alone. This task of staying with the corpse, especially overnight, was fulfilled by the shamoshim of the Chevro Kadisho, who took turns. For people imbued from their earliest childhood with horrible stories of demons and ghosts, staying alone at night with a corpse was rather a ghastly task, and well-to-do shamoshim did it often through a hired proxy. Certain poor shamoshim in the brotherhood were satisfied to do this for a remuneration.

Preparing for the Burial . . . Burial took place as soon after death as possible. If death occurred on Friday or on the day preceding a holiday, burial took place the same day. Otherwise it would have had to be delayed until after the Sabbath or the festival.

However poor the survivors, they had to make payment for the grave even if it was only a token payment. The Chevro

Kadisho exacted larger prices for graves from well-to-do families, particularly if the deceased had not contributed sufficiently to charity during his lifetime.

The corpse was prepared for the burial by a process of purification called *taharo* prescribed in detail by custom, and done by the shamoshim of the Chevro Kadisho. The members of the brotherhood performed this task only in the rare cases when the deceased was highly distinguished for his learning and piety.

The tachrichim were made exclusively of stainless white linen. No knots were permitted anywhere on the garment. Contrary to the tendency of Talmudic times to reduce the shroud to a single garment, every corpse was now clothed in no less than three garments, usually in breeches, shirt, cap, sargonas (shroud) and a girdle. The talis with one of the fringes torn from a corner was placed over these garments. In the case of a woman, an apron took the place of breeches and the talis was not used. The garments for the grave were supposed to correspond with the garments worn by the High Priests in ancient times. Sometimes it was not necessary for the women of the Chevro Kadisho to prepare the tachrichim, for they had been prepared many years before death. Aged people, particularly women who were scrupulously pious, spent a great part of their time reciting prayers and psalms, confessing their sins and preparing the shrouds in which they would be buried. They prepared tachrichim of genuine white linen for themselves, aired and washed them from time to time, and held them in constant readiness. Many men wore a white kittel during the synagogue services on the Days of Awe and at the seder on Pesach night. This kittel was used as the sargonas of the tachrichim, for to clothe the deceased in the kittel which he had worn when reciting prayers was regarded as most advantageous.

Funeral . . . Usually the funeral took place after the morning services on the morning after the day of death. A shamosh of the Chevro Kadisho went from house to house, knocking on windows and calling, "Go to the funeral." Soon, almost the entire community was gathered in front of the house.

In the house numerous candles burnt. The recitations of psalms and prayers which accompanied the "purification" of the corpse partially drowned out the sobs of the survivors. The bier, or in some communities a large black casket, was placed outside of the house, close to the entrance. The corpse was carried from the house in a sheet and placed on the bier. Just before that was done all the kinsfolk begged the forgiveness of the deceased for any possible offenses they might have committed against him. The corpse was carried out with his feet toward the door, and no person was allowed to precede the corpse through the door, the pall-bearers walking at the side of it.

Although the cemetery was usually a long distance from the town, no vehicle was used. The bier was carried the entire distance on the shoulders of the shamoshim of the Chevro Kadisho. Many lent a hand and shoulder to these actual pall-bearers because of the religious merit earned thereby.

The utmost quiet and simplicity characterized the funeral procedure. The bier was carried in front of the procession, followed by the men who attended the funeral. The women brought up the rear. The mourners walked among the crowd. In some cases, the children of the Talmud Torah (elementary free school for poor children) marched in front of the bier, chanting the verse from Psalms, "Righteousness shall go before Him, and shall make His footsteps a way" (85:14). Shamoshim of the Chevro Kadisho mingled with the throng in the procession, carrying small tin boxes in their hands, clanking the coins deposited in them, and calling out intermittently, "Ts'doko tatsil mimoves!" (Charity delivereth from death. See above, p. 258.) Almost everyone dropped a coin in the charity box, the proceeds of which went to the *Chevro Bikur Cholim.*

A funeral discourse eulogizing the deceased was delivered only at the death of a distinguished person, at the cemetery or at the entrance of the synagogue. Only in exceptional cases, at the death of a famous rabbi, was the bier brought inside the synagogue or beis ha-midrosh and placed in front of the Holy Ark while the eulogy was delivered. Funeral discourses were uniform, always citing the same verses of the Bible and the same passages of the Talmud. The text of the discourse embellished by the preacher was usually Isaiah 57:1. "The righteous perisheth, and no man layeth it to heart, and godly men are taken away, none considering that the righteous is taken away from the evil to come." The preacher inferred that disasters and evil decrees were impending because of the death of the righteous man resting on the bier and he reminded the people that "Repentance, prayer and charity avert the evil decree."

The funeral procession always chose the longest way, and proceeded slowly. At a distance of thirty ells from the open grave, the pall-bearers halted at every four ells, in order to make seven stops, at each of which Psalm 91 was recited. This psalm refers to the refuge and protection granted by God against "the terror by night, the pestilence that walketh in darkness and the destruction that wasteth at noonday," and was appropriate to the mood of the funeral rites. In the Hebrew original, the eleventh verse (For He will give His angels charge over thee, to keep thee in all thy ways) consists of seven words. At the first stop, the psalm was recited as far as to include the first word of this verse, at the second stop until the second word was included and so forth. At the seventh stop the psalm was recited to the end. Some regions retained the old custom of making seven encirclings around the bier.

Because the corpse was interred uncoffined, a built-in box had been made to fit inside the grave by placing boards along both sides of it. After the body was lowered into the grave another board was placed over the corpse.

In some rare instances a rabbi left a will instructing that he should be laid in a box made from the lectern on which he had spent his days and nights learning Torah in the beis ha-midrosh. Occasionally a man expressed the wish that the receipts for the money he had paid to charity funds be laid in his grave.

Burial . . . The most ardent desire of every Jew was burial in the Land of Israel, although few were fortunate enough to realize this ambition. One had to be satisfied to be buried among Jews, in accordance with Jewish custom, with a bag filled with earth from the Holy Land placed in one's grave. Once in a great while a pious stranger from Jerusalem visited the town. He told quaint and wonderful tales of sacred graves and holy sites, and sold bags of white sand from the Holy Land. Aged men and women seized this opportunity to provide themselves with earth from Erets Yisroel. The Chevro Kadisho, too, provided itself with a stock of this burial accessory.

The corpse was placed in the grave in the manner prescribed by custom. The act of placing the corpse in the grave was considered of such great religious merit that a certain elderly member of the Chevro Kadisho had the option on this service. On the death of this member his chosen deputy succeeded him. At the burial of a woman, an elderly female member had the option of this privilege.

It was not permitted to close the hands of the dead. The fingers were bent a little to hold tiny sticks called "little forks," which were popularly believed to be the sticks on which the dead would lean on the day of resurrection, when they must roll themselves under the ground until they reached the Land of Israel. Potsherds were placed on the eyes and the mouth. Some earth, preferably from the Holy Land, was sprinkled over the body of the corpse and a bag of it placed under the head. When the member of the burial brotherhood completed these rites in the customary order, he announced that death had now withdrawn the deceased from all brotherhoods of which he was a member. All who stood around the grave took leave of the deceased with the Hebrew words prescribed in the Talmud, "Lech l'sholom" (go in peace). Some added the last verse of the Book of Daniel "but go thou thy way till the end be; and thou shalt rest and shalt stand up to thy lot, at the end of the days."

The first shovels of earth were placed in the grave with the convex side of the shovel by those who wished to attain the religious merit which accrued to those who performed this task. The shamoshim of the Chevro Kadisho hurriedly filled in the grave, taking great care that no one take the shovel from the hand of another. Each shamosh placed the shovel on the ground from which another picked it up.

Before closing the grave, the mourners made a three-inch rent in their coats and said, "Blessed be the true Judge." They also took off their shoes. Then, at some distance from the grave, the prayer *tsiduk ha-din* (the justice of the judgment) was recited, expressing the belief that God's ways are right-eous, and the son (or, in the absence of a son, the daughter of the deceased, or some other close relative) recited the special funeral version of the Kaddish. All who were present then arranged themselves to form two rows. The mourners passed between them, receiving the comforting words, "The Lord shall console you among the other mourners of Zion and Jerusalem."

After the funeral, certain customs were observed before the return home. On leaving the cemetery, each one plucked some grass with the earth attached, throwing it behind him and re-citing the words from Psalms, "And may they blossom out of the city like grass of the earth," and "He remembereth that we are dust" (72:16; 103:14). After leaving the cemetery every-one washed his hands and recited the verse from Isaiah:

> He will swallow up death forever;
> And the Lord God will wipe away tears from
>   off all faces;
> And the reproach of His people will He take
>   away from off all the earth;
> For the Lord hath spoken it.—25:8.

Returning from a funeral, one did not enter a house before washing his hands. The water had to be drawn into a vessel. The vessel was not handed by one person to another, but each one placed it on the ground, from which the next picked it up. The custom forbade wiping the hands with a cloth or rag, unless the latter could then be discarded. Hands were usually dried in the air. After washing the hands, each man sat down three or seven times, each time reciting Psalm 91 (including the last verse of the foregoing psalm).

Suicides and Apostates . . . In all Jewish communities suicides were commonly buried near the fence in a secluded part of the cemetery. Whenever possible, however, an act of suicide was interpreted as resulting from permanent or temporary aberration, and the victim was given a decent burial. If an apostate was killed by accident, Kaddish might be recited for him, because his unnatural death atoned for his sins.

The Meal of the Mourners . . . After the funeral, only the first meal was brought in by strangers, usually by the neighbors. The main food of the meal consisted of hard boiled eggs and *beigel* (hard rolls shaped like doughnuts). The custom of providing the mourners with food from a communal fund during the week of mourning was no longer practiced.

In the House of Mourning . . . For seven days a candle burned in the room where death had occurred. A glass of water and a towel were placed beside the light, in spite of the fact that religious authorities denounced the latter custom as heathenish. The popular explanation offered for this practice was that the Angel of Death might wash his sword in the water and wipe it with the towel.

All mirrors were covered or turned to the wall.

All day the mourners sat on low benches or boxes. They were allowed to read only if the books they read were religious books with sad content. The book most often read in the house of mourning was Job, or the ethical book M'noras Hamo'or in its Yiddish version.

Almost all the people of the community visited the house of mourning to offer comfort to the mourners. Bringing food to the house of mourning was practiced only in some regions. In America people usually bring cakes, boxes of candy and baskets of fruits to the house of mourning. On entering, no greetings were spoken. On leaving, the established formula of consolation to the mourners was voiced, "The Lord shall console you among all the mourners of Zion and Jerusalem."

Custom forbade taking anything from the house of mourning.

During the seven days of mourning, services were held in the house of the deceased. On these days Psalm 49 and a prayer for the dead were recited after the services. This psalm is appropriate for a house of mourning. It speaks of death as the leveler of all distinctions between the rich and the poor, and of God who redeems the soul from the power of the nether world. On the following Sabbath, the mourner visited the synagogue. At the Friday night services, the mourner stood in the anteroom of the synagogue until the end of *L'cho Dodi* (Come, my friend, to meet the bride). Then the sexton tapped the bimo with his hand calling loudly, "Go to meet the mourner!" The whole congregation arose and walked toward the door to meet the mourner, who entered the synagogue at this moment. In most American synagogues mourners are in the synagogue for Mincho and the first part of Kabolas Shabos, but step out just before L'cho Dodi, to reenter at the end of L'cho Dodi.

Even on the Sabbath a mourner changed his place in the synagogue during the twelve months of mourning for the death of a parent, and during thirty days of mourning for the death of other relatives.

Visiting the Graves . . . As in the Middle Ages, the practice of visiting the graves and praying to the dead during crises was observed. Especially were the graves of Chasidic rabbis and miracle men visited by people in distress, who left slips of paper on which their wishes were written. Visiting the graves of parents on the anniversary of their death was a prevailing custom.

There were also certain days and seasons of the year when almost the whole community visited the field of graves. On Tisho B'Ov, after the morning services, the entire congregation encircled the cemetery. During the month of Elul everyone visited the graves of his ancestors and kindred. On those days, the women came more frequently than the men to weep at the graves of those who had been near and dear to them.

The unveiling of the tombstone also provided an occasion for a visit to a grave. This took place twelve months after death, preferably on the first anniversary of the death. Sometimes tombstones were not unveiled for a number of years after death; and there were even some graves without any matsevo (see p. 254). In America, however, the unveiling ceremony has gained in importance and has become an occasion when all relatives and friends of the deceased come together.

The Ma-ane Loshon . . . Visiting the graves and praying to the dead became so important in recent times that a special handbook was written for this purpose, entitled *Ma-ane Loshon* (the Answer of the Tongue, cited from the sentence in Proverbs 16:1: "The preparations of the heart are man's but the answer of the tongue is from the Lord").

The Ma-ane Loshon was, like the Ma-avar Yabok, a product of the same period in Jewish history (the beginning of the seventeenth century), and in the last three hundred years was printed in even more numerous editions than the latter, with a German, a Yiddish, and, in this country, an English translation.

The Ma-ane Loshon was a kind of sequel to the Ma-avar Yabok. The latter, a manual of the ritual of death and burial, contained at its close only a few prayers to be recited on visiting the cemetery. The former was exclusively for this purpose, containing specific prayers to be recited at the grave of each relative.

Women recited the prayers of the Ma-ane Loshon at the cemetery with loud moans and hysterical wailing that could be heard far and wide.

Tales about the Dead . . . Gruesome tales about the apparitions of the dead were wide-spread. People believed the dead occasionally appeared to the living. If a bride and groom were orphans, they visited the graves of their dead parents and invited them to the wedding. There was a popular belief that the dead appeared to the living in dreams, giving them advice, and warning them of impending dangers. Thus they believed that a dead father or mother might appear to his or her children in a dream and choke the child because of some misconduct. Anyone was thus liable to be choked in his sleep for dishonoring or disparaging the deceased.

The medieval belief that ghosts of the dead assembled at night in the synagogue and held services there still prevailed. The popular belief was that anyone who passed the synagogue late at night was liable to hear his name called summoning him to the reading of the Torah, and was sure to die soon. In some communities it was customary for the sexton, who came to the synagogue before dawn, to knock on the door three times before he entered, signaling the ghosts to disappear. Young and old shunned the vicinity of the synagogue late at night.

Among the Oriental Jews . . . In Jerusalem, the S'fardim bury their dead without delay, allowing only enough time between the occurrence of death and the funeral for the purification of the corpse. They even hold the funeral at night, adhering to the ancient law that a corpse cannot remain overnight within the limits of the Holy City (see p. 231).

In the short interval, before the members of the burial

brotherhood come into the house to prepare the corpse for the burial, the women of the family, seated in a circle, bewail and eulogize the deceased in the Oriental manner. With shrill voices, they lament loudly, beating their heads, foreheads and breasts with their fists. After the corpse is carried from the house, the women, standing by the windows, continue their loud lamentations, but they do not attend the funeral.

As the corpse is carried from the house, a member of the burial brotherhood breaks an earthen vessel on the threshold and announces that the wife and children of the deceased are forbidden to follow the bier or leave the house until the members of the brotherhood have returned from the cemetery.

The bier, shaped like a ladder, is carried on the shoulders. A distinguished man's bier is carried lower, near the earth. Two beadles of the community march on either side of the bier, each carrying a large black wax candle. After leaving the gate of the city, the whole throng chants Psalm 91 (see p. 265).

At the cemetery seven encirclings are made around the bier. The participants clasp each other's hands, forming a closed circle. During each encircling, one of the encirclers recite Psalm 91 in addition to prayers for the deceased. Seven silver coins are placed on the corpse. After each encircling is completed, one man in the circle takes one coin, throwing it far away, as he recites the sentence from Genesis 25:6.

The grave in which the uncoffined corpse is laid is plastered inside with thin, smooth stones. No sargonas is used, and the talis is removed when the corpse is placed in the grave.

The relatives and friends bring food for the first meal. After the meal, the benedictions of mourning of the Talmud quoted in a previous chapter are recited, and the Kaddish follows (see p. 241).

In the S'fardic synagogue a special place is reserved for mourners who attend services on the Sabbath.

The Moroccan Jews still scratch and cut their faces as a sign of mourning, notwithstanding their rabbis' denunciation of this flagrant transgression of the Mosaic Law.[273]

ברביעי בשבת ארבעה ועשרים יום לירח אב שנת חמשת אלפים

ושש מאות ושבעים ושנים לבריאת עולם למנין שאנו מונין כאן

בוראד מתא דיתבא על נהר מארדש ועל מי מעינות אנא

פ׳ יוסב ן יעקב העומד היום בוראד מתא דיתבא על נהר מארדש

ועל מי מעינות צביתי ברצות נפשי בדלא אניסנא ושבקית

ופטרית ותרוכית יתיכי ליכי את אנתי לאה בת יעקב העומדת

היום בוראד מתא דיתבא על נהר מארדש ועל מי מעינות דהוית

אנתתי מן קדמת דנא וכדו פטרית ושבקית ותרוכית יתיכי ליכי

דיתהוויין רשאה ושלטאה בנפשיכי למהך להתנסבא לכל

גבר דיתיצביין ואנש לא ימחא בידיכי מן יומא דנן ולעלם והרי

את מותרת לכל אדם ודן דיהוי ליכי מנאי ספר תרוכין ואגרת שבוקין

פ׳ ... בן ... עד

בנימין בן נפתלי עד

יוסף בן חנוך יהודה עד

THE GET (Bill of Divorcement) is torn across by the rabbi
and retained by him so that it may not be used again.
Courtesy of Prof. Alexander Guttmann of the Hebrew Union College

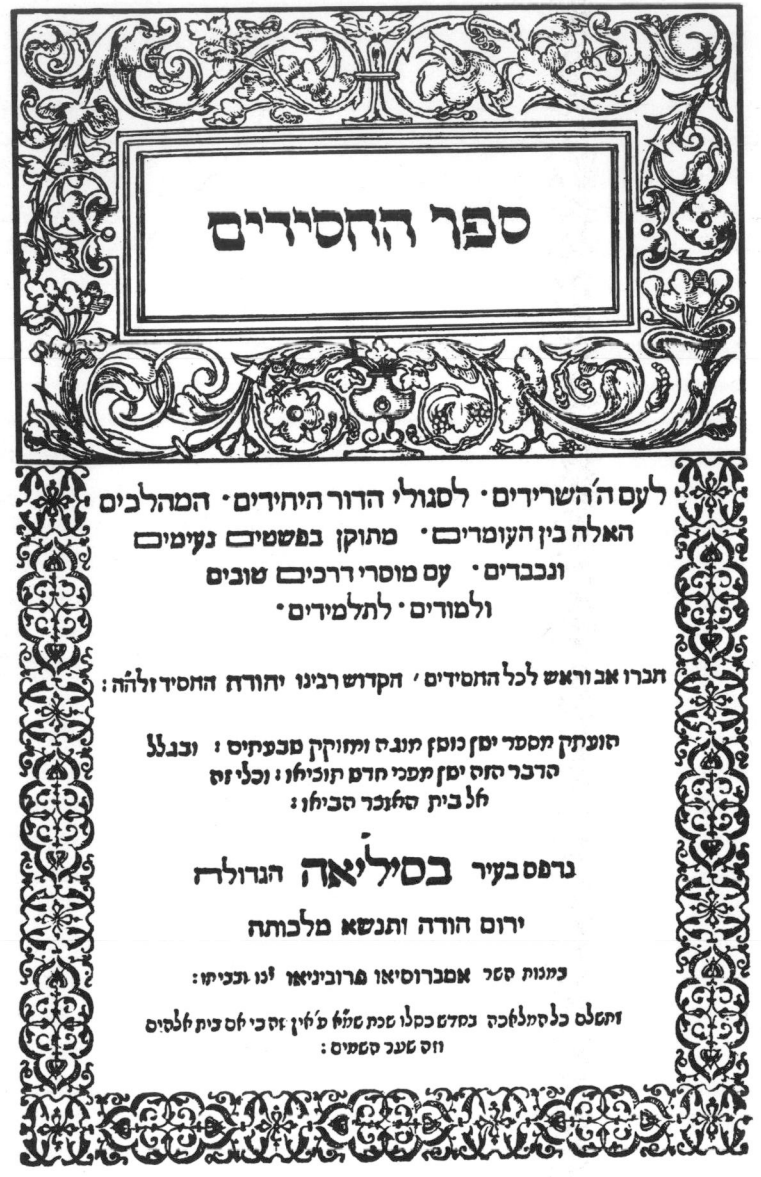

XXII

Beliefs Connected with Death

The Belief in a Future Life . . . In order to completely understand the rites and customs observed at the occurrence of death, it is necessary to have a clear concept of the beliefs developed among the Jews concerning the soul and its existence after death. We have hinted at some of these beliefs in previous chapters; now we shall deal with them at length.

In Biblical times, the Jews, in common with other peoples, believed that man consisted of two components: flesh (bosor) and spirit (ruach) or soul, or as we may also term it, principle of life. Various parts of the body were thought to be the seat of the soul; e.g., the heart, the liver, the kidneys. A current concept was "the life of the flesh is in the blood" (Lev. 17:11), because if the blood flowed from a wound, the vitality decreased and sometimes disappeared altogether. The most popular concept of the soul was that its seat was in the breath, because when breathing ceased, the body became lifeless. In the Bible, the principle of life or soul was called synonymously *ruach*, *nefesh* and *n'shomo*, three words designating breath. (In later times, under the influence of Greek philosophy, the soul was believed to be of a more compound and complicated nature. In the Middle Ages Jewish thinkers interpreted the three Biblical synonyms for the principle of life as distinct names for the three souls, or substances of the soul, functioning in the personality of a human being: the vegetative soul, nefesh; the animal soul, ruach; and the human, thinking soul, n'shomo.)

The soul was conceived as a kind of airy substance which could leave the body either temporarily or permanently. Sleeping was a state of existence in which the soul left the body for a short while, floating through the world, while its experiences in this state appeared as a dream to the slumberer. Dreams played an important part in the life and beliefs of the people in those times. When the soul left the body permanently, the result was death. In the Bible, dying was designated as the departure of the soul (Gen. 35:18).

What happened to the soul after its permanent departure from the body?

There were two ideas among Jews and among various other ancient peoples regarding the soul after death. According to the older notion, the tomb was also the abode of the soul. A current legend related how the mournful voice of Rachel weeping for her children was heard near her tomb. We find this story in Jeremiah (31:14). It was later amplified by the homilists of the Midrash. The Midrash tells how Jacob purposely buried Rachel on the way to Ephrath, because he foresaw that the Jews, when exiled to Babylon, would pass by that spot, and Rachel would be able to invoke the compassion of God for her children. The belief that the soul lingered in the grave was also implied in the age-old practice of praying at the graves, and in many beliefs and customs connected with the dead.

Beside this older notion, the Jews shared with other ancient peoples the belief in a common abode where all souls gathered after death. In the Bible, the abode of the dead was called "Sheol," a proper noun of unknown derivation, translated "grave" in the English Bible.

Sheol, which corresponded to the nether world among other peoples, was believed to be deep underneath the earth, separated from the land of the living by an immense body of water. The Biblical Sheol had gates similar to those of the nether world of the Babylonians. (The nether world of the Babylonians had seven gates.) In the Bible, Sheol was called the land of darkness, silence, oblivion and perdition. In the Book of Job, it is described as "a land of thick darkness as darkness itself, a land of the shadow of death without any order, and where the light is as darkness" (10:22).

In spite of the dissimilarity between the two notions, one of which claimed that each soul remained in a single grave, and the other that all the souls assembled in one abode, both were maintained simultaneously. The belief that the soul lingered in the grave still persists even today, notwithstanding the firm belief that the soul ascends to heaven. Otherwise, visiting the graves to invoke the aid of pious men long deceased would be inexplicable. In general, we must not look for logical con-sistency and accuracy in popular beliefs.

Sheol was called "the house appointed for all living," where all must go, but from which none returned. "As the cloud is consumed and vanished away, so he that goeth down to Sheol shall come up no more," says the author of Job (7:9; 30:23). God excepted only a few favorites such as Enoch and Elijah, who were believed to have been rescued from Sheol and taken to heaven while still alive. The necromancers were also an exception, for it was believed that they possessed the power to summon ghosts from Sheol to answer their questions.

Until long after the Babylonian exile, the Jews cherished no hope of resurrection, nor did they believe in the immortality of the soul. A gloomy, ghastly existence of shadows awaited the souls in Sheol, resting in a state of slumber from which they never awakened. "Till the heavens be no more, they shall not awake, nor be aroused out of their sleep" (Job 14:12). They even lacked the consciousness and strength to praise God. "Sheol cannot praise Thee; Death cannot celebrate Thee; They that go down into the pit cannot hope for Thy truth. The living, the living, he shall praise Thee," says the Biblical poet (Isaiah 38:18–19). "The living know that they shall die; but the dead know not anything, neither have they any more a reward. . . . there is no work, nor device, nor knowledge, nor wisdom in the grave, whither thou goest," says Koheleth (9:5, 10).

This conception of the shadowy existence of all souls in the dark Sheol was devoid of any ethical element. Retribution, belief in reward and punishment after death for the deeds done in life, did not enter into it. Punishments threatened and rewards promised in the Bible refer exclusively to life in this world.

Originally, the concept of Sheol was not an integral part of the Jewish religion, but belonged to the realm of popular beliefs. The religion of the God of Israel was a religion of life, not concerned with the mysteries of the soul after death. Later, when the popular conception of Sheol became imbued with the spirit of the Jewish religion, it assumed a new aspect. The popular conception of the infinite power of Sheol was incompatible with the conception of the omnipotence and the omnipresence of God. The pious worshipper of the God of Israel could not bear to believe that his union with God and his trust in Him ended at the gates of Sheol. The psalmists therefore expressed the ardent hope that God would not forsake them even in Sheol, that "The Lord killeth, and maketh alive; He bringeth down to Sheol, and bringeth up." [274]

The idea of the omnipotence of Sheol and the concept of retribution in this earthly life became untenable in the light of the belief in a righteous God which the Prophets taught. This belief in a rule of justice in a world, which, since the Babylonian exile, had become the orthodox belief of the people, was in glaring contradiction to the facts of life. The orthodox psalmist confidently said, "I have been young and now am old, yet have I not seen the righteous forsaken, nor his seed begging bread (Ps. 37:25). Many skeptics bluntly rejected this pious assertion, declaring that the righteous were actually forsaken and that the wicked prospered. The most telling blow at the orthodox belief in God's retribution within man's lifetime was delivered by the author of Job who vehemently protested, "Wherefore do the wicked live, become old, yea, wax mighty in power?" (21:7). The Book of Job left this burning question without a satisfactory answer.

The inner development of Jewish religious ideas postulated

the belief in retribution after death. Many centuries elapsed before the old popular conception of the dark Sheol was superseded by the new belief in "a world to come," to which this world could be compared as a vestibule at the entrance to the parlor, the world to come, according to the expression of a Jewish sage of the second century c.e.[275]

Retribution after death was first connected with the belief in the resurrection of the dead. In the Book of Daniel, a literary product of the time of the persecutions in the reign of Antiochus Epiphanes, belief in a twofold resurrection was clearly expressed. "And many of them that sleep in the dust of the earth shall awake, some to everlasting life, and some to reproaches and everlasting abhorrence" (12:2). This expectation of the resurrection of the dead in the Messianic Era spread and took root in certain pious circles, in the absence of a belief in the next world. It could hardly remove the conflict between the concept of a God of justice, and the actual injustice prevailing in the world. This problem, found in the Book of Job, was solved later when the people began to believe in the direct continuation of the spiritual life of the individual after death, with the immediate reward for good conduct in Paradise, and punishment for bad conduct in Hell.

These two beliefs, the belief in the resurrection of the dead, and the belief that the soul continued its spiritual existence in the next world, were mutually exclusive. If the soul never died, there was no need for the dead to rise from their graves. But this is not the only inconsistency which we meet in the beliefs concerning the Messianic days and the world to come.

The two beliefs had not been accepted by all the Jews in the days of the Second Temple. There were certain circles, like the sect of the Essenes, who accepted the belief in the immortality of the soul but rejected the belief in the resurrection of the dead. The Sadducees rejected both. The Pharisees accepted both, and through them these two beliefs have become an integral part of the doctrine of the Orthodox Judaism of the present day.

Gan Eden and Gehinom . . . Although the idea of the im· mortality of the soul and retribution after death was an inner postulate of the development of the Jewish religion, the imagery and the terminology for a place of bliss for the right- eous and an infernal region for the wicked, though Hebrew, was apparently influenced by the Persians. The place of bliss was called *Gan Eden,* Garden of Eden, after the legendary garden in the story of Genesis. The inferno was given the name of *Gehinom,* the valley of Hinom, a valley in Jerusalem where in the time of Manasseh, King of Judah, the adherents of the Moloch cult offered up their children as burnt offerings to God. In English, the name is distorted into Gehenna.[276]

The dark Sheol of the Bible now became synonymous with Gehenna, and all the passages in the Bible referring to Sheol were interpreted in the terms and imagery of the new belief in Gehenna. There was a vast difference between Sheol and Gehenna. Gehenna was a place for the wicked only, while Sheol had been the ultimate abode of all souls, righteous and wicked alike. There was no exit from Sheol, but the tortures of Gehenna were not everlasting. Only very wicked men, heretics who spread false doctrines, and tyrants who terrified the world, were condemned to eternal Gehenna. According to the predominant view of the Talmudic rabbis, transgressors were usually kept in Gehenna no longer than twelve months.[277]

Since the beginning of the Common Era, the feeble shadows of the souls of the dead were not supposed to have been locked up in a dark abode from which there was no return, but were believed to retain full consciousness, which made them capable of all the spiritual activities of a human being. According to the Talmud the dead were exempt from all religious precepts. Therefore, the ritual fringes of the talis in which the corpse was dressed were made defective and disqualified. Yet people believed that the dead earnestly craved ability to fulfill the precepts of the Torah, and felt hurt when a man wearing tsitsis or t'filin or carrying a Scroll of the Torah walked close to their graves.[278]

Notwithstanding the belief that the soul ascended to heaven, the primitive notion of the soul lingering in or near the grave persisted. Souls were thus free to hover between heaven and earth, to converse with one another and even to give advice and information to the living. For some time after death, it was believed that the soul longed for the body and lingered near it. According to various versions, this period lasted three days, seven days, thirty days, or even twelve months. It was thought that the soul listened to the funeral discourse and resented improper manner of burial. Ghosts were said to be in contact with this world even many years after death.[279]

At the Departure of the Soul . . . In the first section of this book, a Midrashic tale is told about the prenatal life of man under the tutorship and supervision of a special angel. Afterward this angel delivers to the child the decree of God to go out into the world. We now continue this story to its end.

When the time arrives for a man to leave this world, the very angel who guarded his soul in his prenatal existence appears and asks him, "Do you recognize me?" The man replies, "Yes, but why do you come to me today when you did not come to me on any other days?" The angel says, "To take you away from the world." Then the man begins to weep, and the sound of his voice travels from one end of the world to the other, yet no creature hears his voice except the cock. Man argues with the angel, "From two worlds did you take me and into this world did you bring me." But the angel retorts, "Did I not tell you that you were formed and born against your will, and that you would die against your will, and that against your will you will have to give an account of yourself before the Holy One, blessed be He?"

This angel quotes a popular sentence of the Mishnah tractate, *Sayings of the Fathers* (Ovos). This is not the only angel whom the dead man sees when his soul departs. Three companies of angels accompany the dead on their departure from this world, each one quoting an appropriate sentence from the

Bible. There are two sets of such quotations, one for the right-eous, the other for the wicked. At the departure of his soul, man is accorded a glimpse of the Divinity. This is based upon the passage in the Bible, "Thou canst not see My face, for man shall not see Me and live" (Exod. 33:20). This passage was interpreted to imply that the moment life ends man sees the Divine presence.[280]

Death itself, the moment of the departure of life, is personi-fied in the Angel of Death, who is the subject of many stories and phantasies.

Angel of Death and Angel Dumo . . . Before the Babylonian exile, the old Jewish belief in angels as intermediaries between God and man did not play an important role, for God himself was believed to intervene in the affairs of human life. Since the Babylonian exile, God, in the religious concept of the Jews, became more and more supermundane, aloof from the earth which "He hath given to the children of men" (Ps. 115: 16). Human affairs on earth were believed to be largely in charge of holy and mighty angels, ministers of God who ful-filled His word and carried out His desires.[281]

Although the great prophet of the Exile proclaimed in the name of God, "I form the light, and create darkness; I make peace and create evil, I am the Lord, that doeth all these things," yet in the belief of the people, the angels in the service of God were divided into two categories—friendly angels, full of light and goodness, and evil ones, who acted as God's messengers to bring punishment and calamity to men. "Mes-sengers of evil," they were called by the Psalmist. The "angels of death" belonged to this category.[282]

In time, the angels of death were reduced to one angel, the personification of destruction of human life. Later this angel was identified with Satan or Samael, the prince of the demons, and also with the *Yetser Horo*, the personification of the evil impulse in man.[283]

In imagination and fable, the Angel of Death was represented as a being, consisting of wide open eyes, standing during the last moments of life at the head of the dying person, a drawn sword in hand. On the point of the sword there was a drop of gall, at the sight of which the dying person opened his mouth in terror. The instant he swallowed this drop of gall, death came. This bitter drop caused the alteration of the countenance that followed death.[284]

In the phantasy of the people the Angel of Death had become so thoroughly personified that fables were told about conversations which certain illustrious men held with him while they were still alive. These conversations were given verbatim in the popular tales of the Talmud.[285]

The power of the Angel of Death was not unlimited. He was merely the messenger of God who carried out His decree. According to the popular phantasy, God, in ancient Biblical days, excepted some of His favorites from falling into the hands of the Angel of Death. Six are mentioned who died by a kiss from God instead of the sword of the Angel of Death (the three Patriarchs and Moses, Aaron and Miriam). A large number of exceptionally meritorious persons did not suffer the common fate of all men, but were said to have entered Paradise during their lifetime.

The power of the Angel of Death was further limited by his inability to approach any man who was entirely absorbed in the study of the Torah. There are numerous tales in the Talmud and Midrash about illustrious rabbis whom the Angel of Death could not approach because they constantly studied the Torah. The Angel of Death had to devise means to divert the mind of those rabbis from the Torah in order to take their souls. There is a fable in the Talmud which tells of an entire city over which the Angel of Death had no power. When the aged inhabitants were ready to die they went outside the city. This fabulous city was Luz, built by the man who showed the entrance to Beth-El to the house of Joseph, according to the first chapter of the Book of Judges.[286]

Even the limited power of the Angel of Death was only

temporary. In the world to come, after the resurrection of the dead, the office of the Angel of Death would be abolished, for there would be no sense in dying after the dead have arisen from their graves. According to the Jewish belief, God would then "slaughter the Angel of Death who slaughtered the slaughterer," and the words of the prophet would come true, "He will swallow up death forever; and the Lord God will wipe away tears from off all faces." [287]

In addition to the Angel of Death another angel was prominent in Jewish belief, the Angel Dumo, in charge of the souls of the dead. In the Bible, Dumo, silence, was a synonym for Sheol. The Angel Dumo (the angel of the world of silence) thus played the same role as Nergal, the Babylonian god of the nether world. [288]

The "Beating and the Sling" . . . The Cabalists did not consider the torments of Gehenna sufficient punishment for sinful souls. They added a preliminary torment to Gehenna, called *Chibut ha-Kever*, beating of the grave.

Immediately after burial, the Angel of Death (or according to another version, the Angel Dumo) places himself upon the grave and strikes the deceased with a fiery chain, asking him his Hebrew name. If the Hebrew name has slipped his memory, the angel returns the soul to the body, to be submitted for judgment. For three successive days the deceased is then beaten with a chain of fire or a stick of iron.

None were exempt from Chibut ha-Kever. Only two exceptions were made. They were for those who had lived always in the Holy Land, and for those who died on Friday before sunset and were buried at the moment when the Sabbath rest was heralded. The Cabalists devised means of protection from Chibut ha-Kever for those who lived outside the Land of Israel and for those who were not fortunate enough to die on Friday before sunset. These means consisted of doing benevolent works, showing hospitality and reciting prayers with excessive fervor. Reciting at the end of the Eighteen

Benedictions a Biblical verse in which the first and last letters were identical with the first and last letters of the name of the person for whom it was intended, was a very efficient safeguard against the suffering of Chibut ha-Kever. Since the Eighteen Benedictions were recited three times a day, this verse was engraved in the memory and regarded as an efficient means of remembering one's Hebrew name. The Hebrew prayer book contained a list of Biblical verses corresponding to the Hebrew names used most frequently.[289]

In the Jewish beliefs regarding death, Chibut ha-Kever and Gehenna did not exhaust the possibilities of torments for the sinful. One more punishment was mentioned in the Talmud. The expression of the Bible, "and the souls of thine enemies, them shall he sling out, as from the hollow of a sling" (1 Sam. 25:29), was factually interpreted. When a wicked person died, one angel stationed himself at one end of the world and a second angel at the other end, and they hurled his soul to each other as a stone is thrown from the hollow of a sling. In the popular idiom, this torment was called *Kaf ha-Kala* (hollow of the sling).[290]

Transmigration of Souls . . . In addition to these punishments of the sinful souls, another punishment, though an esoteric mystery, was conceived of in recent centuries by the Oriental and the East European Jews. This was the belief in the transmigration of souls (also called metempsychosis) in which certain souls passed into another body after death. Jews called it by the Hebrew term *gilgul* (cycle, rotation).

The belief in the transmigration of souls, common to primitive tribes, was shared by many ancient peoples and especially developed in India. Originally a foreign element, an exotic mystery, mentioned neither in the Bible nor in the Talmud, it infiltrated into certain circles of Jewish mystics. With the spread of the Cabala in the later Middle Ages, it spread among Jews, although the Jewish thinkers attacked it as a heathen superstition.

Among the Cabalists of the school of Rabbi Isaac Luria (died 1572), the belief in gilgul became a basic doctrine of their teaching, and Rabbi Chayim Vital, the famous disciple of Rabbi Isaac Luria, wrote a whole book on this theme, *Sefer ha-Gilgulim* (the Book of the Transmigrations of Souls).

According to this belief, one's soul after death passed into another body, passing from body to body until it ultimately atoned for the sin for which it had suffered the punishment of gilgul. The soul might pass into a human body, the body of an animal, or even into an inanimate substance, depending upon the degree of sinfulness of the person, and the type of sin he had committed. The soul of the conceited community leader passed into the body of a bee; that of one who had been cruel to the poor passed into the body of a crow; the soul of a denunciator passed into the body of a barking dog; that of one who neglected to wash his hands before meals was transferred to a river, etc.

This doctrine of the Cabalists played a great part in the beliefs and phantasies of the people in recent centuries.[291]

Good and Bad Omens . . . There were good and bad death omens. A good death omen was a sign that the deceased was righteous and would enter Paradise, and vice versa.

The day on which death occurred might be auspicious or inauspicious. Even in early Talmudic times, to die on Friday was a good omen, to die after the departure of the Sabbath was a bad omen. The flaming Gehenna was quiet on the Sabbath, so death on that day was auspicious, while death on the day it reopened was inauspicious. To die at the departure of Yom Kippur was regarded as a good omen because of the advantage of dying with all one's sins forgiven. Conversely, to die on the day preceding Yom Kippur and miss forgiveness of one's sins, which the Day of Atonement bestowed, was a bad omen. In recent popular belief, the entire month of Nison was regarded as an auspicious period for death.

There were many omens attached to the manner in which

man breathed his last breath. Dying with a smile, face upward or with his face toward the people, was regarded as auspicious, and vice versa. Good was portended if one died speaking, especially when speaking words of the Torah.

According to the Talmud, death itself portended evil for the entire family. In the first seven days, the sword of the Angel of Death was still drawn, menacing the family. For thirty days the sword swung back and forth, returning to its sheath only after twelve months. However, if a boy was born in the family, this good omen removed the menace from the entire family.[292]

Origin of the Customs . . . The customs of burial and mourning observed among Jews, as well as among other peoples, are divergent as well as mystifying. Originally, these practices could not have been symbols of mourning, because inherently most of them do not symbolize affliction and sadness. Walking barefooted, strewing dust on the head, sitting on the ground, were not, in themselves, manifestations of grief and mourning. Nor was the music at the funeral or the festive meal eaten after the funeral composed of food brought in from another house. Only in the course of time did they become signs of mourning because of long association with death. Why and how did they become so associated?

Obviously, the customs and practices which later became mere tokens of mourning were originally rites performed for a certain purpose. What was that purpose?

For quite a time this question was a controversial matter, a topic of profound discussion among Bible critics and anthropologists. Various scholars offered various theories to answer this question, but as in the case of the customs of marriage, each theory explained only some of the practices. Even when all these theories are applied jointly, some of the practices of mourning remain unexplained.

Very few of the practices of mourning can be explained as spontaneous outbursts of grief. There are only two theories that adequately explain the origin of most of these customs, i.e., the theory of ancestral worship, and the theory of fearing the ghost of the dead.[293]

The Theory of Ancestor Worship . . . According to the exponents of the theory of ancestor worship, these primitive customs stem from pre-Mosaic times. In those early days, the Jews did not worship the God of Israel, but like many other primitive tribes and peoples worshipped the spirits of their dead ancestors, paying them divine honors and offering sacrifices to them. The later religion founded by Moses embodied belief in the almighty God of Israel, superseding and suppressing the primitive cult of the ancestral spirits. Traces of that cult persisted in later times, and can be found in the customs connected with burial and mourning.

This theory explains why, at the outset, the Jewish religion was so sternly antagonistic to many practices of mourning, and why a corpse could not be touched without defilement. The Hebrew word *to-me*, which the English Bible translates "unclean" or "defiling," originally did not imply physical uncleanliness, but implied that the person or the thing was taboo, banned, interdicted, ritually unfit. "He that touched any man's dead body was *to-me* seven days" (Num. 19:11), because a dead body was a reminder of a prohibited rival cult. The priests who were devotees of the cult of the God of Israel, therefore, avoided any contact with a corpse, with the exception of that of a very close relative. The High Priest avoided contact with any corpse, even those of his own father and mother. The priests were also restricted in regard to the customs of mourning. Ordinary priests were enjoined "they shall not make baldness upon their head, neither shall they shave off the corners of their beard, nor make any cutting in their flesh," customs generally prohibited to all Jews. Priests were particularly enjoined against this practice, lest in so doing, they profane the name of their God. Ordinary priests were not forbidden to rend their garments and let their hair grow long. Only the High Priests were forbidden these two customs of mourning.[294]

There were two alternatives in regard to the hair—cutting it very short, to the point of baldness or allowing it to grow long and loose. The latter, more simple alternative, was less obnoxious to the teachers and spokesmen of the Jewish religion and has been an established custom in Orthodox Jewry since Tannaitic times. According to the theory of ancestral worship, cutting the hair was originally a sacrifice to the spirit of the dead, for sacrificing the hair to a divinity was a current practice among many ancient peoples. But this theory fails to explain the alternative custom of allowing the hair to grow too long. It is also difficult to explain cutting the flesh as a rite of initiation into the cult of the dead. Nor is it easy to explain the custom of wearing coarse sackcloth as a sign of submission to the honored ghost, because sackcloth was worn by slaves.

The theory of ancestral worship explains the festive meal after burial as an original participation in a sacrificial meal in honor of the ghost of the dead, but fails to explain why the food must be brought in from a strange house. Many other practices of mourning cannot be explained by the theory of ancestor worship.

The Theory of Fearing Ghosts . . . More of the burial and mourning customs were explained by the theory of the survivors' fear of the ghost of the dead. Basically, this theory of the anthropologists has much in common with the theory of ancestor worship. Both assumed that the customs of mourning stemmed from the pre-historic age, when the belief that the soul of the dead lingered in the grave still prevailed and that the customs were originally practiced because of the ghost of the dead. The theory of ancestor worship originally motivated the customs by affection for the dead, while the theory of fear of the ghost ascribed the customs to precautions on the part of the survivors to prevent the unwanted return of the ghost.

When a death occurred, the first thing to be done was to

bury the corpse. The ghosts of the unburied were regarded as exceedingly dangerous, especially to their undutiful and disrespectful relatives. This additional motive for immediate interment was added to that of defilement.

Burial alone was an insufficient means of guarding against the return of the ghost. Numerous other precautions and devices were used by primitive man to prevent its return.

The Jews and many other peoples threw sticks and stones or handfuls of grass with earth attached, on the graves. The original motive of this practice, which was a Jewish custom as far back as the early Middle Ages, was to force the ghost to return to the grave in case he attempted to leave. Grass was believed a safeguard against evil spirits. Later, the origin of the custom was forgotten and new meanings were read into it, interpreting the practices as a symbol of the verses of Psalms, "And may they blossom out of the city like grass of the earth," and "He remembereth that we are dust." In addition, the grass which withered and died, and then sprouted again with new life, symbolized the resurrection of the dead.[295]

The theory of fearing the ghosts of the dead also explained the rush to fill the grave with earth. An open grave from which the ghost could easily escape was considered extremely dangerous. The tombstone was originally employed for the same reason. Among some peoples the custom prevailed of even piling a mass of heavy stones on the grave. Later the tombstone became merely a manifestation of affection for the deceased on the part of the survivors.

Primitive man used numerous devices to outwit the ghost, making it impossible for him to find his way home. The eyes of the deceased were closed immediately after death occurred, for many peoples believed that the ghost might return if this was not done. Some closed the eyes even before death. Originally it was a mild form of blindfolding so that the deceased might not see the direction in which he was carried to the grave, for according to the primitive belief, a ghost could find its way back to the house only by the same route by which it had left. The original motive was completely forgotten, and Jews read a new, symbolic meaning into it. They now believed that as long as the eye gazed on this world it was incapable of perceiving the next world. At the moment of death, man had a glimpse of the Sh'chino, the Divine Presence, and he ceased to look at this world. In the late Middle Ages (seventeenth century) this custom of blindfolding the eyes was done with potsherds which were placed on the eyes after the corpse had been laid in the grave. Other nations employed various methods of blindfolding the eyes of the dead. The Russians placed coins on the eyes. In Korea, binders made of black silk and tied with strings at the back of the head were placed over the eyes of the dead.

For the same reason, the corpse was carried from the house feet foremost, for if it had been carried head foremost, the eyes would have been towards the door and his ghost might find his way back. The Jews apparently adopted this custom from the Germans in the Middle Ages. This explains also why a Jewish funeral procession took the longest way to the cemetery, for the longer and more tortuous the way to the grave, the more difficult for the ghost to return.

These precautions prevented the return of the ghost, but in addition, the ghost was made to feel as comfortable as possible in the grave. Foods and various utensils were placed therein to induce him to stay in the grave.

As in the attempt to control evil spirits on other important occasions in the life of man, so at death, deceit was employed to forestall the return of the ghost. Covering the head of the mourner was a precaution taken to hide from the ghost. The custom of the mourner's changing his place in the synagogue might also have been motivated by a desire to hide from the ghost. The custom was recorded as far back as the fourteenth century.[296]

The survivors also endeavored to disguise themselves in order that the dead might not recognize them. They mutilated themselves by making cuts in their flesh, cut their hair too short or let it grow too long. They wore sackcloth, the attire of a beggar, or clothes of an unusual color: black among the Jews and Romans and white and red among other peoples. They strewed ashes on their heads, walked barefooted and sat on the ground. In the house, all beds were inverted. In brief, ordinary life was reversed to make the survivors and the house of death unrecognizable to the ghost of the dead.

Primitive man also took precautions in case the ghost was not deceived. If he reappeared in spite of all means of prevention, a warm conciliatory welcome was given him. After the burial, a festive meal was served in which he was believed to participate. The food had to be brought from another house in order to make sure that the ghost did not cling to it. Appeasing the ghost motivated the custom of keeping a burning candle in the house of death during the seven days of mourning. A religious authority of the thirteenth century said that this was done expressedly for the contentment of the soul, which returned to the house during those seven days.[297]

This theory also explained the custom of pouring out all the water immediately after the occurrence of death. The later interpretation given above, connecting it with the Angel of Death, was invented when the origin was no longer known. This custom was practiced among many peoples, for primitive man believed that spirits could not cross water and therefore the ghost was in danger of falling into it. (Cf. above p. 215.) It was therefore removed from the house in order that it should not annoy the ghost of the dead and hinder its departure.

Guarding the Corpse . . . We have spoken of safeguarding the survivors against the ghost of the dead. The survivors feared also that the corpse might be penetrated by evil spirits. According to the primitive belief, the evil spirits, having no material body, were anxious to become corporate, and sought to enter the corpse. The dead body was believed to be beset by demons, and had to be guarded against them.

This explains the queer phenomenon by which the rites of a funeral so strikingly resembled the rites of a wedding. In both ceremonials, a procession took place in which music, torches, encirclings, aromatic odors, and branches of myrtle were prominent features. Both processions were followed by a festive meal at which legumes were eaten. The bride and groom, like the corpse, were never left alone, and in the attire of the bride and groom, knots were loosened before the wedding ceremony and knots were also avoided in shrouds. The days of mourning numbered seven, the same number as the days of the wedding feast. These similarities are adequately explained by the common origin of both rites—the fear of evil spirits.[298]

Guarding the corpse against demons could not play any significant role in the customs observed in the seven days of mourning, but played a great role in the rites and customs observed from the moment of death until the funeral was concluded. This period was believed the time when the evil spirits infested the corpse as well as the people who participated in the burial.

The Gaon Sar Sholom, head of the academy at Sura (about the middle of the ninth century), explicitly stated that the seven stops made on the return from the grave were made because evil spirits clung to those returning from a burial, one of which hastened away with every halt. Rashi, the greatest of the commentators on the Bible and the Talmud, repeated this explanation two centuries later. About five hundred years after Rashi, this same explanation was again repeated by Rabbi Moshe Isserles, co-author of the Shulchan Aruch (the accepted code of civil and religious laws in Orthodox Jewry). The same explanation also may apply to the stops made by the funeral procession on the way to the grave. So motivated, the stops appropriately went with the recitation of Psalm 91. called in the Talmud, "The Song of Evil Spirits." [299]

Later Customs . . . On the foregoing pages we have applied indiscriminately the theories of modern anthropologists concerning the customs of death in Biblical, Talmudic and post-Talmudic times. A few explanatory remarks must be added about these later customs, which arose in medieval and recent times under the influence of the non-Jewish environment.

The motive of blindfolding the dead is not an adequate explanation of the custom of putting potsherds on the eyes, for it does not explain the potsherd placed on the mouth. We must add a second motive, that of closing the openings in the body of the corpse to forestall penetration by evil spirits.

The custom of covering mirrors or turning them to the wall was known among many nations, originating in a primitive belief that man's soul was in his shadow, and also in his reflection in water, or in a mirror. It was feared that the soul projected in the mirror might be snatched away by the ghost of the deceased.[300]

The above cited Gaon Sar Sholom declared that the custom of washing the hands on returning from a funeral was something new, and not obligatory. In the fourteenth century this practice was still optional, and only in the long course of time did it become a universally accepted custom.[301]

The candle burning in the house of death during the seven days of mourning was mentioned as far back as the thirteenth century. Later, a glass of water and a towel were added. These customs were practiced also among other nations. The religious code of Rabbi Abraham Danzig, noted religious authority at the beginning of the nineteenth century, approved of the lighted candle, but condemned the glass of water and the towel as non-Jewish. This same authority strongly condemned the custom of placing little sticks, called little forks, in the hands of the corpse. In spite of the severe condemnation of this great religious authority, even in this country, these two latter customs are still practiced among Eastern European Orthodox Jews.[302]

In conclusion, it must be remarked that the customs related to death are not homogeneous, but are a product of different times and different stages of religious thought. The various explanations offered for them do not exclude one another, but should be jointly applied. A single custom may have originated or have been sustained through the ages by a concurrence of several motives. However, as already previously remarked, all the joint explanations do not cover the origin of all the practices connected with death. Some of them defy explanation.

Originally these practices were rites with definite objectives. Later the origin faded from memory, and the practices became mere tokens of mourning, manifestations of grief, and expressions of respect and affection for the departed.

Prayers for the Dead . . . As stated in a previous chapter, the belief in a future life after death, in Gan Eden for the righteous and Gehenna for the wicked, was universally accepted among Jews during the early centuries of the Common Era. But there was yet no unanimity in regard to atonement for the sins of the dead in order that they might be redeemed from Gehenna. In the centuries following the second destruction of Jerusalem, we find two contrasting trends of thought in this regard, and we are unable to ascertain which predominated. One trend declared that every man must repent and do good deeds during his life and that there could be no atonement after death. The other school of thought believed in atonement for sins of the dead after death, and the efficacy of prayer to deliver sinful souls from Gehenna. Numerous passages of the Talmud and Midrash reflect both tendencies. In the Middle Ages the latter trend became universally accepted in Jewish religious thought and practice.[303]

The predominance of the belief in atoning for the sins of the dead caused the evolution of three religious institutions which at present are most prominent in the ritual of the synagogue: Kaddish, Yahrzeit (anniversary of the death) and *Hazkoras N'shomos* (memorial service). They will be treated separately.

Kaddish . . . The *Kaddish* (holy in Aramaic like *kodosh* in Hebrew) is popularly thought of as a prayer for the dead,

although its contents have no link with death or praying for
the dead. This ancient Jewish prayer offers praise and adoration to God. Originally, the nucleus was the doxology recited
by the whole congregation, "May His great name be praised
for all eternity!" We find this doxology in a Hebrew version
(in Psalm 113:2, "Blessed be the name of the Lord from this
time forth and forever") and in an Aramaic version in the
Book of Daniel (2:20, "Blessed be the name of God from everlasting even until everlasting; for wisdom and might are His").
Another Hebrew version was used as a congregational re-
sponse in the Temple service ("Blessed be the name of His
glorious kingdom forever and ever"). This praise of God, em-
phasizing the sanctity and glory of His name, had its proto-
type in the verse of Ezekiel, "Thus will I magnify Myself and
sanctify Myself, and I will make Myself known in the eyes of
many nations; and they shall know that I am the Lord" (38:
23). In Ezekiel's magnificent vision, this universal recognition
of God's glory, which will usher in the era of eternal peace
and bliss, will occur after the miraculous defeat and downfall
of the last heathen world power of Gog, of the land of Magog.
No wonder that the praise of God's name was expanded by
the addition of a prayer for the speedy arrival of God's Kingdom, and later enlarged for liturgical purposes.

In the days of the Second Temple, more than one version of
this hymn, consisting of the doxology and a prayer for the
arrival of the Kingdom of God, was current among Jews.
Thus, the Christian Paternoster, which like Kaddish is a prayer
for the sanctification of God's name and the arrival of His
Kingdom, is not something unique and unparalleled, as Christians believe, but is merely one among many versions of an
ancient Jewish prayer.

In Talmudic times this holy praise of God was an integral
part of the liturgy. Recited as a conclusion to public readings
of the Holy Writings and religious discourses in the synagogue or house of study, a mystic power was ascribed in certain circles to the recitation of this prayer, particularly to the

doxology responded by the congregation. The whole world was sustained by merit of this holy praise of God's name. He who recited the prayer was assured of his share in the world to come, and it was thought the recital had power to annul an evil decree passed in heaven. In the course of time, the power of redeeming the dead from Gehenna was also attributed to the recitation of Kaddish.[304]

In the epoch of the *G'onim* (seventh to eleventh centuries), we first meet the term Kaddish and two innovations in connection with its recital. Kaddish was already a part of the services at the synagogue and linked with the occurrence of death, but recited by a stranger, not by the son. It was the chazan who recited it at the synagogue on the first Sabbath of mourning.[305]

Since the belief prevailed that the religious merits and pious deeds of the son could atone for the sins of his deceased parents, only one step was necessary to establish a redeeming power for the parents through the son's recital of prayers to which the congregation responded with the sanctification of God's name. To strengthen this belief, a basis was found for it in the verses of Isaiah, "Therefore thus saith the Lord, who redeemed Abraham, concerning the house of Jacob: 'Jacob shall not now be ashamed, neither shall his face now wax pale; When he seeth his children, the work of My hands, in the midst of him, That they sanctify My name; Yea, they shall sanctify the Holy One of Jacob, And shall stand in awe of the God of Israel'" (29:22–23). In addition, several versions of a story were told with either Rabbi Akiba or Rabbon Jochanan ben Zakkai as the main character, accentuating the fact that the orphan's recital of Kaddish and Bor'chu (the two prayers to which the congregation responds with praise of God) had the power to rescue the most wicked man from the tortures of Gehenna. Here is the story in brief.

Once Akiba (or Rabbon Jochanan ben Zakkai) met a ghost, in the guise of a man carrying wood. He told Akiba that the wood was for the fire in Gehenna in which he was burned daily for his sins committed when he was a tax collector. He could be released from his terrible punishment if he had a son to recite Bor'chu and Kaddish before a congregation of worshippers who would respond with the praise of God's name. Rabbi Akiba, learning that a son had been born to the man after his death, cared for the youth and educated him, so that at last one day he stood in the assembly of worshippers and recited Bor'chu and Kaddish. The dead man then appeared to Rabbi Akiba, telling him that he was now released from Gehenna.[306]

The son's recitation of Kaddish after the death of a parent spread during the Middle Ages, until, in the course of a few centuries, it was universally accepted in all Jewish communities. Some religious authorities disliked the idea of relying too much on the prayers of the sons for redemption from Gehenna, but their opposition was overcome. It is the opinion of scholars that the custom began spreading in Germany during the time of the wide-spread persecutions against the Jews. A great many Jews perished as martyrs for Kiddush ha-Shem, the sanctification of the name of God. It is therefore easy to understand why the prayer sanctifying the name of God became more precious among the people.

At first Kaddish was recited for twelve months after death, corresponding to the period in which wicked people were kept in Gehenna, according to the predominant view of the rabbis of the Talmud. Later, the Kaddish period was curtailed to eleven months, in order that the dead parent should not appear wicked.[307]

At first, only the sons recited Kaddish; later daughters also were permitted to recite Kaddish if there was no son. Grandchildren were allowed to recite Kaddish for their grandparents, parents for children, pupils for teachers, and even distant relatives and complete strangers. This latter custom of reciting Kaddish for a stranger led to the recent commercialization of the custom. Many elderly people do not have sons or are not sure that their sons will be able and willing to go three times daily to the synagogue to recite Kaddish. They pay a certain amount to the study circle at the house of study or to a pious individual, with the stipulation that Kaddish be recited for them after their departure. Hiring a stranger to recite Kaddish has become an ordinary practice.

Yahrzeit . . . As far back as Talmudic times, Jews memorialized the anniversary of the day of their parents' deaths and also of great teachers' deaths. Some people fasted on this date. In the G'onic times, on the anniversary of the death of great scholars, large throngs gathered at their graves. We may assume that the custom of visiting the graves of parents on the same occasion was also practiced in those times.[308]

Although observing the anniversary of the death of parents went back to the first centuries c.e., the word Yahrzeit and most of its concurrent observances are of a late origin.

The word Yahrzeit was not mentioned before the sixteenth century, and was derived from the German word Jahrzeit used in the Christian Church to denote the occasion for honoring the memory of the dead. Fasting on the anniversary of the death of the parent was not obligatory. The above-mentioned Judah the Pious of Regensburg (died 1217) recommended this custom. Rabbi Moshe Isserles, a co-author of the Shulchan Aruch (sixteenth century), also recommended it for its religious merit. In recent times it became customary that, if one fasted once on the Yahrzeit day, he was obliged to fast on that day every year.[309]

The word Yahrzeit (as well as the custom of reciting Kaddish) originated among the Jews of Germany. Both are mentioned in the book of Maharil, the illustrious Rabbi of Mayence (beginning of the fifteenth century), with whom the readers of this book are already well acquainted. At first the Spanish and Oriental Jews were opposed to the recital of Kaddish on the Yahrzeit day, maintaining that this implied that the deceased parent had remained in Gehenna more than a year. Later, the opposition of the S'fardim was overcome by their acceptance of the explanation given by the great

Cabalist, Rabbi Isaac Luria, who maintained that even the soul which was already in Gan Eden was elevated every year to a higher sphere by the recital of Kaddish on the occasion of the Yahrzeit. Both name and custom were ultimately accepted by the S'fardim. Even the Persian Jews, who use their own Judeo-Persian vernacular, call the observance of the anniversary of the death by its Yiddish name Yahrzeit.[310]

In order to avoid quarrels about the right of precedence, the practice in which all mourners and observers of Yahrzeit at the services recite Kaddish together, was introduced among the S'fardim and, more recently, among some Ashk'nazim.[311]

The liturgical part of Yahrzeit is not confined to the recital of the Kaddish. If the person observing the Yahrzeit has the opportunity, he also reads the prayers before the congregation, and if he is a learned man, he recites a chapter in Mishnah or a section of some other standard religious work, concluding it with the longer version of Kaddish recited after a religious discourse (*Kaddish D'rabbonon*, Kaddish of the Scholars). Everyone who observes Yahrzeit is called up to the reading of the Torah on the Sabbath on which the Yahrzeit falls or on the preceding Sabbath. Since a reading from the Scroll of the Torah also takes place on Monday and Thursday, the mourner may be called on either of these two days, although the Sabbath is preferable. The prayer for the dead on the occasion of Yahrzeit will be discussed in the following topic.

In the seventeenth century, burning a "Yahrzeit light" for twenty-four hours was still considered a strange custom. Jewish scholars ascribe it to the influence of the Christian Church. But the custom soon became Judaized, because Jews saw in the burning light a symbol of man's soul.[312]

Besides the Yahrzeit of the individual, there were national traditional anniversaries of famous men in Jewish history. Most popular was the seventh day of the month of Ador, the traditional anniversary of the death of Moses. This anniversary dates back to the time of the G'onim and is still observed as a fast day in many Jewish communities.[313]

Among the Chasidim, the observance of Yahrzeit was transformed from an occasion of mourning to an occasion of joy. Chasidism arose in Poland in the eighteenth century and, about a century ago, the Chasidim constituted nearly half the Jewish people. They preached piety through joy, and celebrated the Yahrzeit of their respective rabbis with hymns, religious dances and general rejoicing. Their individual Yahrzeit was an occasion of joy on which the person observing the Yahrzeit passed brandy and cakes among the worshippers in the house of study. This custom spread in America among *Misnagdim* (opponents of Chasidim). In Eastern Europe among Misnagdim, there were regions where the observer of Yahrzeit provided himself with a box of snuff which he passed among the people assembled for the services.

Among the S'fardim, the observer of Yahrzeit invites relatives and acquaintances to his house, foremost among them the chacham (rabbi) and the communal functionaries of the synagogues, who honor the memory of the departed by studying Torah. This performance is called "limud" (study). The invited guests study Mishnah and Zohar and the chacham delivers a discourse on Torah. The only refreshment served is coffee.[314]

Yahrzeit is the anniversary of the day of death, not of burial, and it is observed according to the Jewish calendar. People believe the day of Yahrzeit is an unlucky day for any enterprise.

Hazkoras N'shomos . . . The custom of performing a memorial service for the dead developed among the Jews in Germany in the time of the Crusades, when thousands of Jews were massacred by mobs. Originally, a communal service was performed once in a year, on Yom Kippur, when lists were read of men and women, who during persecutions had become martyrs to the "Sanctification of the Name of God." These lists were called "memor books" (from the Latin memoria) and the German Jews called the performance of this service "memern." The earliest "memor book" extant is that of Nuremberg, containing the names of the martyrs who died between 1096 and 1349 (from the First Crusade until the Black Death). The communal service of Hazkoras N'shomos gradually has become an individual service in which each individual remembers his dead parents and prays for their souls.[315]

In recent times it has become customary to have memorial services on the three festivals. For individuals the services are held on any Sabbath, Monday or Thursday, on which the Yahrzeit falls, or on the Sabbath preceding the Yahrzeit. At the services of the synagogue, this latter occasion is marked by the chazan or sexton's chant of the prayer *El mole rachamim* (O God, who is full of compassion, etc.), a prayer for the dead, mentioning the name of the deceased, which came into vogue in the seventeenth century. Recently, this prayer has become as popular as Kaddish, and since it was chanted by a hired stranger, it has also been commercialized. During the month of Elul, especially on the Sundays, when everyone visits the graves of his or her parents and other kindred, the Jewish cemeteries in this country resound with the prayer El mole rachamim, chanted by someone who is competent to do so, for the benefit of those who do not know Hebrew and cannot recite the prayers themselves. He chants the prayer on behalf of every individual of the family who visits the grave, receiving a coin from each. This prayer is also recited at the unveiling of a tombstone.

Among the S'fardim, the memorial service is called *Hashkabah* (praying for the repose and peace of the dead).

Conclusion

Through several hundred pages, the panorama of the life of the individual Jew has unfolded through long stretches of time and through many lands and climes. We have seen how much Jewish life has changed under the impact of new environments and new civilizations, and how much it remained unchanged throughout the ages. Moving swiftly through three thousand years of Jewish history, we have come to a Jewish cemetery here in America. The cycle of the life of the individual Jew has thus come to an end. But the way of life of the Jewish people, based on the Jewish monotheistic faith, will not perish from the earth, though it may undergo many more transformations.

Notes

Glossary

Index

Notes

The sources as well as the scientific literature referred to in the following notes are merely selective.

All Talmudic tractates mentioned below refer to the Babylonian Talmud, unless preceded by a Y. This symbol is used to indicate Yerushalmi.

The books and treatises in the following list which are referred to repeatedly throughout the notes are given there under the name of the author only:

Benzinger, *Hebraeische Archaeologie*, 3rd ed.
Berliner, *Aus dem Leben der deutschen Juden im Mittelalter.*
Frazer, *The Golden Bough*, one volume ed.
Guedemann, *Geschichte des Erziehungswesens und der Kultur der abendlaendischen Juden waehrend des Mittelalters und der neueren Zeit.*
Krauss, *Talmudische Archaeologie.*
Loew, *Die Lebensalter in der juedischen Literatur.*
Mann, Jacob, "Rabbinic Studies in the Synoptic Gospels," *Hebrew Union College Annual*, 1924.
Samter, *Geburt, Hochzeit und Tod.*
Scheftelowitz, Isidor, Alt-Pal.—*Alt-Palaestinensischer Bauernglaube.*
Scheftelowitz, Isidor, altper.—*Die altpersische Religion und das Judentum.*
Smith, W. Robertson, *Lectures on the Religion of the Semites*, 3rd ed.
Wuttke, *Der Deutsche Volksaberglaube der Gegenwart*, 3rd ed.
J.E.—*Jewish Encyclopedia.*

[1] See Tosefto Shabos 6–7; Shabos 67a–b.

[2] We are not sure whether the birth-stool was already in use in Biblical times, because we cannot be sure about the original meaning of the Hebrew word *mashber* in the Bible (Isa. 37:3; Hos. 13:3). The fact that in Talmud (Shabos 129a; Mishnah Nido 10:5) mashber is used for a birth-stool does not prove that it had this meaning also in Biblical times. Neither are we sure

about the meaning of the Hebrew word *ovnoyim* (Exod. 1:16; Jer. 18:3). See Loew, p. 74, Krauss II, p. 6 and note 53, p. 426. See also the hypotheses of Sarsowski in *Hakedem* I, p. 23 and Spiegelberg in *Zeitschrift fuer Assyriologie* XIV, p. 269.

[3] Exod. 1:19.

[4] Gen. 35:16–18; I Sam. 4:20; see also B'reshis Rabo 82:9.

[5] Jer. 20:15. It is evident from this that in the days of Jeremiah it was customary for the father to be absent from the place where his wife was in labor. Among many other peoples the custom prevailed to place the child at birth on the knees of his father, who thereby acknowledged it as his. We do not have any conclusive proof that, barring cases of adoption, this custom had ever prevailed among Jews. The expression "that she may bear upon my knees" (Gen. 30:3) refers to the adoption of Bilhah's children by Rachel. A case of adoption may also be implied in the expression "the children also of Machir the son of Manasseh were born upon Joseph's knees" (Gen. 50:23). It may imply the adoption of Machir's sons by Joseph. See *The International Critical Commentary*, and Gunkel, *Genesis*, on these two passages. The expression "Why did the knees receive me?" in Job 3:12, being a later source than the time of Jeremiah, does not refer to the knees of the father but rather to the knees of the midwife or some other woman. See Stade in *Zeitschrift fuer die alttestamentliche Wissenschaft* VI, pp. 143 ff. and Benzinger, p. 123.

[6] Pss. 127:3; 128:3; Ruth 4:10.

[7] Ezek. 16:5. This custom of rubbing the new-born babe with salt was still practiced among Jews in Talmudic times (Shabos 129b) and it is still in vogue at the present time among the Arab peasants in Palestine who continue this practice for weeks in succession. They believe that the salt invigorates the child. See *Zeitschrift des Deutschen Palestina—Vereins*, IV, p. 63. The origin of this custom is the primitive belief that salt, as well as garlic, is a safeguard against demons and the evil eye. See Immanuel Loew, "Das Salz," in *Jewish Studies in Memory of G. A. Kohut;* Ploss, *Das Kind* ⁴ I, pp. 227 ff.; Samter, pp. 151–161; I. Scheftelowitz, Alt-Pal., pp. 78–79. Cf. Wuttke, p. 281.

[8] Ruth 4:14–15; Luke 1:58.

[9] The father chooses the name: Gen. 4:26; 5:3, 29; 21:3; 41: 51–52; Exod. 2:22; II Sam. 12:24; Hos. 1:4, 6, 9. The mother chooses the name: Gen. 4:25; 29:32–30:24; 38:4–5; Judg. 13:24; I Sam. 1:20; Isa. 7:14. Relatives and friends suggest a name: Ruth 4:17.

[10] Deut. 25:6; Ruth 4:10. Boaz married Ruth in a levirate marriage "to raise up the name of the dead upon his inheritance, that the name of the dead be not cut off from among his brethren." But the son born of this marriage was not named Mahlon but Obed.

[11] The father performed the operation: Gen. 17:23, the mother, Exod: 4:25. About a knife of stone, see also Josh. 5:2–3.

[12] See Richard Andree, "Die Beschneidung," *Archiv fuer Anthropologie*, Vol. XIII; Ploss, *Das Kind* ³ II, pp. 157 ff. For a brief account of the diffusion of circumcision and of the divergent theories offered by scholars to explain its origin, see article "Circumcision" in *J.E.* and in *En. of Religion and Ethics*.

[13] See Gressmann, *Mose*, pp. 56–61; Ed. Meyer, *Die Israeliten*, p. 59; W. Robertson Smith, p. 328.

[14] See Gunkel "Ueber die Beschneidung im alten Testament," *Archiv fuer Papyrusforschung* II, pp. 13–21; Kautzsch, *Biblische Theologie*, pp. 34–35; Ed. Meyer, *Die Israeliten*, p. 449.

[15] Gen. 34:14 ff.; II Sam. 1:20. The uncircumcised could not belong to the "congregation of Israel" and was forbidden to eat from the Pesach sacrifice, Exod. 12:47–48.

[16] Jer. 4:4; 9:24 and Deut. 10:16; 30:6. Scholars disagree as to whether this metaphor is original to Jeremiah or to Deut. In Lev. 19:23, the Hebrew word for uncircumcised ones, *arelim*, connoting *taboo*, is applied to the fruits in the first three years of newly planted trees. Metaphorically the word *orel* is also used for hardness in speech and in hearing, Exod. 6:12, 30; Jer. 6:10.

[17] Ezek. 31:18–32:32.

[18] Gen. 9:8–17; 17:1–14; Exod. 31:16–17.

[19] Gen. 21:8; I Sam. 1:24.

[20] It is not mentioned anywhere in the Bible that the redemption of the first-born son took place at the sanctuary. The only place where it is mentioned is the Gospel of Luke (2:22–23). But Luke was not a Jew and was liable to err in matters of Jewish usage. He may have used as a pattern for his account the story of Hannah, who when she had weaned Samuel brought him into the house of the Lord in Shiloh. However, we have to presume that in the ancient pre-Josianic days, when the local shrine, the *bomo*, was near at hand, the ceremony of redeeming the first-born son of the mother took place at the local sanctuary. See Jacob Mann.

[21] Exod. 13:13–15; 22:28; 34:20; Num. 3:11–13; 8:16–18.

[22] The theory that pidyon ha-ben was a substitute for human sacrifices goes back to German scholars in the nineteenth century. They, in their zeal to vilify "the religion of the Old Testament," endeavored to "prove" that the God of Israel was in pre-exilic times a Moloch like Chemos, the God of the Moabites to whom Mesha, king of Moab, offered his eldest son as a burnt-offering (II Kings 3). According to these scholars human sacrifices were a legal part of the cult of the God of Israel. They applied this view to the interpretation of Exod. 22:28: "The first-born of thy sons shalt thou give unto Me," and maintained that it was only after the Babylonian exile that "the religion of the Old Testament" was reformed and the Moloch cult prohibited (Lev. 20:1–5; Deut. 18:10).

This rather superficial and ill-founded position was properly rejected by competent authorities. It can hardly be questioned that human sacrifices occurred in the heathen stage through which the ancestors of the Hebrews passed in pre-historic times. It was a practice which had prevailed throughout Semitic heathendom. As far as the Bible is concerned, human sacrifices are not mentioned anywhere as a legal part of the cult of Israel. The moral of the tale of the sacrificing of Isaac is that the forefathers of the children of Israel rejected human sacrifices already in pre-Mosaic times. Jephthah, like Samson and the other Judges, was a hero of the sword, not a religious leader. It is not at all surprising that this "mighty man of valor, the son of a harlot," who had been a leader of a band of marauders in the desert, expressed his devotion to his God in the manner of the neighboring heathens. The slaying of Zebah and Zalmunah by Gideon (Judg. 8), of Agag by Samuel (I Sam. 15), and of the children of Saul by the Gibeonites (II Sam. 21) were executions of war and blood revenge and do not belong to the category of sacrifices. It was only in the Assyro-Babylonian times that the heinous Moloch cult penetrated to the Jews from Mesopotamia, along with many other strange heathenish rites of the Assyrians and Babylonians, and was practiced publicly in Jerusalem in "the valley of the son of Hinom" (II Kings 16:3; 21:6; Jer. 7:31; 19:5; Ezek. 16:20; 36; 20:26–31; 23:37–39). It seems from Micah 6:7 that there were in those days many Jews, apparently of the higher classes, who, under foreign influences, misconstrued the above cited verse 28 in Exod. 22 to mean that the first-born should be sacrificed as burnt-offerings, exactly as it was misinterpreted by some modern Bible critics. It was apparently in allusion to these Jewish Molochists and their misinterpretation of Exod. 22:28 that Ezekiel said: "Wherefore I gave them also statutes that were not good and ordinances whereby they should not live; and I polluted them in their own gifts in that they set apart all that openeth the womb, that I might destroy them, to the end that they might know that I am the Lord" (20:25–26). Ezekiel could not have meant that as a punishment God commanded his people to sacrifice their first-born sons. This would have been a flat contradiction of verse 2 in the same chapter where it says that God gave to Israel His statutes and ordinances in order that the man who keeps them shall live by them. Ezekiel could only mean to say that as a punishment God so formulated His law in Exod. 22:28 to give cause to the Jewish Molochists to misinterpret it.

Thus, competent scholars are agreed that the first-born was redeemed from service in the sanctuary, for the first-born preceded the Levites as the servants of God in His sanctuary, as it is explicitly stated in Num. 3:41 and 8:16–18. Compare the same expression for the sacredness of the Levites in Num. 8:16, "given unto Me," and the sacredness of the first-born in Exod. 22:28, "shalt thou give unto Me." See Benzinger, p. 357; Evaritus Mader, *Die Menschenopfer der Alten Hebraer und der Benachbarten Voelker;* W. Robertson Smith, pp. 464–465 and 688–689. See also Hugo Gressmann, *Die aelteste Geschichtsschreibung und Prophetie Israels,* 2te Auflage, p. 256.

[23] Lev. 12:1–8.

[24] See Frazer, pp. 207–208; Ploss, *Das Kind* [3], pp. 381 ff.; Samter, pp. 22 ff.

[25] Shabos 129a; Mishnah Nido 10:5; Mishnah Shabos 18:3; Mishnah Rosh Hashono 2:5; Bovo Kamo 59a; Avodo Zoro 26a; Soto 11b; Tosefto Y'vomos 9:4; Tosefto Makos 2:5; Y. K'subos 5, Halocho 6.

[26] Vayikro Rabo 27:7; Shabos 129b; B'reshis Rabo 34 at the end.

[27] Tosefto Shabos 6.

[28] Tosefto Makos 2:4; Tosefto Kelim, Bovo M'tsio, 1–12; 8:4; Tosefto Kelim, Bovo Basro, 7–12; Shabos 58b. See article "Birth, Jewish" by M. Gaster in *En. of Religion and Ethics.*

[29] Josephus, Apion II, par. 25; Gitin 57a. See Ploss, *Das Kind* [3], pp. 61–63; Scheftelowitz, Alt-Pal., pp. 25–27.

[30] II Macc. 6:10.

[31] See Schuerer, Geschichte III, pp. 164 ff.

[32] Josephus, Ant. XX, chaps. 2–4.

[33] See Schuerer, Geschichte III, p. 552.

[34] Book of Jubilees, chap. 15; Sanhedrin 32b; Bovo Basro 60b; N'dorim 32a. About the expression *Sh'vuo ha-ben,* see Krauss II, pp. 11–12 and Jacob Mann.

[35] Mishnah Shabos 19:1; M'nochos 42a; Shabos 130b, 137b, 156a.

[36] Ruth Rabo 6:5; Y. Chagigo 2, Halocho 1.

[37] Tosefto M'gilo 4:15.

[38] Koheleth Rabo 3:4; D'vorim Rabo 9:1. See A. Buechler, *The Political and Social Leaders of the Jewish Community of Sipporis.*

[39] See Krauss II, p. 439, note 123.

[40] Book of Jubilees 11:15 (Terah named his son Abram after the name of his mother's father); B'reshis Rabo 37:10 (a discussion between two Tannoim as to why it had become the custom to name children after their dead ancestors instead of naming them according to the events of the time, as they did in former days). A son named after his father or grandfather who was still alive: Eruvin 85b–86a; Y. Nozir 4, Halocho 6; Tosefto Nido 5:15; Luke 1:59. See Buchanan Gray, *Studies in Hebrew Proper Names;* the same author, "Children Named after Ancestors in the Aramaic Papyri from Elephantine and Assuan," *Studien zur Semitischen Philologie und Religionsgeschichte, Julius Wellhausen gewidmet.* See Krauss II, p. 13 and Jacob Mann.

[41] Vayikro Rabo 32:5 (Israel was delivered from Egypt because they did not change their names); Gitin 11b (most Jews outside of Erets Yisroel bear heathen names).

[42] The Aramaic version is first mentioned in the Sidur of R. Amrom Gaon and the Sidur of R. Saadiah Gaon (9th and 10th centuries), the Hebrew version is first mentioned in Shibole Haleket (13th century).

[43] B'choros 51b.

[44] P'sochim 121b; T'rumas Hadeshen, 268.

[45] Book of Jubilees 3:9–14; Nido 31b; B'reshis Rabo 20:17; Mishnah Nido 3:7.

[46] Mishnah Sh'kolim 6:5; Mishnah Soto 1:5; Eruvin 32a. See Loew, p. 111.

[47] Elijah Levita, *Tishbi, s.v.,* Lilith; Isaac Holzer, "Aus dem Leben der alten Judengemeinde zu Worms," *Zeitschrift fuer die Geschichte der Juden in Deutschland,* Jahrgang V.

[48] Machzor Vitri by R. Simcho, a pupil of Rashi, mentions as an established custom, observing the eve of the b'ris by a joyous feast, but does not call it Watch Night. See J. Bergmann, *Monatsschrift,* 1927, pp. 165 ff.; Guedemann, III, pp. 103 ff.; J. Perles, *Graetz Jubelschrift,* pp. 23 ff.; *Filologishe Shriftn* (Yiddish) I (the Watch Night as observed by the Jews of Vienna at the beginning of the 15th century); Wuttke, pp. 386 ff.

[49] The words in Genesis 17:9 "and as for thee, thou shalt keep My covenant" were interpreted by the Jewish homilists to mean that watch shall be kept on the eve of the b'ris (the Hebrew word for "thou shalt keep," *tishmor,* has also the meaning of "thou shalt watch"). Also the words of Koheleth 11:2 "Divide a portion into seven, yea, even into eight" were interpreted to mean that on the seventh day after birth a feast shall be held as on the eighth day. See R. Jacob Chagiz, *Halochos K'tanos,* 169; Jacob Glassberg, *Zichron B'ris Lorishonim,* 65–148.

[50] Loew, pp. 81 ff.

[51] Pirke R. Eliezer 29; Yalkut Shim-oni 71, on Gen. 13:17.

[52] Shabos 67b; N'dorim 56a and Rashi, *ad loc.;* Moed Koton 27a; and Rashi, *ad loc.;* Sanhedrin 20a, 92a and Rashi, *ad loc.;* Shulchan Aruch, Yore Deo 178:3. See Scheftelowitz, Alt-Pal., p. 4.

[53] Tosefto 6:4; Shulchan Aruch Yore Deo 179:17 and commentaries thereon. See Samter, p. 53, and Bergmann, "Der Stuhl und der Kelch des Elijah," *Monatsschrift*, 1927.

[54] See *Birke Joseph* by H. J. D. Azulai on Shulchan Aruch Yore Deo 179:17. It is evident from this commentator, an Oriental rabbi of the 18th century, that it was only in the course of a very long time that the table bedecked with food on the Watch Night and the chair of Elijah were completely disassociated from one another in the popular mind. See also the chapter on Elijah's chair in *Zichron B'ris Lorishonim* by Jacob Glassberg. A different role in the history of the Jewish ceremonial was played by Elijah's cup on the Seder night, the counterpart of Elijah's chair at the b'ris. See *The Jewish Festivals* by the writer, pp. 80 ff.

[55] See Lipman, *Sefer Nitsochon*, 22 and M. Gaster, Ma'asch Book, II, pp. 391–392.

[56] Loew, p. 83.

[57] Shibole Haleket.

[58] See Holzer as in note 47.

[59] Loew, p. 104.

[60] Sefer Chasidim (ed. Wistinetzki), p. 114.

[61] The son of Judah Halevi's daughter was called Judah after his grandfather while the latter was still alive. About the Jews of Yemen see *Even Sapher* I, 51a.

[62] See Guedemann III, pp. 104–105; Holzer as in note 47; A. Landau in *Zeitschrift des Vereins fuer Volkskunde*, 1899; Loew, pp. 104–105; J. Perles in *Graetz Jubelschrift*. About the Teutonic goddess, Dame Holle, see Grimm, *Teutonic Mythology*, pp. 267 ff. See also בער, סדר עבודת ישראל: 494.
פסוקי התורה שאומרים הנערים אצל ילד זכר קודם שיקראו לו את שמו החול (חול קרייש).

[63] נחלת שבעה מ"ה, י"ב.

[64] Yosef Omets, 361 (17th century).

[65] About naming children in general see Ploss, *Das Kind*[3] I, pp. 408 ff. About naming children among Jews see Hershberg, *Hatkufo*, Vols. XXII, XXV; Lauterbach, "The Naming of Children," *Central Conference of American Rabbis*, 1932; Zunz, "Namen der Juden," *Ges. Schriften* II. See also Tylor, *Primitive Culture* II, pp. 4–5, and article "Names" in *J.E.*

[66] T'shuvos Ha-g'onim, Sha-arei T'shuvo, 47.

[67] Shulchan Aruch Yore Deo 305:15 and *Sifse Kohen, ad loc.*

[68] Shulchan Aruch Orach Chayyim 282:17 and *Mogen Avrohom, ad loc.* See Loew, p. 80 and Ploss, *Das Kind*[3] I, pp. 396 ff.

[69] Nido 31b; Onon, *Sefer Hamitsvos;* S. Bernfeld, *R'shumos* I; Lunts, *Jerusalem* I; Almaliach, A., *Hashiloach*, 24.

[70] Pulner, "Zur Volkskunde der georgischen Juden," *Mitteilungen zur Juedischen Volkskunde*, 31 and 32.

[71] Tanchumo, P'kude 3; "Y'tsiras Havlad," Eisenstein, *Otsar Midroshim;* for a detailed bibliography of the sources, with critical remarks, see Ginzberg, *Legends* V, note 20 on Adam.

[72] See M. Gaster, "The Chronicles of Jerahmeel," *Oriental Translation Fund,* new series IV, p. LXIV; Guedemann, "Mythenmischung in der

Hagada," *Monatsschrift*, 1876; K. Kohler, *Jewish Theology*, pp. 215 and 289; Scheftelowitz, altper., pp. 157–158.

[73] See Sota 21b about the sorceress Jochani and Rashi, *ad loc.;* also *Oruch*, *s.v.*, Jochani.

[74] About the magic circle, *Kaporos* and *Shofar* see *The Jewish Festivals* by the writer, pp. 164–167 and 206–207.

[75] See Frazer, *Folk-Lore in the Old Testament* III, pp. 1–18, and Samter, pp. 136 ff.

[76] About sympathetic magic, see Frazer, pp. 11 ff. About untying knots see Frazer, pp. 239–240 and Samter, pp. 121 ff.

[77] See R. Campbell Thompson, *Semitic Magic*, pp. 65 ff.; by the same author, article "Semi-human demons," *En. of Religion and Ethics;* M. Gaster, "Two Thousand Years of a Charm Against the Child-Stealing Witch," *Studies and Texts II;* Max Gruenbaum, *Gesammelte Aufsaetze*, pp. 94 ff.; James Montgomery, *Aramaic Incantation Texts from Nippur*, pp. 68 ff. and pp. 75 ff.; F. Perles, *Orientalistische Literaturzeitung* XVIII, pp. 179–180; Scheftelowitz, Alt-Pal., pp. 5 ff.

[78] Long hair: Eruvin 100b; a man alone in a house in danger of being seized by Lilith: Shabos 151b; a human being born with wings like a Lilith: Nido 24b; Ahriman the son of Lilith: Bobo Basro 73a.

[79] II Alphabet of Ben-Sira, Eisenstein, *Otsar Midroshim*. See Bacher, "Lilith, Koenigin von Smaragd," *Monatsschrift*, 1870; Ginzberg, *Legends* V, note 40 on Adam; G. Sholem, *Kirias Sefer X;* I. Zoler, *Filologishe Shriftn* III.

[80] For pictures of Hebrew amulets to guard against Lilith, see article "Amulets" in *J.E.*

[81] Tosefto Shabos 6; Scheftelowitz, Alt-Pal., pp. 39–40, 66–69; Tylor, *Primitive Culture* I, p. 140.

[82] Cf. Shabos 67b and Rashi, *ad loc.*, and Rosh Hashono 16b.

[83] Pr. 10:2. *Ts'doko* which originally signified righteousness, the right conduct, was interpreted in post-Biblical times to mean especially almsgiving. About changing the name as a magic means, see Sefer Chasidim (ed. Wistinetzki), par. 365; Lauterbach as in note 65; Loew, 107 ff.; Scheftelowitz, Alt-Pal., pp. 55–57.

[84] Machzor Vitri, par. 507. Cf. Rashi, B'reshis Rabo on Gen. 21:8 (on the day when Isaac was weaned, the day when they put him in a cradle).

[85] See Wuttke, p. 385.

[86] Sefer Chasidim, ed. Wistinetzki, p. 106.

[87] See the collection of Yiddish folk-songs by Ginsburg and Marek, pp. 59 ff.; the collection of Yiddish folk-songs by J. L. Cahan, II, pp. 97 ff., and *Jewish Folklore*, edited by J. L. Cahan, pp. 51 ff.

[88] Yomo 38b.

[89] II. Macc. 7:27; Nido 9a; D'vorim Rabo 7:12.

[90] Gen. 21:8; I Sam. 1:24. According to D'vorim Rabo 1:22 and Pirke R. Eliezer 29, the great feast of Gen. 21:8 took place on the day of circumcision. Some Jewish homilists in the Middle Ages have interpreted *hgml* (the Hebrew word for weaned) to mean the eighth day of circumcision. According to these homilists h and g have the numerical value of 8 and ml is the infinitive of the Hebrew verb for circumcising.

[91] See Frazer, pp. 231 ff. and pp. 68–681; Ploss, *Das Kind* [3] II, pp. 64 ff; W. R. Smith, p. 324; Scheftelowitz, Alt-Pal., pp. 149–150.

[92] The prohibition of rounding the corners of the head, Lev. 19:27, is explained by modern scholars as forbidding the heathen cult of hair-offering. See W. R. Smith, pp. 325 ff. and Wellhausen, *Reste Arabischen Heidentums* [2], pp. 198–199. Cf. Apocryphic Book of Baruch 6:30 (Epistle of Jeremiah).

[93] Judah Elzet, "Miminhagei Yisroel," in *R'shumos* I; I. Goldfarb, "Hilulo d'rabi Simeon ben Yochai," in *Luach Achi-osof*, 5664; A. Sh. Hershberg, "Ha-s'fardim b'erets Yisroel," in *Hashiloach*, XVIII; Lunts, *Jerusalem* I.

[94] See F. T. Elinorthy, *The Evil Eye*, and the most comprehensive book on this subject by S. Seligmann, *Die Zauberkraft des Auges und das Berufen*.

[95] Bovo M'tsio 107b

[96] See Ludwig Blau, *Das altjuedische Zauberwesen*, pp. 152 ff.; Almaliach as in note 69; Regina Lilienthal, "Das Kind bei den Juden," *Mitteilungen zur juedischen Volkskunde*, 1908.

[97] Vayikro Rabo 26:7; Tanchumo, Buber, Emor 35.

[98] See Rashi on Num. 12:1.

[99] Mishnah Shabos 6:9–10; Kidushin 73b; Rambam, Resp. (ed. Freimann), p. 5; Berliner, pp. 96 ff.; Guedemann, I, pp. 199 ff.; Almaliach as in note 69.

[100] See Schrader, *Keilinschriften und das Alte Testament* [3], p. 364 and Seligmann as in note 94, p. 410.

[101] Beis Yosef, Tur Orach Chayim, 308.

[102] See Schechter, "The Child in Jewish Literature," *Studies in Judaism* I.

[103] Josephus, Apion II, par. 18; Suko 42a.

[104] See Shulchan Aruch Orach Chayim 4:2 and more at length in *Chaye Odom* 2:1. About nails see *The Jewish Festivals* by the writer, note 33. About water as a charm to forestall harm by evil spirits see Scheftelowitz, Alt-Pal., pp. 71 ff. See also below, p. 215 and p. 290.

[105] Deut. 6:7; 11:19; Judg. 8:14; Isa. 8:1; 10:19; 29:12; Hab. 2:2.

[106] The term *Beis Midrosh* is first mentioned in the Hebrew Ben-Sira 51:22. See R. H. Kennet, *Ancient Hebrew Social Life and Custom;* Klostermann, *Schulwesen im alten Israel.*

[107] Bovo Basro 21a.

[108] Midrash Echo, proem 2; K'subos 5a; Sanhedrin 17b; Shabos 119b; Vayikro Rabo 27:2; 30:1.

[109] Avodo Zoro 3b.

[110] Bovo Basro 21a; Mishnah Shabos 1:3; Mishnah Kidushin 4:13.

[111] Mishnah Bovo Basro 2:3; B'reshis Rabo 65:16; D'vorim Rabo 8:4.

[112] M'gilo 21a; Pirke Ovos 1:4 and Ovos de R. Noson, *ad loc.;* Bamidbor Rabo 21:15; Tosefto Kelim, Bovo Basro, 1:11.

[113] Shir Hashirim Rabo 1:13; 6:17; Horoyos 12:1; Midrash Echo, proem 30; Sanhedrin 95b; B'reshis Rabo 1:5; D'vorim Rabo 8:3; Gitin 60a; Tosefto Yodayim 2:11.

[114] Midrash Echo 2:5; K'subos 50a; M'chilto on Exod. 13:14; Pirke Ovos 5:15; Vayikro Rabo 7:3 ("Why does one begin to teach the children with the Priestly Torah and not with B'reshis? Because the children are pure and

the sacrifices are pure, let the pure ones come and occupy themselves with the pure ones"). The strange custom of beginning to teach the child Pentateuch with the sacrificial laws of Leviticus, which persisted to our day, was discussed by many scholars. The explanation cited here from Vayikro Rabo was thought up in later times, and does not explain the origin of the custom. The most plausible explanation is the one given by Nathan Drazin in his book, *History of Jewish Education*, pp. 82–83. According to this theory the custom sprang up after the destruction of the Second Temple, in order to make the child aware of the significance of the Temple and the glory that was lost by its destruction.

[115] Yalkut on Deut. 32:24; Kidushin 30a; Shabos 119b, 129b; Ta-anis 30a; Mishnah Bovo M'tsio 2:11; Tosefto Suko 2:6; Bovo Basro 21a.

[116] Kidushin 29a; B'reshis Rabo 63:14 ("Until the age of thirteen Jacob and Esau went together to the Beis Sefer; after the age of thirteen one went to the Beis Midrosh and the other went to the heathen temples"). For more details and a full bibliography of sources, see N. Drazin as in note 114; L. Ginzberg, "The Jewish Primary School," in *Students, Scholars and Saints*; Krauss III, pp. 200 ff.; Nathan Morris, *The Jewish School*.

[117] Deut. 33:4; Lev. 1:1; Ezek. 3:3; Pss. 119:99, 103. The translation of verse 99 as given here is the conventional one according to Rashi. The modern translation, "I have more understanding than all my teachers," is according to the interpretation of Ibn Ezra.

[118] The name *cheder* (room) for the primary school was in use already as far back as the beginning of the 17th century. See Simcho Osof, *M'koros L'toldos Hachinuch* I, p. 78.

[119] *Machzor Vitri; Sefer Horokeach.* See Guedemann, I, pp. 50 ff.; Zunz, *Zur Geschichte und Literatur*, pp. 167 ff.

[120] See Emanuel Gamoran, *Changing Conceptions in Jewish Education;* A. M. Lifshitz, "Hacheder" in Hatkufo VII, pp. 294–352; I. Stern, "Baschreibung fun a cheder" in *Schriften für psychologie un pedagogic* I; Simcho Osof as in note 118, Vol. IV.

[121] Bovo M'tsio 96a.

[122] Exod. 30:14; Lev. 27:5; Num. 1:3, 20; 14:29.

[123] Mishnah Nido 5:6.

[124] See Heinrich Schurtz, *Altersklassen und Maennerbuende* II, pp. 83 ff.; article "Age of Majority," in *En. of Social Sciences;* Schechter, *Studies in Judaism* I, p. 307. The verses of the Bible referred to in note 122 belong to the so-called Priestly Writing of the Pentateuch which is, as a whole, a product of post-exilic times. Schechter, rejecting the Higher Criticism of the Bible and maintaining the traditional Mosaic origin of all Pentateuchal laws, was thus forced to ascribe to a Roman influence the Talmudic law of attainment of majority at thirteen for a boy, and twelve for a girl. About 13 as a sacred number among the Oriental peoples and an ill-omened number among Europeans, see Berliner, p. 101, and Scheftelowitz, Alt-Pal., pp. 145–146.

[125] Ovos 5:21. See also K'subos 50a.

[126] B'reshis Rabo 63:14.

[127] Sofrim 18:5.

[128] Suko 42a; M'gilo 23a; Yomo 82a; Sofrim 18:7.

[129] Cf. Tur Orach Chayim 37 and Schulchan Aruch Orach Chayim, *Karo* and *Ramo* and the commentaries thereon.

[130] See *Joseph Omets*, p. 357.

[131] About the Bar Mitsvo feast see Osof, as in note 118, I, p. 102; *Yam Shel Shlomo* on Bovo Kamo 7:37; *Zohar Chodosh* on Gen. 1:14. About the Bar Mitsvo celebration in general see Krauss III, p. 222; Loew, pp. 210 ff.; Yitschok Rivkind, *L'os U'lzikoron;* article, "Bar Mizwah," in *J.E.*

[132] See Holzer as in note 47; Osof as in note 118, I, p. 120.

[133] Almaliach, *Hashiloach*, 24; Lunts, *Jerusalem* I.

[134] *Allgemeine Zeitung des Judentums*, 1839, pp. 278–279.

[135] Ps. 128:6; Prov. 17:6; Gen. 24:4; 28:2; Num. 26:8–11.

[136] Cant. 8:2; I Sam. 18:6–7; II Macc. 3:19.

[137] About the Jews of Yemen see Erich Brauer, *Ethnologie der Jemenitischen Juden*, pp. 120 ff.; about marriage conditions and marriage customs among the Arabs today see Hilma Granqvist, "Marriage Conditions in a Palestinian Village" (*Societas Scientiarum Fennica Commentationes Humanarum Litterarum* III, 8, VI, 8, Helsingfors, 1931, 1935); Elihu Grant, *The Peasantry of Palestine*, pp. 53 ff.; John D. Whiting, "Village Life in the Holy Land," *The National Geographic Magazine*, March, 1914.

[138] See Exod. 22:15–16 and Deut. 22:28–29.

[139] I Sam. 18:25; Josh. 15:16–17; Judg. 1:12–13.

[140] Code Hammurabi, par. 159–160.

[141] Deut. 20:7; 22:23–29; 28:30. See A. Buechler, "Das juedische Verloebnis" (*Israel Lewy Festschrift*).

[142] Cf. Mal. 2:14; Prov. 2:17; Tobit 7:12. This betrothal formula is quoted here from the papyri of the Jews of Elephantine of the fifth century B.C.E., which will be fully dealt with in the following chapter. See A. Cowley, *Aramaic Papyri of the Fifth Century*, p. 44. Cf. Hosea 2:4 in which this betrothal formula is reversed. It is possible that "she is not my wife, neither am I her husband" was the current formula of divorce in the time of Hosea. In Gen. 24:51 and Tobit 7:13 we have also a different formula of betrothal pronounced by the father or brother of the girl. Cf. Kidushin 5b and Tosefto Kidushin 1:1, where it is declared as not valid if she gives him money or anything of value and says to him "I am betrothed to you." See Louis M. Epstein, *The Jewish Marriage Contract*, pp. 55 ff. In Tobit we have a case when betrothal and wedding were celebrated together without the intervening of any time between. About such cases see Buechler as in note 141.

[143] See Crawley and Besterman, *The Mystic Rose* II, pp. 25 ff.; Westermarck, *The History of Human Marriage*, 5th ed., II, pp. 496 ff.

[144] Gideon's Canaanitic concubine also stayed with her folk in Shechem, Judg. 8:31. See Hugo Gressmann, *Die Anfaenge Israels* [2], p. 214 and p. 241. Cf. W. Robertson Smith, *Kinship and Marriage in Early Arabia*, p. 176.

[145] Judg. 14:20; Ps. 45:15.

[146] Cant. 3:6–8 and cf. also I Macc. 9:37–39. The "dread in the night" were evil spirits believed to have great power over the bride and the groom on the wedding night. See about this further below.

[147] K'subos 17a.

[148] Judg. 14:12, 17.

[149] Judg. 14:18. This answer to Samson's riddle sounds rather like a question demanding an answer. See H. Steinthal, "The Legend of Samson" (Appendix to *Mythology Among the Hebrews,* by Ignaz Goldziher), pp. 394 ff. See also Hermann Gunkel, "Simson" (*Reden und Aufsaetze*).

[150] II Kings 4:10.

[151] Cf. Exod. 21:1–11 and Deut. 15:12–17. This same evolution in the attitude towards women can be traced in the two versions of the tenth commandment of the Decalogue. One version, apparently the older one (Exod. 20), says: "Thou shalt not covet thy neighbour's house, thou shalt not covet thy neighbour's wife, nor his man-servant, nor his maid-servant, nor his ox, nor his ass, nor anything that is thy neighbour's." The wife of the neighbor is set on the same level as the other possessions. Only the house of the neighbor is here in a separate category. One's own house was regarded as too precious to be put on the same plane as other property. In a second, apparently a later version (Deut. 5), the commandment reads: "Neither shalt thou covet thy neighbour's wife; neither shalt thou desire thy neighbour's house, his field, or his man-servant or his maid-servant, his ox or his ass, or anything that is thy neighbour's." In this version, the wife, not the house, is in a separate category.

[152] See Cowley as in note 142; *Aramaic Papyri Discovered at Assuan,* edited by Sayce; Eduard Meyer, *Der Papyrusfund von Elephantine.*

[153] Jer. 32.

[154] Par. 128 and 171. Cf. above pp. 127 f.

[155] Prov. 19:13–14; 21:9; 31:10–31.

[156] Ben-Sira 7:24–26; 25:24–25; 36:24–27.

[157] Tosefto K'subos 12:1; K'subos 82b; Y. K'subos 8, Halocho 11. About the various phases in the history of the mohar see Epstein as in note 142, pp. 19 ff. About the transformation of the bride price among other peoples see Westermarck, as in note 143, Vol. II.

[158] Vayikro Rabo 20:7; 27:2. Cf. above p. 97. About Ben Azzai see Y'vomos 63b; Soto 4b. See S. Baron, *A Social and Religious History of the Jews,* I, p. 261 and Botsford and Sihler, *Hellenic Civilization,* pp. 663–664.

[159] Y'vomos 62b, 63:a; Kidushin 29b–30a.

[160] Koheleth Rabo 11:14.

[161] Vayikro Rabo 20:7.

[162] Kidushin 29b; Shir Hashirim Rabo 7:7.

[163] Mishnah Ovos 5:21; Kidushin 29b–30a; 41:a–b; Y'vomos 62b; Sanhedrin 76a–b; Mishnah Y'vomos 13; Tosefto Y'vomos 13.

[164] B'reshis Rabo 49:10; Mishnah K'subos 9:4. See Krauss II, pp. 24 ff.

[165] Mishnah K'subos 7:7–9; Shir Hashirim Rabo 4:3; Ta-anis 24a; B'choros 45b; Bovo Basro 110a.

[166] Mishnah K'subos 7:10; K'subos 22a; P'sochim 4:9a; Derech Erets Rabo 1; Kidushin 70a–b.

[167] P'sochim 49b.

[168] K'subos 28b; Ruth Rabo 7:10.

[169] Kidushin 12b, 44b; K'subos 5a.

170 Mishnah K'subos 13:5; K'subos 52b–53a; Bovo M'tsio 74b.

171 Kidushin 70a. See also Josephus, Apion II, par. 24.

172 Mishnah K'subos, chaps. 1–7; K'subos 12b; Y'vomos 63b.

173 Gitin 89a.

174 Kidushin 5b, 6ab, 7a, 9a. On the relation between the oral and the written declaration of betrothal and the relation of the latter to the K'subo, see Epstein, as in note 142, pp. 55 ff. and cf. Chanoch Albeck, "Ho-eirusin U-sh'toroseihem," in *Kovets mado-i l'zecher Moshe Shur*.

175 Kidushin 2b: "The rabbinical term connotes that he interdicts her to all men as hekdesh" (that which is dedicated to a sacred purpose). Tosafos, *ad loc.*, "Originally the meaning of *m'kudeshes li* was apparently devoted to me to a determined end." See A. Geiger, *Nachgelassene Schriften* III, p. 324, and Jacob Neubauer, *Beitraege zur Geschichte des biblisch-talmudischen Eheschliessungsrechts*, pp. 195–198.

176 See the benediction of betrothal in the Boraiso K'subos 7b (2nd century), which is still in use today.

177 P'sochim 49a and Rashi, *ad loc.*

178 Bobo M'tsio 104a; Y. K'subos 4, Halocho 8; Tosefto K'subos 4:9. Note in this K'subo of Hille's time the formula "according to the law of Moses and Israel," cf. the formula "according to the law of Moses" in the Book of Tobit 7:13, and see Albeck as in note 174.

179 K'subos 7b, 12a.

180 Mishnah K'subos 1:1, 5:2; Gen, 24:55; Mishnah Betso 5:2; K'subos 7a.

181 Y. D'mai 4, Halocho 2; Vayikro Rabo 11:2.

182 K'subos 17a; Ovos D'Rabbi Noson 41:13.

183 B'reshis Rabo 18:12; Sh'mos Rabo 41:6; Mishnah K'subos 2:1; Mishnah Soto 9:14; Mishnah Kelim 23:4; III Macc. 4:6–8; B'rochos 61a; Eruvim 18a.

184 B'rochos 50b; Moed Koton 9b; Soto 49b; K'subos 17a; Gitin 57a; Matthew 25:1; John 3:29.

185 K'subos 17a; Midrash T'hilim 24; Yalkut Shim-oni, Job, 917.

186 B'reshis Rabo 70:17; Vayikro Rabo 28:2; Moed Koton 28b; K'subos 7b–8a; Sanhedrin 101a, citing Rabbi Akiba. *Beis Mishteh* does not mean a tavern or a house of a banquet, but a house of a wedding feast, so in Jer. 16:8; Koheleth 7:2; Mishnah B'rochos 1:1; Mishnah Soto 9:11; Mishnah T'rumo 11:10; Tosefto Bovo M'tsio 8:28, and in many other places.

187 Mishnah D'mai 4:2; Tosefto Bovo M'tsio 8:28. For more detailed discussions on marriage in Talmudic times, see Buechler, "The Induction of the Bride and the Bridegroom" (*Posnanski Memorial Book*); Epstein, as in note 142; A. S. Hershberg, "Minhagei Ho-eirusin V'ha-nisuin" in *He-osid*, V. Krauss, II; Jacob Mann; Joseph Perles, "Die juedische Hochzeit in nachbiblischer Zeit," *Monatsschrift*, 1860, pp. 339 ff., in an English translation: *Hebrew Characteristics*, New York, 1875.

188 Harkavi, Resp. G'onim, 195; Tosafos on Kidushin 41a and K'subos 54b.

189 For a bibliography of sources and literature on this subject, see Krauss II, note 246 on pp. 450–451.

190 K'subos 48b. See Epstein as in note 142, pp. 13–15.

191 Machzor Vitri, pp. 586–588. See Epstein as in note 142, p. 16.

¹⁹² Tosafos on Kidushin 9a; Harkavi, Resp. G'onim, 65; Tikune Zohar 5; Resp. G'onim, Sha'are Tsedek III, 16. It is evident from this latter source that the custom of using a wedding ring first appeared in post-Talmudic times among the Jews of the East. This refutes the theory that among the Jews the custom of using a wedding ring arose in the West under the influence of the Romans, who used an iron wedding ring.

¹⁹³ Tractate Sof'rim 19:9. See Loew, pp. 185 ff.

¹⁹⁴ Karo and Ramo in Shulchan Aruch Even Ho'ezer 55 and Resp. Maharam Mints 109.

¹⁹⁵ Ramo, Shulchan Aruch Yore Deo 391:3 and Even Ho'ezer 61:1. See Loew as in note 193 and also Loew, *Gesammelte Schriften* III.

¹⁹⁶ See above p. 130 and p. 154. See Louis Finkelstein, *Jewish Self-Government in the Middle Ages*, pp. 83–84 and pp. 271–272; S. Osof, "L'chayei Hamishpocho" in *Jubilee Volume of S. Krauss*.

¹⁹⁷ See Josef Ometz, par. 657; *Mogen Avrohom* on Orach Chayim 551:1; Guedemann III, p. 119; Holzer as in note 47; Krauss II, p. 456, note 302.

¹⁹⁸ See Maharil, Eruve Chatseros; Mordechai on Alphas, Betso, chap. 5; Resp. Radbaz IV, 132.

¹⁹⁹ Resp. Maharam Mints, 102. More details about Jewish marriage in the Middle Ages in Abrahams, *Jewish Life in the Middle Ages*, chap. IX; Berliner, pp. 41 ff.; Guedemann III, pp. 119 ff.; Albert Wolf, "Fahrende Leute bei den Juden," *Mitteilungen zur juedischen Folkskunde*, 1908–1909; article "Badhan" in *J.E.*

²⁰⁰ Mishnah K'subos 2:1; 7:6; Yomo 47a. See Aptowitzer and Krauss in *Monatsschrift*, 1923, pp. 67–68 and 186–202; Krauss in *Hebrew Union College Annual*, XIX; Scheftelowitz, Alt-Pal., pp. 153–154.

²⁰¹ See Epstein as in note 142, p. 38; M. Gaster, the Ketubah; Jews' College Jubilee Volume, pp. 101 ff.; Schechter, "Geniza Specimens," *Jewish Quarterly Review*, 1901, pp. 218 ff.; article "Ketubah" in *J.E.*

²⁰² Loew, p. 189.

²⁰³ Maharil, Hilchos N'suin.

²⁰⁴ See Holzer as in note 47.

²⁰⁵ This method of confirming a purchase, or any transaction, was known among Jews under the name of *Kinyan Sudor*, agreement by a kerchief. See article "Alienation and Acquisition" in *J.E.*

²⁰⁶ See Lunts and Almaliach as in note 69 and Hershberg, "Has'fardim B'erets Yisroel," *Hashiloach* XVIII.

²⁰⁷ See Erich Brauer, *Ethnologie der Jemenitischen Juden*, pp. 119 ff.; Tabib, *Golas Temon*.

²⁰⁸ Chulin 7b; Soto 1b; B'reshis Rabo 68:3.

²⁰⁹ B'reshis Rabo 68:4; Vayikro Rabo 8:1.

²¹⁰ Moed Koton 18b.

²¹¹ Tanchumo, Buber, Introduction, p. 136.

²¹² Sefer Chasidim, ed. Wistinetzki, p. 286. See Abrahams, "Marriages Are Made in Heaven." *The Book of Delight and Other Papers*, pp. 172 ff.; Ginzberg, *Legends* V, pp. 75–76.

²¹³ This belief is based on a Midrashic amplification of the story of the

wooing of Rebekah. In Gen. 24, verse 50, Bethuel is mentioned as the father of Rebekah, while in verses 53 and 55, only a brother and a mother are mentioned. The explanation of the Midrash is that Bethuel died suddenly that same night because at the outset he tried to obstruct the match, B'reshis Rabo 60:7.

214 See Berliner, p. 46; Loew, pp. 192–193. Scheftelowitz, Alt-Pal., pp. 135–138.

215 Tur Yore Deo and Shulchan Aruch Yore Deo 179. See Scheftelowitz as in previous note.

216 Resp. G'onim, Shaare T'shuvo 278; Shibole Haleket Hasholem 235; Tur Orach Chayim and Shulchan Aruch Orach Chayim 493. See Biram, "Lagbeomer" in Ost und West, 1906, pp. 307 ff.; Landsberger, "Der Brauch in den Tagen Zwischen dem Pessach—und Schabuothfeste sich der Eheschliessung zu entziehen" in Juedische Zeitschrift fuer Wiss. und leben, 1869, pp. 81 ff.; The Jewish Festivals by the writer, pp. 276–277 and notes thereon. About this belief among other peoples see Westermarck as in note 143, pp. 566 ff.

217 "Three persons require guarding, namely, a sick person, a bridegroom, and a bride. In the Baraitha it was taught: a sick person, a midwife, a bridegroom and a bride; some add a mourner," B'rochos 54b and see Rashi, ad loc.

218 See a variant of this tale in Tanchumo on Deut. 32:10. About this belief among other peoples see R. Campbell Thompson, Semitic Magic, pp. 134 ff.

219 Pirke R. Eliezer 16; K'subos 17b and Rashi, ad loc. See Scheftelowitz, Alt-Pal., p. 80; Thompson as in the foregoing note, p. 171.

220 Bovo Basro 60b; Shulchan Aruch Orach Chayim 560.

221 See Lauterbach, "The Ceremony of Breaking the Glass at Weddings," Hebrew Union College Annual II, and Westermarck as in note 143, pp. 543 ff.

222 Kovets T'shuvos Horambam V'igrosov I, 51; S. Osof, M'Koros L'toldos Hachinuch B'yisroel, Vol. II, 200. See Bergmann, "Ein Hochzeitsbrauch," Monatsschrift, 1927, p. 161; Samter, pp. 90 ff.; Scheftelowitz, Alt-Pal., pp. 54–55.

223 Tsharni, Sefer Hamaso-os B'erets Kavkaz, p. 299.

224 Oruch Com., sub voce לפד; Soto 49b; Tosefto Soto 15:8; Resp. Maimonides as in note 222. See Loew; Samter, pp. 152 ff.; Scheftelowitz, Alt-Pal., pp. 39–40, 67, 78–79, 82.

225 See Lauterbach as in note 221; Heinrich Lewy in Archiv fuer Religionswissenschaft, Vol. XXV, pp. 194 ff.; Vol. XXVIII, pp. 241 ff.; Vol. XXXI, p. 123. For another explanation of the custom of breaking earthenware at weddings, see Westermarck, as in note 143.

226 Tosefto Shabos 7:16–17 and cf. Leonard Whibley, A Companion to Greek Studies, p. 595.

227 Rashi on K'subos 8a.

228 Gitin 57a. See Guedemann III, p. 123.

229 Smochos 8; Shulchan Aruch Yore Deo 391. See Scheftelowitz, Alt-Pal., p. 87 and cf. above in the wedding in Worms, p. 178.

230 See Zunz, Zur Geschichte und Literatur, pp. 300–307.

231 Gen. 18:19; 47:29–30; 49:29; Deut. 31 ff.; Josh. 23–24; II Sam. 17:23;

I Kings 2; 13:31; II Kings 20:1. Cf. also the apocryphal books *Testament of Adam* and *Testaments of the Twelve Patriarchs.*

232 Isa. 15:2–3; 32:11–12; Jer. 48:38.

233 Gen. 46:4; 50:1; Lev. 19:28; 21:5; Deut. 14:1; Jer. 6:26; 48:37; Ezek. 24:15–23; Mic. 1:16; Esther 6:12; and many more passages in the Bible.

234 II Sam. 3:31–35; I Kings 13:30; Jer. 22:18; 48:37; Ezek. 32:16; Amos 5:16–17; Koheleth 12:5; Josephus, War III, 9, par. 5.

235 Lev. 20:14; 21:9; Josh. 7:15; Amos 2:1; Deut. 21:23; Jer. 16:4. The text in I Sam. 31:12 "and burnt them there" is apparently distorted. Cf. II Sam. 21:12–14 and I Chron. 10:12.

236 I Sam. 28:14 (When Saul was told by the witch that the godlike being that was coming up out of the earth had the appearance of an old man covered in a robe, he perceived that it was Samuel); Ezek. 32:27 ("The mighty ones lie in the netherworld with their weapons of war").

237 Jer. 34:5; II Chron. 16:14; 21:19; Josephus, Ant. XV, 3, par. 4; Tosefto Shabos 7:18; Avodo Zoro 11a.

238 See also Ps. 106:28; MacCalister, *The Excavations of Gezer* I, pp. 392 ff.; Kittel, *Geschichte des Volkes Israel*, I, 1923, p. 164.

239 I Sam. 31:13; II Sam. 1:12; 3:35; Jer. 16:7; Ezek. 24:17, 22.

240 Num. 20:29; Deut. 21:13; 34:8; Nahum 3:7; Koheleth 7:2.

241 Lev. 19:27–28; Deut. 14:1.

242 Family graves: Gen. 23:4, 9, 20; II Sam. 21:14. Single graves: Gen. 35:8; II Kings 13:21.

243 Josh. 24:30; I Sam. 25:1; I Kings 2:34; II Kings 21:18; Ezek. 43:7–9. See articles "Tombs" and "Tombstones" in *J.E.*

244 I Sam. 15:12; II Sam. 18:18; II Kings 23:17; Ezek. 39:15. The *matsevo* in Gen. 35:20 is not a gravestone, but a sacred pillar, an object of worship, connected with an ancestral grave. Cf. Gen. 28:18; 31:45; 35:14.

245 Bovo Basro 151a; Tosefto Yomo 5; Sh'mos Rabo 52:3; Tanchumo, Bo, 2; see Abrahams, *Hebrew Ethical Wills* I, pp. 3 ff.

246 Mishnah B'rochos 8:6; Mishnah Shabos 23:4–5; Shabos 105b; Moed Koton 25a–26b; K'subos 17a.

247 Sanhedrin 46b–47a; S'mochos 11; St. John 19:40.

248 B'rochos 18b; Shabos 114a; Moed Koton 27a–b; Y. K'subos 12, Halocho 3; B'reshis Rabo 100:3; Charles, Pseudepigrapha, the Books of Adam and Eve XLVIII, 4; Josephus, Ant. XVII, 8, par. 3.

249 K'subos 17a; B'rochos 18a, 53a; Josephus, Apion II, par. 26; Sanhedrin 20a; Mishnah K'subos 4:4; Mishnah Moed Koton 3:8–9; Josephus, Wars, III, 9, par. 5; Moed Koton 8a, 28b.

250 Shabos 152b–153a; Moed Koton 8a, 25ab; Mishnah M'gilo 3:3; Y. K'subos 12, Halocho 3; B'rochos 62a; S'mochos 3, 8, 14.

251 Moed Koton 29a; Sanhedrin 19a; M'gilo 23b; Bovo Basro 100b.

252 Moed Koton 27ab; K'subos 8b; Josephus, Wars, II, 1, par. 1; Bovo Basro 16b; B'reshis Rabo 63:16. Cf. above pp. 223–226.

253 Mishnah Moed Koton 3:5–9; Moed Koton м4b, 15a–b, 21ab, 22b, 25b, 27b; Ta-anis 30a; Echo Rabosi 1:1; Psikto R. Kahano 15. See Morris Jastrow, "Dust, earth and ashes as symbols of mourning among the ancient Hebrews"

(*Journal of the Am. Oriental Society,* Vol. XX, pp. 133 ff.). About plucking out the hair as a manifestation of grief in this period, see Echo Rabosi, proem 24. Cf. above p. 224 and further below p. 252.

[254] Koheleth 7:2 and Koheleth Rabo, *ad loc.;* Shabos 152a–b; Tosefto M'gilo 4:14; Tosefto Bovo Basro 6: 13; Moed Koton 23a, 22b; K'subos 8b; S'mochos 12; Sofrim 19:9; Vayikro Rabo 23:4; Sidur R. Amrom; Machzor Vitri, no. 248. See A. Buechler, *Der galilaeische 'Am-ha-'Ares,* pp. 210–211.

[255] Sanhedrin 46b, 98b; Y. Kil'aim 9, Halocho 4; Moed Koton 25a–b; K'subos 111a; Y. K'subos 12, Halocho 3.

[256] Mishnah Sanhedrin 6:5; S'mochos 2.

[257] Mishnah P'sochim 8:8; Mishnah Sanhedrin 6:6; Nido 24b; S'mochos 12–13. Cf. Rhode, *Psyche* [4], I, p. 226; Guhl-Koner, *Das Leben der Griechen und Roemer* [5], p. 495. See S. Krauss, *Die Doppelbestattung bei den Juden;* D. Schuetz, "Die Assuarien in Palestina," *Monatsschrift,* 1931, pp. 286 ff.; E. L. Sukenik, "M'oras k'vorim y'hudis b'morad har hazeisim," in *Jerusalem,* in memory of Lunts; "Aronos U-k'sovos," in *Hashiloach,* 42.

[258] Mishnah Sh'kolim 2:5; Tosefto M'gilo 4:15; Mishnah Sanhedrin 2:1; Bovo Basro 8a.

[259] Eruvin 17a; K'subos 84a; Mishnah Bovo Basro 2:9; Mishnah Sanhedrin 6:5; Matthew 27:7.

[260] Isa. 14:18; Job 17:13; 30:23; Koheleth 12:5.

[261] Mishnah Sh'kolim 1:1; Mishnah Moed Koton 1:2; Moed Koton 5b; Eruvin 55b; Sanhedrin 96b; Horoyos 13b; Mishnah Tohoros 3:7; B'reshis Rabo 82:11; I Macc. 13:27–30; Josephus, Ant. XIII, 6, par. 6; Wars, V, 6, par. 2; 7, par. 3; Ant. XVI, 7, par. 1; XX, 4, par. 3.

[262] Tosefto B'rochos 7:6; B'rochos 18b, 58b; Tosefto Trumo 1:3; Ta-anis 16a; Y'vomos 122a, Rashi, *ad loc.,* citing T'shuvos Hag'onim; Nido 17a. For more details about the rites and customs of death and mourning in this period, see S. Klein, *Tod und Begraebnis in Palestina zur Zeit der Tannaiten;* Krauss, II, pp. 54 ff.

[263] B'rochos 18b. See *Monatsschrift,* 1874, pp. 130 ff. and pp. 183 ff.

[264] See Beyer and Lietzman, *Die juedische Katakombe der Villa Torlonia in Rome;* H. Gressmann, "Jewish Life in Ancient Rome" (*Jewish Studies in Memory of Israel Abrahams*); H. J. Leon, "New Material about the Jews of Ancient Rome," *Jewish Quarterly Review,* April, 1930.

[265] Treatise S'mochos of R. Chiyyo (ed. Higger), chaps. 1–2.

[266] Tur Yore Deo, 352, 362; Shulchan Aruch Yore Deo, 352; Chidushe ho-Ran on Sanhedrin 46a. See Guedemann III, p. 131.

[267] Shulchan Aruch Yore Deo 352; Resp. Rivosh, no. 158. See Louis Finkelstein, as in note 196, p. 98.

[268] Machzor Vitri, p. 243; Shibole Haleket, Hilchos S'mochos 21, 27; Maharil; Tur Yore Deo 387; cf. Karo and Ramo in Shulchan Aruch Yore Deo 386; Danzig, *Chochmas Odom.* About cutting the flesh see Finkelstein as in the previous note.

[269] Mishnah Midos 2:2; S'mochos 6, 10; Sofrim 19:9. Resp. G'onim, Sha'are Tsedek 4; Maharil.

[270] See Abrahams as in note 199, p. 94; Berliner, p. 118; David Philipson, *Old European Jewries,* pp. 76 ff.; Zunz, *Zur Geschichte und Literatur,* pp. 390 ff.

271 Sanhedrin 47b; Ta-anis 16a, Tosafos, *ad loc.;* Sefer Chasidim, ed. Wisti-netzki, 271. See Berliner, p. 119; J. Perles as in note 187. Joshua Trachtenberg, *Jewish Magic and Superstition,* pp. 61–68; Wiesner, "Die Leichenbestattung in thalmudischer und nachthalmudischer Zeit," *Ben-Chananja,* 1861, pp. 277 ff. and pp. 405–6.

272 Moed Koton 27b, Rashi, *ad loc.;* Resp. R. Osher 13:12; Resp. Tashbats 3:13. See Abrahams as in note 199, pp. 357–359; Leopold Loew, *Gesammelte Schriften* II, pp. 150 ff.

273 About the S'fardim see Almaliach, Hershberg and Lunts as in notes 70 and 205. About the Moroccan Jews see Jacob Tulidanu, *Ner Hama'arov,* p. 215.

274 Cf. Ps. 88 and Job 10:21–22 with Pss. 16:10; 23:4; 49:16; I Sam. 2:6.

275 Ovos 4:21.

276 II Kings 21:6; Jer. 7:31; 19:5–6. Cf. note 22. For descriptions of Paradise and Hell in Jewish literature, see M. Gaster in *Transactions of the Royal Asiatic Society,* 1893, pp. 571 ff. and Ginzberg, *Legends* I, pp. 15–16, 19–23 and note thereon. About Persian influences see Scheftelowitz, altper., pp. 187 ff.

277 Rosh Hashono 17a and see Scheftelowitz as in the preceding note, pp. 184 ff.

278 B'rochos 18a; Shabos 30a; S'mochos 12.

279 B'rochos 18b; Shabos 152b; B'reshis Rabo 100:7. See Scheftelowitz as in note 7, pp. 177 ff.

280 See Ginzberg, *Legends* I, pp. 55–59 and notes thereon and V, pp. 95–96.

281 Pss. 89:8; 103:20–21; Job 1:6; 38:7. See Kautzsch, *Biblische Theologie des A. T.,* pp. 99 ff.; Stade-Bertholet, *Biblische Theologie des A. T.* II, pp. 374 ff.; David Neumark, *Toldos Ha-philosofia B'Yisroel,* 20–21.

282 Isa. 45:7; Ps. 78:49; Prov. 16:14.

283 Bovo Basro 16a; Pirke R. Eliezer XIII.

284 Avodo Zoro 20b.

285 B'rochos 51a; Suko 53a.

286 Bovo Basro 17a; D'vorim Rabo, end; Shabos 30b; Moed Koton 28a; Bovo M'tsio 86a; Makos 10a; Sanhedrin 97a; Soto 46b. See Ginzberg, *Legends* IV, p. 30 and p. 175, and VI, Judges, note 28.

287 Isa. 25:8; Mishnah Moed Koton 3:9.

288 Pss. 94:17; 115:17; B'rochos 18b; Shabos 152b; Chagigo 5a; Sanhedrin 94a; P'sikto Rabosi 23. See Scheftelowitz, altper., p. 157, and Alt-Pal., p. 6.

289 See Ber, Seder Avodas Yisroel, pp. 106–107.

290 Tractate "Chibut Hakever" in *Otsor Midroshim* (Eisenstein); Shabos 152b; see Bender, *Jewish Quarterly Review,* 1893–94, pp. 669–670.

291 See article "Transmigration" in *En. of Rel. and Ethics,* Vol. XII, also "Transmigration of the Souls" in *J.E.,* Vol. 12.

292 K'subos 103b; Ovos d'R. Noson 25; Y. Moed Koton 3, Halocho 7.

293 See Elhorst, "Die israelitischen Trauerriten" (Wellhausen Festschrift); Fray, *Tod, Seelenglaube und Seelenkult;* Frazer, "On Certain Burial Customs" (Journal of the Anthropological Institute of Great Britain and Ireland, Vol. XV); Grueneisen, *Der Ahnenkultus und die Urreligion Israels;*

Hoelscher, *Geschichte der israelitischen und juedischen Religion,* pp. 17–18; Kautzsch, *Biblische Theologie des A. T.,* pp. 8 ff.; Matthes, "Die israelitischen Trauergebraeuche" (Vierteljahrschrift fuer Bibelkunde II).

[294] Lev. 10:6; 19:27-28; 21:1–6, 10–11; Deut. 14:1. See Scheftelowitz, altper., pp. 32 ff. (parallels among the Persians).

[295] Cf. above p. 267. See Machzor Vitri, hilchos ovel and Marmorstein in *Zion* II.

[296] Tur Yore Deo 393.

[297] Shibole Haleket, Hilchos S'mochos 21.

[298] See B'reshis Rabo 100:14; Samter, p. 128; Scheftelowitz, Alt-Pal., p. 82.

[299] See note 217; Y. Eruvin 10, Halocho 11; Bovo Basro 100b and Rashi, *ad loc.;* Sh'vuos 15b; Sha'are Tsedek, Resp. G'onim, Shaar IV, par. 19–20. Shulchan Aruch Yore Deo 376:4. See Marmorstein in *Zeitschrift Neutest. Wiss.,* 1931, pp. 277 ff.; Scheftelowitz, Alt-Pal., p. 74.

[300] See Frazer, p. 192; Samter, pp. 134–135.

[301] Sha'are Tsedek as in note 299 and Tur Yore Deo 376.

[302] See Shibole Haleket; Danzig, Chochmas Odom; Berliner, p. 100. See also Bodenschatz, IV, chap. V, p. 174.

[303] No atonement: Z'vochim 9b; Koheleth Rabo 1:36. Souls can be delivered from Gehinom: B'reshis Rabo 63:2; Sifri on D'vorim 21:8; Tanchumo, Ha'azinu 1.

[304] B'rochos 3a, 57a; Shabos 119b; Mishnah Yomo 6:2; Ta-anis 16b; Soto 49a.

[305] Sofrim 16:9; 18:10; 19:9; 21:6.

[306] See M. Gaster, *Ma'aseh Book* I, p. 286; L. Ginzberg, *Ginze Schechter* I, pp. 235 ff.; Krauss in *Bitsoron* I, no. 2.

[307] Maharil, Hilchos S'mochos; Beis Yosef on Tur Yore Deo 376. See Elbogen, *Der Juedische Gottesdienst,* pp. 92–98; Idelsohn, *Jewish Liturgy,* pp. 84–88; David De Sola Pool, *The Kadish,* pp. 100 ff.

[308] N'dorim 12a; Y'vomos 122a and Rashi, *ad loc.;* Sh'vuos 20a.

[309] Sefer Chasidim (ed. Wistinetzki) 68, 290–291; Shulchan Aruch Yore Deo 376:4; Danzig, *Chochmas Odom* 171. See Guedemann II, p. 132.

[310] Menasseh Ben Israel, *Nishmas Chayim,* ma-amar sheni, perek shiv'o v'esrim; Emanuel Ch. Riki, *Mishnas Chasidim,* Maseches G'milus Chasodim. See Bacher, *Zeitschrift fuer Heb. Bibliographie,* Vol. V, p. 154.

[311] Ber, Seder Avodas Yisroel, p. 17.

[312] Guedemann III, pp. 128 and 132; Abrahams as in note 199, p. 156. See above p. 292.

[313] See *The Jewish Festivals* by the writer, p. 278 and note thereon.

[314] See Bernfeld as in note 69, p. 260.

[315] See article "Memor Book," *J.E.* Vol. 8.

Glossary

The following Glossary lists certain non-English terms used in the book. Those omitted are either explained where they occur in the text or may be found in the regular English dictionary.

AFIKOMON, name for the piece of matso with which the meal of the Passover night is concluded.

ALEPH, first letter of the Hebrew alphabet.

AMORA (pl., Amora-im), sage of the Talmud, from the third century C.E. on.

BADCHON (pl., badchonim), public merrymaker and entertainer.

BAR MITSVO, *son of commandment;* man of duty; boy reaching the age of religious majority; the ceremony marking that occasion.

BEHELFER, assistant of the m'lamed, *q.v.*

BEIS, second letter of the Hebrew alphabet.

BEIS MIDROSH, *house of study.*

BEIS SEFER, elementary Jewish school.

BEN ZOCHOR, *male child;* celebration on the Friday night following the birth of a boy.

BIMO, reading dais in the center of the synagogue.

B'RIS, *covenant* (of circumcision); circumcision ceremony.

CHACHAM, rabbi among the S'fardim, *q.v.*

CHAMISHO OSOR, *fifteen;* the fifteenth day of the months of Sh'vot and Ov, two minor Jewish festivals.

CHASIDIM, Jewish sect which arose in Eastern Europe in the eighteenth century.

CHAZAN, cantor or precentor; in olden times the sexton of the synagogue.

CHEDER, elementary Jewish school.

CHES, eighth letter of the Hebrew alphabet.

CHEVRO, *society;* brotherhood.

CHEVRO BIKUR CHOLIM, *society to care for the sick.*

CHEVRO KADISHO, *holy brotherhood;* burial brotherhood.

CHUMASH, Pentateuch.

CHUPO, *wedding canopy;* bridal chamber; wedding.

DROSHO, discourse on Torah.

ESROG, a citron used with the festive wreath on the Feast of Booths.

GABAI (pl., gabo-im), director, manager.

GAN EDEN, *Garden of Eden;* Paradise.

GET, legal declaration of divorce.

HAFTORO, portion of the Prophets read at the conclusion of the reading from the Pentateuch.

HALLEL, psalms of praise, consisting of Psalms 113–118.

HAVDOLO, *division* (between sacred and profane); the benediction recited on the exit of the Sabbath or a festival.

HAZKORAS N'SHOMOS, memorial services.

KABOLAS PONIM, *reception;* welcome; greeting.

KABOLAS SHABOS, *greeting of the Sabbath;* prayers recited Friday evening before the evening services.

KADDISH, *holy;* prayer of praise and adoration to God, popularly thought of as a prayer for the dead.

KAPOROS, ceremony of atonement practiced with a fowl as scapegoat before the Day of Atonement.

KIDDUSH, benediction sanctifying the Sabbath or a festival.

KIDDUSH HA-SHEM, *sanctification of the name* (of God); martyrdom for the Jewish faith.

KIDUSHIN, *betrothal.*

KITO (pl., kitos), *class* in the Jewish elementary school.

KLEZMER or KLEZMORIM, *musicians.*

KNAS MAHL, *engagement feast.*

KOHELETH, *Ecclesiastes.*

KOHEN (pl., Kohanim), *priest;* descendant of the priestly caste.

K'RIAS SH'MA, reading of Sh'ma Yisroel, *q.v.*

K'SUBO, *marriage contract;* sum of money written in the contract due to the wife on her husband's death or on being divorced.

LAG BO-OMER, minor Jewish festival on the eighteenth day of the Jewish month Iyor.

MA-ARIV, evening services.

MAFTIR, person called up in the synagogue to read the Haftoro, *q.v.*

MATTON, gifts given by the bridegroom to the bride.

MAZOL, *star of destiny;* destiny; luck; with Tov, **good** luck.

M'GILOS, *Scrolls* (The Song of Songs, Ruth, Lamentations, Ecclesiastes, Esther).

MINCHO, afternoon services.

MITSVO, *religious precept;* religious act; religious merit.

M'LAMED, *teacher* in an elementary Jewish school.

M'NORAS HAMO'OR, The Candlestick of the Light, name of an ethical book.

MOHAR, price paid by the groom or his father to the bride's father.

MOHEL (pl., mohalim), *circumciser.*

MUSOF, additional morning prayers for the Sabbath and festivals.

M'ZUZO, a slip of parchment containing Deut. 6:4–9 and 11:13–21 in a container which is nailed to the door-post of a Jewish home.

OLENU, prayer in the Jewish liturgy named after its first word, "Olenu."

Peos, *ear-locks.*

Pesach, *Passover.*

Piyut (pl., piyutim), poetical additions to the original prayers which liturgical poets composed in the Middle Ages.

P'ruto, smallest copper coin.

Rashi, abbreviation of Rabbi Solomon, the son of Isaac, most popular commentator of the Bible and the Talmud (eleventh century).

Rebe, distorted from rabbi; title of the m'lamed, *q.v.*

Rebitsin, wife of the rabbi or the rebe, *q.v.*

Rosh Chodesh, New Moon.

Sabbath Nachamu, the Sabbath following Tisho B'Ov, so called because on this Sabbath the fortieth chapter of Isaiah is recited as the Haftoro, beginning with *Nachamu, Nachamu Ammi* (Comfort ye, comfort ye My people).

Sandek, he who holds the child on his knees for circumcision.

Sarver, *waiter;* general handyman.

Seder, order of service; home ceremony of the Passover night.

Shadchon (pl., shadchonim), *matchmaker.*

Shamosh (pl., shamoshim), *sexton* of the synagogue; assistant who did the menial work of the burial brotherhood.

Sh'ma Yisroel, *Hear, O Israel;* the declaration of the Jewish monotheistic faith, *see* Deuteronomy 6:4.

Shovuos, the Feast of Weeks; Pentecost.

Simchas Torah, *rejoicing with the Torah;* the last day of the Sukos festival, *q.v.*

Simon Tov, *good omen.*

Sukos, Feast of Booths or Feast of Tabernacles.

Tachrichim, *shrouds* of the dead.

Talis, *garment;* prayer-shawl.

Talmud Torah, communal free Hebrew school.

Tanna (pl., tannaim), sage of the Talmud, in the first two centuries C.E.

T'filin, *phylacteries.*

Tisho B'Ov, ninth day of the Jewish month, Ov, commemorating the first and second destructions of the Temple in Jerusalem.

T'no-im, *stipulations;* engagement celebration.

Tov, last letter of the Hebrew alphabet.

Tsadik, *righteous, pious, holy man;* Chasidic rabbi.

Vov, sixth letter of the Hebrew alphabet.

Yahrzeit, anniversary of the day of death.

Y'shivo, Talmudic academy.

Yud, tenth letter of the Hebrew alphabet.

Zuz, silver coin; one-fourth of a shekel.

Index

in Eastern Europe, 268; in the first centuries c.e., 237f.; in the Middle Ages, 252; among the S'fardim, 272
Mi Sheberach, 58f.
M'ni, see Gad
Moabites, 13
Mohar, 126ff., 141f., 144, 203
Monotheism, monotheistic, 3–5
Morocco, Jews of, 31, 119, 272
Moses, anniversary of the death of, 260, 298; and Joshua linked with the beginning of circumcision among Jews, 15f.
Mourning, benedictions in the house of, 241f.; in Biblical times, 223–226; connected with the synagogue, *see* Synagogue; customs of, in the Middle Ages, 252f.; in Eastern Europe, 268f.; in the first centuries c.e., 238–240; gestures of, 223f.; among the Moroccan Jews, 272; period of, 225f.
M'zuzo, 34, 93

n

Names, adding of, changing of, hiding of, magic power of, *see* Belief, in the magic power of names
Naming a child, after dead ancestors, 27f., 43f.; after living relatives, 28; in Biblical times, 12f.; among Chasidim after a deceased tsadik, 52; with dual and double names, 44–48, 56; in the Middle Ages, 43ff.; with non-Jewish names forbidden to Jews, 52f.; in post-Biblical times, 27ff.; in recent times, 51ff.; in the State of Israel, 52; use of foreign names for, 28, 44
Naming a girl, in the home among the S'fardim, 61; soon after birth, 27; in the synagogue, *see* Synagogue

o

Omens, connected with, a child, 79f., death, 284f., marriage, 217–219
Orient, Jews of the, 7, 36, 44, 6of., 86, 88, 93, 118f., 161, 163, 167, 204, 214, 218, 252, 271f., 297

p

Palestine, Jews in ancient, 7, 15, 17, 27f., 36, 76, 82–84, 147f., 153f., 235, 243–245
Paradise and Hell, *see Gan Eden* and *Gehinom*
Passover, *see* Pesach
Persia, Jews of, 203, 298
Persians, 242, 278
Pesach, 54, 84, 120, 209f., 263
Pharisees, 144, 206, 230, 277
Philistines, 13, 16, 127
Phoenicians, 13
Phylacteries, *see T'filin*
Pidyon ha-ben, abolished by the Karaites, 60; in America, 62; in Biblical times, 18; in the Middle Ages, 48–50; origin of, 18, note 22; in Talmudic times, 29
Poland, Jews of, 47, 115–117, 163f., 187
Poles, 82
Popular medicine, among Jews, 90
Prayer-Shawl, *see Talis*
Priest, priests, *see* Kohen, Kohanim
Purim, 52, 104

r

Redemption of the first-born, *see Pidyon ha-ben*
Reform Jews, confirmation among the, 119f.; controversy about circumcision among the, 51; name sons after a living father, 43; shifted the marriage ceremony from the courtyard back to the synagogue, 164
Resurrection of the dead, belief in, 277
Rhineland, Jews of the, 4of., 252f.
Rising from childbed, in Biblical times, 18f.; in Eastern Europe, 59f.; in the first centuries c.e., 29f.; in the Middle Ages, 43, 45, 50; observance discarded in America, 61
Romans, 6, 21, 36, 148, 210, 244f., 290
Rome, Jews in, 39f., 248f.
Rosh Chodesh, 210
Rosh Ha-shono, 53
Russians, 289

§

Sadducees, 277
Samaritans, 169
Sandek, 37–43, 58, 60
School, the Jewish elementary, 95ff.; in America, 110f.; in Eastern Europe, 102ff.; in the Middle Ages, 100–102; in recent years, 109–111; in tannaitic times, 98ff.
Seven days of the feast, 133, 136f., 156f., 201f., 204f.
S'fardim, 7, 43, 60f., 84, 91, 118f., 169f., 198ff., 201–203, 205, 216, 218f., 254, 271f., 297f., 299f.
Shadchon, Shadchonim, see Matchmakers
Shehecheyonu, 29, 49, 201
Sheol, 225, 274ff.
Shir Hamaalos, 55
Sholom Zochor, 56
Shovuos, 101, 120, 209f.
Shrouds and Coffins, 231–233, 251, 263
Simchas Torah, 92, 115
Simon Tov, 218f.
Slavs, 5
Societies, *see* Brotherhoods
Spain, Jews in, 93, 252–254
Spinholz, 166, 175
Sukos, 115
Synagogue, bar mitsvo celebrated in the, 116; ceremony in the, when changing a sick person's name, 76; ceremony of the first haircut in the, 84; the child in the, 91f.; circumcision in the, *see* Circumcision; circumcision reverted to the home from the, 51; confirmation in the, 121; connected with wedding, *see* Wedding; the elementary school attached to the, 97; funeral orations delivered in the, 235f., 265; ghost stories connected with the, 256, 271; the head of a, 149; Kaddish as part of the services in the, 294–297; key of the, to ease childbirth, 53; memorial services in the, 299f.; mourner changes his place in the, 269; mourner visits the, 269; naming a girl in the, 43, 52, 59, 62; observance of Yahrzeit in the, 299; rites of mourning in the, 253; rushing to the, to pray for a woman suffering in labor, 53f.
Syrians, 13

t

Tachrichim, see Shrouds and Coffins
Talis, 58, 118, 120, 172, 200, 213, 263, 278
T'filin, 34, 93, 114–116, 119f., 278
Tisho B'Ov, 209, 255, 270
T'no-im, see Knas Mahl
Tombstones, *see* Graves
Transmigration of souls, 283f.
Trousseau, 154, 199
Ts'doko, see Charity
Tsitsis, 34, 93, 200f., 248, 263, 278

u

Unlucky days and seasons, *see* Days and Seasons
Unterfuerers, 187
Unveiling the tombstone, 270

w

Walk, aiding the child to, 81f.
Watch Night, 32f., 36f., 56, 60f., 74
Weaning the child, 18, 81
Wedding, benediction, 156f., 161, 177, 194; in Biblical times, 131ff.; ceremony in America, 164f.; ceremony in the synagogue of Mayence, 170–173; ceremony in the synagogue on the Sabbath following the, 162, 174, 177, 195f., 202; preceding the, 175, 184f.; in the courtyard of the synagogue, 164f.; in the courtyard of the synagogue in Eastern Europe, 192–194; cutting the bride's hair before the, 168f., 202; drosho delivered by the bridegroom at the, 177, 196, 200; in Eastern Europe, 183ff.; feast, *see* Seven days of the feast; festivities on the Sabbath following the, 157; in Mayence, 170ff., 212, 217; in the Middle Ages, 160ff.; for the paupers, 185; per-

formed in the synagogue, 161–165; preceding the, 154, 199; preliminaries, in Eastern Europe, 183ff., in the Middle Ages, 165ff.; songs, 132–135, 156; in Talmudic times, 154–157; in Worms, 174–178, 217
Weighing the child, 80f., 90
Witchcraft, *see* Evil spirits

ย

Yahrzeit, 293, 297–299
Yemen, Jews of, 44, 126, 130, 203ff.
Yom Kippur, 192, 213, 260, 299
Yortseit, see Yahrzeit

Z

Z'miros, 34, 43